MADE IN INDIA

Made in India

BIDDU

First published in India in 2010
by HarperCollins Publishers India
a joint venture with
The India Today Group Copyright © Biddu 2010

Second Edition published globally by Read Out Loud Publishing LLP in 2015
ISBN: 978-15-168537-5-5

Formatted by E.M. Tippetts Book Designs

emtippettsbookdesigns.com

To
my mother, Sue, Zak and ZaZa,
the four pillars of my inner temple

CONTENTS

PREFACE

WHAT PROPELS SOMEONE TO WRITE AN AUTOBIOGRAPHY?
I BELIEVE THERE are three main reasons why one does so.

The first is a monumental and almost leviathan-sized ego that lives in the self and assumes the world wants to know every tiny morsel of information about you, which you are only too willing to reveal with the ease of a nightclub stripper.

The second reason is money. The paucity of wealth or the nearness of poverty urges you to throw your principles and caution to the wind, in a final spin of the roulette wheel. However, only an autobiography containing chapters that include goblins, elves, witches on broomsticks, fairies and creatures from Middle Earth would captivate the reader and sell in sufficient quantities to allow one to contemplate the lifestyle of a Russian oligarch. On second thoughts, sleeping with a string of B-list celebrities can enhance sales and your bank balance while it mows down your reputation.

The third reason – and probably the most altruistic – is because you have a story to tell, which could be curiously interesting or mildly entertaining, or perhaps even inspirational, with a modicum of human interest. In exceptional cases it may be a life worthy of merit and distinction that demands to be told to the world at large.

But writing a biography of the self is a hazardous challenge, as one is always writing in the first person singular. So page upon page is filled with 'I', 'me' and 'my', and no matter how disparaging the style of writing or self-deprecatory the prose, the nearness of overbearing pride is only a step away, so one could easily come across as a pompous and egoistical so and so.

I always told myself, I would never write my autobiography. Not that I'm a deeply private man or diffident by nature but the naked parade of my hidden emotions was anathema to me and like most people I did not want my private life to become public property. Neither did I consider my journey through life worthy of print, let alone anything else.

'I'll never write my story,' I repeated like a spiritual mantra. 'There's no harm if three of four people get to know more about you. It wouldn't sell any more, would it?' my waggish friend quipped.

I truly believed I did not have the ego to write two or three hundred pages about myself. Also, never having kept a diary of my journey through life, I would have to delve deep into my memory. All this from a guy who has been having 'senior moments' from the age of seven!

It all started, I suppose, at dinner parties, when conversation around the meal occasionally ebbed into a brief silence as it sometimes does, and to pick up the slack, I would reveal little anecdotes, interesting or attention-grabbing revelations about something that happened to me many years ago. Like my early career as a singer in India or how I managed to get out of the country (I'd made more attempts at leaving than the prisoners at Colditz) despite being robbed of every penny by a cunning devil. The funny yet rather daring escapade (for the time) by boat to the Middle East and my penniless walkabout through that part of the world, when it was little more than just a pile of sand, till I finally came to the Mecca of music and hedonism, the Sodom and Gomorrah of rock and roll. Yes! Great Britain – the country that once ruled my India and now, I was coming to collect.

I would also tell friends about my brief sorties in Bollywood and Hollywood, which always sounded more interesting in the telling of the yarn than when they actually occurred. Thus, I would weave and embroider a story or two that close friends found marginally amusing, especially after a bottle and a half of cheap Bulgarian wine.

Over the years my friends would say, 'Oh! You must write about that.'

'Who would want to read it?' I would ask. 'Not many,' the chorus would reply.

'And don't forget to spell my name right,' another would insist, while friends round the table would fall about laughing.

WHEN MY WIFE THREATENED ME WITH DIVORCE IF I DIDN'T write the autobiography, I deduced it would be infinitely cheaper to write than to pay her alimony.

So finally, I fell into the slipstream of the idea and though I was a closed book, I began the first chapter as a cathartic exercise, even though there were no demons to exorcize. Gradually, my pen developed a mind of its own, while my mind reconciled to the opening of the sluice gates of my reminisces and the story began to unfold like the unrolling of a carpet, till eventually the dam of thoughts was released and words and events began to spew forth like a gushing oil well.

And you, the reader, may be inquisitive enough to want to know what happens to the author. Does he get his comeuppance, does he do Class-A drugs, does he find God and religion? Or, then again, you may just be looking for a literary serum for insomnia.

1

THE SON ALSO RISES

I WAS BORN AT A TIME WHEN MAN HAD finally learned to walk upright. The year was 1945.

My mother, bless her, told me my birth had brought good luck to the world, as a few months later the Second World War came to an end and peace reigned over the planet. Gullible fool that I was, I believed her and for a considerable part of my life I thought I was the 'special one'. To say my mother doted on me excessively is akin to describing Michelangelo as a painter of ceilings. As my present wife (she's been present for the last thirty-eight years) once said, 'If you were driving and your car climbed the kerb and ran over a bunch of school children, in your mother's eyes it would be the fault of the children for being on the pavement.'

It was only later on – in my adolescence – I noticed that when it came to talking up her children (I have an elder brother and a sister), my mother was an inveterate liar and no praise was deemed enough. I also realized she was a gambler par excellence and she had a rummy session once a week at home till her ninety-fourth birthday, when three other cronies would come to her place, leave their Zimmer frames parked in the hallway and sit down to a leisurely game of cards with tea and biscuits for accompaniment. Mother also played the horses every day of her life: a bookie would pop round to the house and take her bet, often leaving some biryani that the man's wife had cooked for her. My mother invariably won her bets. She knew her horses as well as she knew a pack of cards.

Mom was a very attractive woman in her day. A gregarious, garrulous lady, with the spirit of a thousand flames. She passed away recently, ninety-five years young, from a fall that broke her thigh bone and the resultant coma and operation sucked that wonderful life force out of her. She had spent the last fifty years on her own but was helped to a great degree by my sister-in- law, Jamuna, and my elder brother Kuts, who lived with her. My father, who was a doctor, passed away suddenly from stomach cancer when I was still in school. I do not remember too much about him except that he was a shy, retiring man, subdued even. He was the yin to my mother's yang.

MY PARENTS WERE ORIGINALLY FROM THE STATE OF COORG, NOW part of the bigger state of Karnataka. Coorg was about 220 km from Bangalore and, at one time, had its own raja. It is a place of infinite beauty and abundance, with continuous hills and valleys. Almost all the coffee grown in the south of India comes from Coorg, where it grows on the gentle slopes, shaded by pepper and orange trees, while all around, the valleys are blanketed by paddy fields. The Coorgis, or Kodavas as we are called, are a tribal race of people, made up of clans very much like the Scots. We are supposed to be a warrior race, remnants of Alexander's battalion of soldiers who wandered south and mingled with the populace, intermarried and produced a race of people who are marginally different to other south Indians. There could be some truth in this myth about us being warriors, as many of my uncles were generals and brigadiers in the British Indian Army.

However, it was a time when most Indians had heard of the Queen of England's corgis but not of us Coorgis. There are only 90,000 of us left in the world, a tiny minority in a land of one billion two hundred million people.

I was born in Bangalore, when it was a pleasant little haven of 700,000 people, with tree-lined roads, parks, gardens and sublime weather. In fact, Bangalore was known as 'the garden city'. That was then. Today it has a population of nearly eight million whizzing around like dervishes in the chaos and bedlam of an overgrown city with no thought towards order or planning. Bangalore was a British cantonment, and a residue of the Raj still does exist in certain government buildings, clubs, gymkhanas and public schools. But in the early 1950s, it was a town where every home was a bungalow – a lovely low-built house with a garden in front and a small backyard. When my friends ask me about Bangalore, I tell them the name comes from the word 'bungalow' and they shake their heads sagaciously. It could be true or all myth, but it sounds plausible enough to me and, anyway, I can't be arrested for it, unless Bangalore was in Iran or Myanmar, where loose talk can land you in leg irons.

I STUDIED AT TWO FAMOUS SCHOOLS; FIRST AT ST JOHN'S School till I was eleven years old and then at Bishop Cotton Boys School. How I hated them. School was as appealing to me as radioactive waste. I think I sleepwalked through most of my academic life. The subject I hated the most was Hindi, which was to eventually become our national language. At that time, though, it was as foreign as Aramaic or Bantu, especially to us in the south of India. I always spoke English with my family and amongst friends. At school we had an hour's lesson once a week in Hindi. So every Tuesday, we would learn a smattering of words, and a bit of grammar from a rather uninspiring teacher and by the following Tuesday, we would have forgotten every word, syllable and nuance of the previous week. We were forever entering a cul-de-sac of learning.

At that young and impressionable time in my life, everything Indian except for the food was anathema to me. India was not the best place to be in the 1950s; the country was stagnant in its evolution, burdened with new rulers and old poverty, trying to find its way towards progress. Let no one tell you any different. I grew up in a cultural vacuum, because the country was caught up in the sterile and claustrophobic environment that socialism creates. America, that firebrand of democracies, was, ironically, more interested in Pakistan, Iran and various tinpot dictators and military regimes in Latin America, and not in the biggest democracy that Partition had created. So the Soviet Union became our new best friend and role model. We rocked with Khrushchev, not Kennedy. Which was a shame, because America had everything a young lad longed for: the glamour of film stars, rock 'n' roll heroes, hamburgers, and blue jeans. We never had anything foreign in our shops. In fact, we hardly had shops in Bangalore. They were more like glorified stalls that sold rice, ghee, dhal, butter, fruit and vegetables. One or two places sold local baked beans and cornflakes, but never chocolates or jeans, perfumes or Marks and Spencer's underwear. Whatever we saw occasionally in magazines was a distant dream, which could only come true in another incarnation, or via a job – such as a pilot's or flight purser's – that would take us abroad briefly.

WE LIVED IN A RATHER BIG WHITE HOUSE IN RICHARD'S Town. It wasn't a bungalow like the other homes, as ours had a ground and first floor to it. It was, if I remember right, the finest house on the road. Obviously, there was a time when Dad had money. But how he managed to keep the place going, I'll never know, because he was just about hanging in there, as his dispensary was not doing well. He doctored to the poor in a fairly derelict section of Bangalore, and half the time, the people he treated played Moses and put him in the Promised Land about paying their bills. It was always tomorrow. But tomorrow rarely came, and Dad, who empathized with his patients, never pushed them for payment.

Instead, as the money dried up, he decided to sell the lovely big white house we so enjoyed and grew up in, and the family moved to a smaller place on Spencer Road in Cleveland Town, which cost far less money. The savings kept us going for the next year or two.

As a twelve-year-old, I would dream of America, that distant Garden of Eden, the land of temptation, seduction and the good life. My first big hero was the actor James Dean. How I tried to emulate him in pose, mood and hairstyle. I swear that from a certain angle and if the lighting was right I looked a dead ringer for him. I had 500 pictures of my hero in a cellophane-wrapped album and twenty posters up on my bedroom wall. Imagine my ecstasy when I learned that James Dean and I shared our birth date, 8 February. My love affair with Dean lasted for many years, even after his death in a car crash and in some ways, my hero worship of the man bordered on the blasphemous. But around the same time as my fascination for James Dean began, another American star would inveigle his way into my affections.

An American fieldworker (who was involved with a non-governmental organization) brought back a vinyl record of Elvis Presley from his trip to the States and presented it to one of my school friends. One Saturday afternoon, after a bunch of us kids had finished cricket practice, we went back to a friend's place and hung out in his bedroom. The four of us yapped away until we were bored and then we decided to play the record my friend had been given. We wanted to hear what this Presley guy sounded like. It was love at first hearing. The music was pulsing with a vibrancy I had never heard before. His voice and the songs' primeval rhythms resonated within us and cut through to the very heart of our juvenile desires. It was an awakening and I can only assume it was like being on acid. We played the record till the vinyl nearly wore off.

Elvis made a lasting impression on me. Well, at least till the Beatles and the Rolling Stones came along a few years later. But at that time, Elvis was the Man. I thought I looked a bit like him. He had jet-black hair, so did I, I learned to sneer like him, walk like him, talk like him and I wore my hair and sideburns just like him, but I never learned to sing like him. That would have been too easy. I think Elvis inspired in me a burning desire to become a singer.

So I began to sing at local talent shows, held at the Catholic Club or the Bowring Institute and other similar venues in Bangalore. The lure of prize money worth Rs 20 to the winner did not go unnoticed to my all-seeing third eye. At these venues, the crowd was mainly comprised of Christians. The Anglo-Indians of Bangalore were fun-loving, and most of them could hold a tune. Some of them, like Cliff Richards and Gerry Dorsey (Englebert Humperdinck), who had migrated to Britain went on to bigger and better things.

I WAS THIRTEEN YEARS OLD WHEN I ENTERED MY FIRST talent show. I didn't bother telling my mom or dad about it. Not that they would have stopped me, but as sure as night succeeds day and day follows night, my mom would have asked me a hundred-and- one questions about the contest. I don't think she would have objected, but I decided to be like Dad and keep mum about it.

At that show, I was stiffer than a corpse. I clutched the microphone stand with the tenacity of an anaconda winding itself round its victim. Call it stage fright or what you will, but when the lights suddenly beamed on me and the piano man hit the opening chord, I forgot all about my sneer, my look, my wiggle; in fact I almost forgot my voice, which fortunately was awake to the crisis and followed a few beats behind the piano. I was like a rabbit forced into statue-like immobility by the blinding lights of a car. On a bare stage, with 200 people in the hall watching me, it was a nerve-wracking and terrifying experience. Suffice it to say I did not win the Rs 20. It wasn't all disaster though, as I had given a false name when entering the competition and nobody in the hall knew who this kid was. But that first show at the Catholic Club lit the flare to my wanting to become a singer, not as a hobby but as a career. This was unheard of at the time. Idyllic as it was, Bangalore was little more than a one-horse town, and most youngsters studied to become doctors, engineers, chartered accountants or whatever else it was that their parents wanted them to be. Wanting their son to be a pop singer was way down the parental wish list. Just above funeral director.

2

ELVIS WHO?

'MA, I NEED A GUITAR,' I SAID, USING MY whining, pleading voice which could sometimes work miracles in getting what I wanted, like an extra gulab jamun after lunch or two biscuits instead of the statutory one during morning tea.

'You mean you want a guitar,' my mother replied, emphasizing the word, 'want'. As if there was a world of difference between 'want' and 'need'.

'No ma,' I kept up the attractive whine. 'I need a guitar. Otherwise I can't become a singer.'

'You don't need a guitar to sing, son. You already sing beautifully.'(Like I said, my mother never tired of showering me with praise. The sun had one purpose and one purpose only, to shine on her son.)

'Everyone thinks you sing just like that Pat Boone.' My mother was referring to the American crooner who had a rich baritone, wore white buckskin shoes, was religious, faithful to his wife and had four daughters.

'Who is everyone?' my ego wanted to know. 'Uncles and aunties,' Mom replied most casually.

Her reply had punctured my pride a tad, but, undaunted, I went on.

'But I want to be like Elvis,' I replied.

'Who?' my mother asked, not really interested. There was so much more for her to do in the house than listen to a whingeing thirteen-year-old. My sister Dechu, who was a few years older than me, was becoming quite a tennis player. She was winning tournaments around the state and country and would eventually become the national tennis champion of India. So Mom had her hands full, sorting out my sister's daily sporting itinerary and the usual household chores.

Anyway, when I finally convinced my mother to buy me a guitar, she did so with the understanding that, 'I'll pay half and you earn the other half. Otherwise no guitar. Money is tight.'

I knew my mother would stand firm on her resolve.

So I NEEDED A WAY TO EARN MONEY FOR THAT guitar. A tube light clicked on above my head. There was one shop, D'Mello's, that sold musical instruments and the cheapest guitar on sale was Rs 50. It's less than a pound in today's money, but was, at the time, a fortune in my eyes. This cheap guitar was good for one thing only – firewood! But I was determined to buy it.

My plan was to buy sweets from the local kiosk and I bargained with the kiosk owner for two free sweets for every twenty that I bought. After much coaxing and using that whining voice of mine, the man agreed. Probably to get rid of me! I then sold the sweets to my brother, sister, cousins and friends and for every twenty-two sweets sold, I made a profit on two of them (which were given to me gratis by the kiosk owner. Are you with the programme?). At this rate, I soon realized I would have enough money saved to buy a guitar by my fiftieth birthday. Fortunately luck smirked, if not smiled, at me in the form of a distant uncle who came to visit us. He was in the Indian Army and, when he heard about my guitar fetish, promptly furnished Rs 50 from his khakis.

'Here you are, young man,' my distant uncle said in his clipped British Army accent. 'I want to hear you play that damn thing one day. Okay?'

'Yes uncle,' I said bashfully, grabbing the loot with one sweep of my hand.

'Oh! No! You can't take it,' my mother pleaded with embarrassment, knowing all the time that refusal was the last thing on my mind … after death.

Gradually, I began to win a contest or two and my confidence grew. No longer the rabbit, I was now downright foxy on stage, moving my pelvis and all parts south, the sneer perfected to beyond perfection. For a thirteen-year-old, I was giving Elvis a run for his money. Notice how Presley never came to India – was it sheer coincidence, I ask you? Slowly, I began to master the art of playing the guitar. Well, I use the word 'master' purely as a euphemism. I learned to stroke it in a fashion, but on stage it was an alluring and sexy appendage.

While I was walking down the rocky road of music, my sister was going great guns with her tennis. Every morning at six, on our way to school, we would head for the tennis courts at Bowring Institute where sis would be coached for two hours by a Mr Khan. In that early-morning crispness with a benign sun basking over the city and Bangalore not totally awake, my sister would hit the ball a thousand times as her coach spoke and coaxed her into the right shots and the right footwork, while I sat on the sidelines and watched, my head continuously moving from left to right and then right to left as my eyes followed the ball. This became a ritual for about two years, and when she became the Indian champion, it was deemed that sis was good enough to play at Junior Wimbledon. Father somehow managed to scrimp the airfare together (along with some financial assistance from that distant army uncle of mine, who chipped in with Rs 2000), and in 1959, my sister was given a rousing send-off to the UK, with a shopping list from me for chocolates and a pair of blue jeans.

Once again the money was beginning to run out, or maybe my father just liked moving house. But soon enough we moved from Spencer Road to a bungalow in Mc'Iver Town. In fact, the house we moved to was in the heart of town and just a stone's throw from my school, Bishop Cotton. It was also a lot closer to many of my school friends, so the move was in no way detrimental. All weekend the house would fill up with my boisterous noisy chums – both boys and girls – just yapping the day away or playing hide-and-seek or snakes and ladders. My best girlfriend at the time was a sweetheart called Lorraine Dozey, an ingénue gifted with a golden complexion and long chestnut-brown hair around an extremely attractive face. Her English parents had both been born in India. Larry (her pet name) went to Bishop Cotton Girls School and lived just 200 metres from our new home. It was an innocent age, untouched by the complexities of today.

Sadly, Lorraine committed suicide eight years ago, unable to live with the ravages of breast cancer and the resultant mastectomy which disfigured her body and, ultimately, her mind.

At school I had two other close friends and we were a gang. One friend was called Gautam, a lad of great sartorial style, similar in height and build to me, and the other was Arun, who, due to his lean and almost emaciated appearance, would forever be called Skinny. The three of us would hang out together, talking films and music and plotting ways to avoid school and the forthcoming exams on a permanent basis. None of us were into books of an educational nature; comics like Captain Marvel and Superman were more our form of reading material. So, in desperation, we three decided to run away from home. Yes, we would flee the town and country and head for some destination abroad. Where? We had not yet thought of that, but there was a whole wide world out there. We decided on facta non verba or in plain English, 'action not words'. Unfortunately, another school friend somehow overheard our clandestine whispers and wanted in on the mission. His name was Uday, and we had no choice but to let him run away with us, otherwise he was going to blow the whistle on us.

So one Tuesday morning around 8:30, the four of us met at the main railway station in Bangalore city. Four young guys, middle class in appearance with four suitcases in tow, boarded a train that was heading out of Bangalore.

'Where are we going, Bidz?' Skinny asked as we got inside the compartment. It was a question left too late, yet better late than never.

It was also a matter I had not given any thought to. As we lugged our suitcases on the upper shelves, I finally replied, 'Er, Japan.'

Uday, the gatecrasher to the party, thought it was a great idea. 'I've always wanted to go to Tokyo. They have Geisha girls, you know.' A childish leer on his face.

'Since when have you had this desire for damn Japan?' Skinny asked, surprised by Uday's in-depth knowledge of that country.

'Listen, how do we get to Japan by train?' Gautam wanted to know. It suddenly dawned on him and us that going by train was probably not the right way of getting to Tokyo. But we had bought our tickets to the next big town, we were in our carriage and our dislike of school plus the fear of failing our exams impelled us into continuing with our adventure.

By this time other travellers were getting on the train and the platform was alive with the commotion of people running frantically in search of an empty compartment, coolies with luggage on their heads shouting for people to move out of their way, hawkers selling tea and coffee, beggars without arms asking for alms and the general melee of an Indian railway station, which I was watching for the first time in my life.

'We can't turn back,' I said nervously. 'We've come too far.'

The 'too far' was approximately four kilometres – the distance from our homes to the station. As we started a discussion that was turning into an argument, a large head popped in through the half-open window.

'So there you are,' the voice thundered. It was Uday's father. 'I knew something was bloody up, when I saw a suitcase missing.'

He walked into the carriage and yanked his sheepish son and suitcase out onto the platform. 'You boys better get back to school, otherwise I'll tell your parents. Understand?'

He glared at us, then turned and, with suitcase in one hand, walked off with Uday, whose tail hung limply between his legs.

We sat for a few minutes in silence and shock at what had just happened. Uday's father was smarter than Sherlock Holmes. He deduced his son was running away just by noticing a suitcase missing from the cupboard. The man must have been a tantric! Or Uday must have made a habit of running away from home. We could not believe our bad luck.

'It was a mistake to take him along. I knew this would happen,' said clairvoyant Skinny.

'In that case you should have told us before the event, not now,' I replied crossly.

We got up, our shoulders drooping, and offloaded our suitcases onto the platform. A minute later the station master blew his shrill whistle, and with steam escaping from the engine like a cappuccino machine, the train slowly chugged its way out of Bangalore station, minus four boys and their suitcases.

With the ignominy of our failure hovering above us, we headed back to school. The class we had missed that Tuesday morning was Hindi, so in a way the morning wasn't a total disaster, and if we were lucky we could slip into the next lesson as inconspicuously as a crow at a raven's party and no one would be the wiser. Later, we would discreetly put our suitcases back into cupboards at home without being found out.

3

HOLD THE FRONT PAGE!

LET ME THROW SOME LIGHT ON TONY BRENT.
'Tony who?' I hear the collective shout. Well, I don't blame you, dear reader, for your bewilderment, your nonplussed expression or your ignorance.

Tony Brent was a singer born in Bombay in 1937. He left India and went to try his luck first in America and then the UK. In the early 1950s, he had a small hit on the British charts with a song called 'Cindy Oh Cindy'. Not much else was known about him. Then one day I scrutinized a piece on him in the 'What's On' section of my Sunday newspaper. It said Tony Brent, the internationally famous pop singer from England, was coming to Bangalore to do a show at the Bowring Institute. It mentioned briefly his Indian roots and his hit song 'Cindy Oh Cindy'.

I could not believe that a famous and internationally known pop star like Tony Brent (whom I had not heard of till the moment I read that paper) was visiting Bangalore. At the time, Bangalore was a great place to come from, not go to. But as a youngster I was deeply impressed because finally my home town would be on the world map of entertainment and rock-and-roll. How cool was that?

Soon the buzz around town built up: 'Tony Brent is coming',

'Tony Brent is coming.' All I could think of was TB. I knew I could not afford a ticket to his show. The prices were set way above a schoolboy's pocket money, but I found out the day and time he was arriving at Bangalore airport, and I was determined to be there to greet my latest hero. I asked my friends Gautam and Skinny if they wanted to come along.

'Who he?' they asked and passed on the idea.

However, one or two of the schoolkids were planning to be at Bangalore airport to greet the great man, but some goody-two-shoes snitched to the headmaster, who banned anyone from bunking school that day and promised fire and brimstone to whosoever disobeyed his order.

The day of Tony Brent's arrival saw me at the airport. It was 9:30 a.m., and a small coterie of newsmen and photographers were on hand to capture the momentous occasion. Only one Anglo-Indian girl from Bishop Cotton Girls School was there; else, it was mainly grown-ups. Someone handed out black-and- white pictures of Tony – a 10×8 head-shot of him gazing at the camera with a limpid smile.

I saw him get off the plane, wave to the small group of us onlookers and pose for the two photographers. He was copiously garlanded and a gentleman from some association or the other made a welcome speech, and TB said a few words of thanks in return. He cracked a weak joke about returning to India like a boomerang, which we sycophants found utterly hilarious. More photographs were taken with the crowd; he signed a few prints of his head-shot and then gave one final wave before he was herded into someone's Austin Morris.

The car travelled about forty metres and then suddenly shuddered to an ignominious halt. The motley crowd of well-wishers stood transfixed at this abrupt stoppage. We heard the engine being revved and then silence. Again we heard the turn of the ignition, a lot of wheezing and gasping, followed by another bout of silence. We looked at one another as a few giggles broke out. Then like an army of ants we moved towards the vehicle. I could see Tony Brent inside the car, a wan smile on his face, a picture of embarrassment, as he waved half-heartedly at his fans.

'Somebody give us a bloody hand,' the car owner shouted, rolling down his window and sticking his head out. As if on cue, about six of us lay our hands on the car and began pushing. I was near the rear passenger side and could see my hero visibly perspiring. The car began gathering speed as we pushed for India and the world. Suddenly, the engine lurched into life with a subtle roar and a cheer went up from all of us as the Austin Morris slowly sped away in a trail of bluish-white smoke. Tony Brent did not bother to look back or wave at us. But we kept waving on the slight chance that the superstar just might glance back at us.

I WALKED THE SIX KILOMETRES BACK HOME AS I DID not have any money for the bus fare. But it was worth every footstep of that journey. It had been a fabulous day. Bunking school and meeting a real live pop star from the UK. I could easily have died with nary a protest.

When I got home, I slowly broke the news to Mom. I did it in bits and pieces. First, I told her I would need a sick note.

'What for?' she asked, rather puzzled by my demand. 'I didn't go to school today,' I mumbled.

'Aren't you feeling well?' she enquired, touching my forehead.

'I'm fine, ma,' I said, pulling away.

'Then why a note to your teacher?' she wanted to know. 'Because ...' I replied, a thimble of exasperation in my voice.

'Because of what?' she demanded, a bucketful in hers. 'Because I went to the airport,' I finally gave in.

'What for?'

Honestly! Mothers can sometimes be so unnecessarily inquisitive.

'I went to see Tony Brent,' I said, spilling the beans. I could not take any more of her questioning. Guilt is far more fragile than the truth. So I surrendered.

'I cannot believe you would skip school to go and see a third- rate singer,' she said, walking away. She had also read about Tony Brent in the local papers. 'You go on like this and you will fail in school.' By now she had entered the dining room and her attack was softened by the distance.

'I need a note', I yelled in her direction.

The next day I went to school with my sick note and all was well. But the day after that all hell broke loose. The morning papers had a huge photograph on the front page with the caption, 'TONY BRENT COMES TO BANGALORE'. There was this picture of a beaming Tony Brent – 'surrounded by well-wishers' as the paper called us – his arm around my shoulder as I wore a smile that outshone the sun. I was in my school uniform to boot. The boy next to the star was undoubtedly me for all of Bangalore to see. The game was up. I had been outed by the press.

The headmaster called me into his office later that morning. The bottom line: the cane flashed three times on my derrière.

'I hope this never happens again,' the headmaster said ominously, as he held the cane in his right hand and slowly flexed and arched it with the index finger of his left hand. He removed his fingertip, the right hand brought the cane down, whacking me three times. My eyes turned red with restrained tears. I walked away clutching my buttocks but the pain, while excruciating, was quite worth it.

A short while after this episode, I met two young boys in short trousers, bicycling around my area. I was by now nearly fifteen years old and had made the transition to wearing long trousers with turn-ups. The boys seemed a little lost and we struck up a conversation which turned into a friendship that has lasted till today. A few years younger than I was, Suresh and Ashok had come down from Bombay to spend their vacation at Suresh's uncle's house which happened to be around the corner from my place. We seemed to hit it off rather well. I was enamoured with the glamour that Bombay exuded, especially to those of us who lived in smaller towns. I also had dreams of going there one day, as Bombay was the next best thing to New York and London. They, in turn, were looking for something to do during their time in Bangalore. I introduced them to my crowd and they fell in love with the city, especially with some of the attractive girls like Larry and Christine and Elizabeth, two beguiling twins, whom one could hardly tell apart. In fact the boys repeated their annual holiday in Bangalore the following year. Such was the enticement of the twins! Suresh was also learning the guitar so a glue-like bond developed between the two of us.

Although I hated the academic part of school life, I actually excelled in athletics and boxing. I won quite a few trophies in track and field, not because of any great practice I put in, but perhaps due to a certain amount of natural athleticism that was already in my genes, being a Coorgi and all that. Although, on reflection, I did build a jumping pit in my garden to practice my long and high jumps. It was a crude pit made of course sand and the constant running, taking off in the air and landing on the hard sand did eventually take its toll on my back, the painful and debilitating effects of which I only began to feel when I entered my thirties. At home the cupboard in the front room was full of silver cups and medals we had won as a family. My boxing trophies were won out of a natural desire of not wanting to get hit in the face. Call it fear or paranoia, but I had never come across an American pop star with cauliflower ears and a broken nose. So in the ring, I danced and moved with the adroitness and skill of a Nijinsky or a Nureyev. I couldn't bear to be touched by a velvet glove, let alone a pair of leather boxing gloves!

To supplement my non-existent pocket money, I often used to work at the Bangalore Race Course during the racing season. To get this job took great influence, and Dad managed to get me a job working behind the ticket counter selling win or place tickets for each race. I got paid Rs 32 for the weekend during the months of June and July when we had our school holidays, a not inconsiderable sum of money in those days, which helped me to buy my make-up and high-heeled shoes. Okay, I'm kidding about the last two items, but it helped me to stay solvent, especially if I didn't win a talent contest. During my stint at the race course I met a jockey called Alford, who took a shine to my music. I'd meet him quite often on race days and sometimes he'd give me tips on certain horses that looked like certs, which I'd pass on to Mom.

'If you ever come to Calcutta, look me up,' he said and wrote his number down on a piece of paper, which I scratched on the back of my guitar when I got home. Had I not done so, I'd still be looking for that piece of paper today.

But more than ever I wanted to get out of the confines and constraints of a small town to try and make it in the music world out there. When you are young, failure is not an option. It is not even on your horizon. There are no barriers, cynicism or disillusionment to assault and peel away your confidence and prevent you from reaching your Holy Grail, because youth gives you the freedom to fly close to the sun. I now had a new destination and it was London, the capital of the world, as far as I was concerned. And to this end I hatched another plot along with my comrades in crime, Gautam and Skinny. We were basically frustrated youngsters with our wants and desires firmly entrenched in everything American or British. We were privileged kids leading unprivileged lives.

So we decided we would run away once more, but this time unlike the previous year it would be just the three of us and to this end, we spoke about our venture only after school hours, and, that too, after making sure no one was around eavesdropping, especially not that Uday or his father. We would not leave first thing in the morning as we did last time. That was a huge operational error; instead we would leave straight after school at around 3:30 p.m., which would give us a few hours of getaway time, as our parents would assume we were at sports practice. Also, no large suitcases were allowed; only smaller ones that were easy to cart around. We would have to shiver away our first few days in London.

IT WAS FIVE IN THE EVENING WHEN WE BOARDED THE train. Where this train was headed to we really didn't know. On hindsight, planning and preparation were not our forte, but this time the train did leave with the three of us on board. There was a certain frisson of excitement as it left the platform and slowly gathered speed. The tapestry of village life whizzed past our window as dusk cast its riveting chiaroscuro over the land. The earth was arid, yet green fields chequered the landscape periodically. It all looked so biblical, yet it was in the present. Slowly dusk turned to darkness, as the train rolled through the countryside. There was nothing to see outside our window, no street lights, no car headlights or the light from houses, only the faint kiss of stars, which failed to illuminate the almost inky darkness outside. So in the muted amber light of our carriage and to the monotony of the train's rhythm we relaxed and, gradually, sleep overcame us.

Suddenly the train came to a shuddering halt; the abruptness of the stop and the sound of the braking iron wheels woke us from our sleep. I looked out of our window and all I could see was a small platform and a ramshackle old building. It was a village station that I'm sure wasn't meant as a stop on the schedule. Anyway, the three of us were awake and, rubbing the sleep from our eyes, we got out of the carriage to have a look around. It was a deserted outpost, with just the faint glow from one or two oil lanterns, which gave the place an eerie feel. It looked like something out of a Clint Eastwood Western. A few people came out of their carriages, wanting to know why the train had stopped. Then I heard someone further down the platform mention that the police were looking for some runaways. The three of us looked at one another, and even in the semi-darkness of our surroundings, the panic showed on our faces. We jumped back into the carriage wondering what to do next.

'I know,' I said, as a worry line began to form on my (at the time) unblemished face. 'Let's give ourselves different names, so they won't think we are the guys who ran away.'

'Great idea,' the other two chorused, and we sat in our carriage awaiting the inquisition.

'It's dicey,' I declared.

Shortly, two policemen entered our carriage. They were carrying their batons, or lathis, and one had a sheet of paper from which he read.

'We are looking for three boys who have absconded from their homes. Their names are...' He looked at us and then back again to the sheet in front of him. 'Their names are Master Biddu, Master Gautam and Master Arun. Please to give me your good names.'

In our hearts we knew the game was up, but we fought on gamely or should I say foolishly.

'My name is Dilip Kumar,' I replied with a stutter. 'My name is

Ashok Kumar,' Gautam said hesitantly. 'My name is Raj Kapoor,' Skinny answered timidly.

We had picked the names of three of the most famous film stars in the firmament of Hindi cinema. We weren't going to fool anyone with this act of naïve stupidity. Obviously, our brains (what little we had) had been parked at home, forgotten in the thrill of running away.

'I am sorry,' the policeman replied, not looking one bit remorseful. 'But you boys will have to come with us.'

'Where to?' we asked, a tremor belying the defiance in our voices.

'We have received a telegram from the assistant DIG of Police in Bangalore....' He rattled on. This was serious stuff and at 11:30 that night we were bundled into a van and taken by road to Bangalore. Waiting in the van was my brother Kuts. He had been sent as an emissary by the three families.

We reached Gautam's house at two in the morning, and there was a reception committee to greet us even at that unearthly hour. All our parents were there, waiting in the lounge. The mothers had tears in their eyes, while the fathers had murderous, baleful looks on their faces.

Yes, we got a humiliating telling-off by the mob as they examined our suitcases and asked us a hundred questions. To pour more salt on our wounds, it turned out that Gautam had packed underwear and a new pair of socks that belonged to his father.

'You packed my socks and chuddies!' his father cried, holding up the damn things with a look of incredulity on his face. If someone had handed us boys a shovel, I know what we would have done with it. This was a night to forget, although I'm afraid I will always remember it.

4

DESTINY RIDES A FIVER

THE FAMILY ONCE AGAIN MOVED HOME, AS MONEY – like Plutonium – was in short supply. This time we went back from McIver Town to Richard's Town, where Dad bought a bungalow fairly close to our old white house. Again, there was some money left over from the sale, so destitution was still light years away. It was our fourth move in as many years, and often I would leave school for home, and have to make a detour when I realized I was heading for the wrong house.

Then one day the world caved in on my mother's life. The year was 1961. My father had complained of some pain in his stomach, and being a doctor, he did nothing about it. Within a week the pain worsened, and thinking it might be appendicitis, Dad went to a hospital to have it removed. When they cut him open they found he had advanced stomach cancer and, within two weeks, he passed away. It was the suddenness of his passing away that devastated my mother, who found herself a widow at just forty years of age. The protective bubble of a breadwinner in the family had burst and with his death, the money stopped instantly, like a tap turned off. In India, people are not given social security or a financial safety net. Since Dad was a doctor and a private one at that, there was no state or government pension to fall back on; so overnight, with the abruptness of his death, our lives would go through another chameleon-like change.

Somehow my mother managed to make ends meet and feed the three of us. But I knew that soon a change of dwelling would occur, but it didn't matter to me. I was too caught up in the callousness of my youth, when the mirror of vanity reflects only on the self. It was only much later in life when I became a parent that I realized what my mom must have gone through on her own.

Is destiny pre-written or do we orchestrate our destinies? Do incidents that define our future happen by accident or is it karma? Is a coincidence really a coincidence or part of a bigger picture? While mulling over this conundrum, a seminal moment took place that probably changed the boulevard or route map of my destiny, and it was of my own making.

There appeared an advertisement in our local paper, the Deccan Herald, for young men and women wishing to join Air India. At that time it was the only airline in India. They were looking to recruit future pursers and hostesses. To work for Air India was a dream job that few could achieve – it was like winning a lottery. The catch to this advertisement was that you had not only to fill in a questionnaire but send in a five-rupee postal order along with it. This was the bit that wheedled the haves from the have-nots, the learned from the unlearned, and, quite frankly, the middle class from the poor.

My cousin Ashok, who was two years older than I and was staying with us at the time, planned to apply for the job. The salary was decent but the icing was the trips abroad and the goodies one could bring back for oneself or sell for a profit. As I mentioned earlier, foreign goods were as rare a sighting as an eclipse. While my cousin filled in his form, my mother thought it would be a good idea if I also tried for the job of a purser. I had just scraped through my final exams, with Cs in all subjects except for a lowly E in Hindi. My friends Gautam and Skinny also skated through with just the minimum requirement of grades. Now school was a thing of the past and it was obvious to my family that I had an allergy to shellfish and higher education. So Mom thought she would cajole me into trying for this job.

'I'll have to cut my hair, Ma,' I said reluctantly.

'You'll look so handsome in a uniform and all those trips abroad son …' Mom was making it sound quite tempting. 'Think of all the chocolates and perfumes you can bring back.'

'I'm not really cut out for serving people,' I argued. 'But think of the money, son.'

I understood the subtext of that line.

'And all those trips to Rome, London and Paris,' she enthused. I had to admit there was a certain allure about these places.

I had seen Audrey Hepburn in Roman Holiday a few times and I thought it was magic, plus the fact that I could visit London, the city of my dreams, and who knows …

'Okay!' I said, not totally convinced but since cousin Ashok was applying for the job, I fell in with the prevailing mood. It was a 'ho jaye' moment, as they say in India.

MOM GAVE ME THE Rs 5 FOR THE POSTAL ORDER, as did cousin Ashok's mom for him. We walked down to the local post office, clutching our forms and money and stood in line behind the counter, cousin Ashok in front of me. The post office was a pale yellow bungalow with a courtyard in front. All the windows, shutters and woodwork were painted a deep vermillion red. The counter faced the road, so the queue stood out in the courtyard just yards from the entrance. It was finally cousin Ashok's turn and he gave the form and the money to the clerk behind the counter, who took the money, examined the form and then duly stamped the receipt and handed it back to him. Then it was my turn and as I was about to hand the form and the money to the clerk I heard the beep–beep honk of a scooter and my name being called out. I turned round, still holding the form and money in my hand. It was my friend Darius Sagar.

'We're having a party tonight, Bidz,' he yelled to me. 'We need money for the food and drinks. Have you got any cash on you?'

His scooter engine was idling noisily by the kerb and he seemed in an almighty hurry.

I looked at the fiver I was holding. I looked at cousin Ashok, then at Darius, who had an impatient look on his face, as he revved the engine. It was only a nanosecond at the most, but in that briefest interval of time I had made up my mind. I was sure Air India would not let me keep my hair long, and frankly I wasn't a uniform kind of guy. There was only one thing I could possibly do.

'Okay,' I shouted from the courtyard. 'I've got a fiver.' 'That'll do,' he yelled back.

I walked away from the counter and went down the steps towards the pavement.

'See you at seven,' Darius said, grabbing the note as he zoomed away on his little phut-phut.

As we walked back home, I turned to my cousin and said, 'Tell Mom I sent off the form too, okay?'

A crescent of a smile crossed his lips. 'Sure,' he said softly. Three months later, cousin Ashok received a letter from Air

India in Bombay asking him to appear for an interview. Six months later, he got the job and remained with Air India for over twenty-five years, flying prime ministers, presidents and you and me. My mother could not understand how her son, around whom the planets revolved, did not get the call from Air India. Twenty years later, while we were having a pot of tea and a chat, I told her the story of the five-rupee postal order. Twenty years after the event, she found it amusing.

It was now approaching the tail end of 1962, and television was still largely unknown in India; it would remain so until 1982 when the Asian Games held in Delhi necessitated the country stepping into the twentieth century. There were no radio stations either, except for one government-owned national station called Akashvani, which played classical Indian songs interspersed with prehistoric Hindi film songs, which were a brew of screeching violins, twanging sitars and stratospheric, wine-glass-shattering female vocals. The station and music were as stultifying and starched as a barrister's collar. No

English music ever got played on this station. To hear Western music I had to twiddle the dial on my radio till I could find Radio Ceylon. On that station, every Sunday between the hours of 7:30 and 8:00 p.m., was a programme called the Binaca Hit Parade, playing the top twenty songs from the UK. I would spend hours trying to locate the station on my radio. At times the static was so bad you could hardly listen to anything at all, but behind that curtain of crackle you could just about hear the Rolling Stones belting out 'Come On' and 'I Wanna Be Your Man' and the Beatles wailing 'Love Me Do' and 'Please, Please Me'. Their music was the soundtrack to my youth and I would go through six days of hellish anticipation and nervous waiting, for on the seventh day, there was rock-and-roll.

This weekly window of sound forever remained an unforgettable capsule of excitement for me. The animal magnetism of the Stones and the rich harmonies and uplifting melodies of the Beatles were now an even greater influence on me than Elvis Presley, whose star was waning, and like a fair-weather friend I had already begun to forget what's-his-name.

Now more than ever, I had been seduced by the raw energy and the riot of sounds emanating from my crackling radio. I knew that music was my mistress and forever I would dance to her tune.

Sure enough, within a year of my father's passing away, we sold up and moved to a tiny bungalow that was also in Richard's Town but towards the outskirts of the area. At this rate I could see ourselves living in a broom cupboard pretty soon. However, during these metaphorical days of darkness, a scintilla of light shone on my brother Kuts. He had some months back applied for a job on a tea estate in Kerala, and in a sea change of fortune, he got the call to work as an estate manager. It was a fairly well-paid job, but the downside of working on a tea or coffee estate is the loneliness that goes with the job. Your nearest neighbour can be miles away, and it's only on Sundays, when all the planters meet for drinks and more drinks at the country club, that a semblance of social activity takes place. My brother, like our mother, was a gregarious person who loved the company of people. I wondered how he would take to this imposition of isolation.

It was also in this diminutive bungalow that I knew I had to do something with my life. One day I would have to support my mom financially. There were only so many houses she could move, before she'd be checkmated. It played on my mind. There could be no more faffing around, it was time to get serious. To be a singer in Bangalore, the glory road would end at the Catholic Club or Bowring Institute with me singing my heart out for prize money of Rs 50, or sometimes a box-set of books by some author or the other, or a bottle of cheap Indian rum, which I always thought of as a strange prize, especially if the winner was a juvenile.

I had set the parameter of my goals a little higher than that and so I decided on a modus operandi. Step One was to form a group. Step Two was to get the hell out of Bangalore. Step Three was world domination. And, to this end, I put together a group with myself and Skinny, plus a new guy I had met called Ken, a soft-spoken chap who played the guitar rather better than I did. I decided to call the group 'The Trojans', a name that was plucked off the top of my head without any great thought or deliberation. It was only a few years later I found out that Trojan was the name of a famous brand of condoms in the United States, which was why we often got some wild guffaws from American sailors in the audience. I'm sure we would have got less of a ribbing had we called ourselves 'The Prophylactics'.

So, the Trojans began to practise in earnest, honing our trade, sculpting our vocals and polishing our harmonies till we rose from mediocrity to a semblance of adequacy. We had a small cache of Beatles songs, plus songs by the Searchers and a few other Mersey Beat groups, but the pièce de résistance were our clothes and hair. Skinny and I were each armed with a serious head of hair. We had enough hair to lend some to Yul Brynner and Kojak and still not miss it. Our collarless suits were cut just like those the Beatles wore; the material we used was bleeding Madras cotton which had a plethora of psychedelic colours embossed on the print and to top it all, a local cobbler made us black Cuban-heeled boots. It was a cheap imitation of what the Fab Four wore. We just could not miss with this ensemble. Skinny, with his full mop of hair that resembled a crow's nest and Toucan-shaped nose, was the Ringo Starr of the group. The silent musician Ken was obviously George Harrison, while I, the wildly ambitious spokesperson with the pudding-bowl haircut was probably McCartney. We had to do without a Lennon, as talent was thin on the ground in Bangalore. I think it would have been easier to find a Lenin than a Lennon.

We began to play at the only cool cafe in town, The Three Aces on Mahatma Gandhi Road, and promptly made a name for ourselves as there was no other group around in those days. In the field of one, we were number one.

What we lacked in musical talent we more than made up with shaking our mop tops and by screaming 'Yeah! Yeah! Yeah!', which always brought a banshee of a scream from one or two of the girls in the front row. We played at little parties and events, charging Rs 50 for a twenty-minute programme of five songs. After deducting the taxi fare and ancillary expenses, we came out with Rs 12 per head. It was a meagre amount, but as the saying goes, we were paying our dues. I just prayed we didn't owe too much.

In a pale imitation of John Lennon, I would shout, 'Where are we going boys?' Skinny and Ken would answer back with a modicum of enthusiasm, 'All the way to the top!'

So we practised and played our little gigs and as Bangalore fell under our musical spell, we charted a course towards world domination.

By a stroke of providence or good luck, a gentleman approached us at one of our gigs at Three Aces. He was short, fat and balding but with an attractive and charming demeanour.

'I'm Kishore,' he said, a smile winging its way from ear to ear. 'Would you boys be willing to play at a wedding in Hyderabad?'

'Yeah! Sure,' I said, not knowing what to expect.

'My niece is getting married next month and I just saw you boys.' He still had that engaging smile. 'I think you'll go down terrifically with the crowd.'

Hyderabad was not Bangalore. That was good enough for us.

Step Two was about to happen.

'I'll pay you boys to come and play,' he continued.

This came as a relief. Being the sharp cookie I was, I probably would have settled just for train tickets. Remember, I came from a clan of warriors, not businessmen.

'How much?' I asked, in surprise.

'Four hundred rupees, plus train fares and two nights' stay at the YMCA.'

I looked at the other two Trojans. Like the Three Stooges we shook our heads with a muted grin, unanimous in our decision to go to Hyderabad.

'It's a deal,' I replied, extending a hand.

'Wonderful,' he replied, that smile of his not losing a millimetre of its width. 'I'll organize everything. Call me.' He then wrote out his telephone number on the back of a napkin and gave it to me.

The three of us pumped each other's hands amidst cries of 'Too good ya!' 'Wow, Hyderabad!' and 'Four hundred bucks, can you believe it?'

The first thing we needed to do was check out where the hell Hyderabad was. The second, and probably the most important – was telling our parents. How was my mom going to take it?

We found out that Hyderabad was approximately 700 km from Bangalore – a giant step for the group, let alone mankind. I told my mom about the impending trip and initially she was quite receptive to the idea. We began feverishly working on our songs till they shone like polished silver. Every day we'd meet in my bedroom, practising a dozen songs for the wedding, while Mom made us nimbu pani to keep our voices and throats well lubricated. Skinny and Ken told their parents, who were also au fait with the idea of going to Hyderabad.

Come the day of departure, my suitcase was neatly packed and my guitar rested in its soft canvas case. I shuffled about the house as a confluence of thoughts hurtled through my mind, nervous and tentative, yet determined and resolute. I could subliminally feel my mother's worries and fear. Then she came into my room and I could see she had been crying. Her eyes were just that shade of red from one too many wipes with the end of her sari.

'Play well and come back safe,' she said, as she reached up and kissed me gently on the forehead.

I could not look my mother in the eye. I stood silently looking at the floor. Then I bent down and touched her feet.

'Remember, friends can never replace family, my son,' she said, holding back her tears. 'Friends will disappear like dried-up leaves in a gust of wind. Only the family will be there for you.'

It was quite unlike my mother to talk this way. It was almost as if she had some premonition of my going away forever.

'Yes ma,' I replied, trying to look busy in looping my guitar over my shoulder, and grabbing my small suitcase. There was a momentary silence that lasted a lifetime.

'Come back soon,' she said finally, trying to sound cheerful, as I walked towards the door.

I did not reply. It was better not to say anything than to end with a lie.

5

GO EAST YOUNG MAN!

THE WEDDING BASH IN HYDERABAD WASN'T LAVISH BY INDIAN STANDARDS. Indian wedding ceremonies have a tendency to last longer than some Western marriages. Even so, we played, got paid and then we laid plans to move on. To us Hyderabad was just a station on the way. We could head for Bombay or even Calcutta, that other major city which, I had heard, had a vibrant pop music scene. I also remembered the jockey I had met a few years ago at the Bangalore Race Course.

I looked at the back of my guitar. Jockey Alford's number was still etched on the wood. I picked up the phone and dialed him in Calcutta.

After a few tries:

'Jockey Alford,' I yelled into the phone, trying to be heard above the static. 'It's Biddu.'

One thing you have to understand is that in those days the telephone service was so bad that it was impossible to hear one another unless you bawled at the top of your voice. It always seemed you were arguing or fighting with the person you were in conversation with.

'Who?' the voice yelled back. It sounded distant, faint and echoing.

'Biddu,' I hollered once more. 'You know, the singer from Bangalore who used to work at the race course.'

There was a moment's silence. I thought he was paying his respects to the dead.

'Oh! Biddu,' he bellowed finally. 'Why the bloody hell didn't you say so? How are you, you old bugger?'

'It's Calcutta or bust,' I said to Skinny and Ken after I put the phone down on jockey Alford. Again, a Saturn-like ring of excitement buzzed around our heads. This was the big league we were heading to. 'Let's go, fellas.'

LIKE AN IRON CAGE ON WHEELS THE TRAIN RATTLED ACROSS 1600 km of Indian heartland all the way from Hyderabad to Calcutta on the eastern side of India. It was a journey of forty-one hours, including delays and, if you added the nineteen from Bangalore, we were about to complete a total of sixty hours – long by Western standards but a snip for us Indians. The journey wasn't too bad. Our carriage had two rather attractive Muslim sisters. They said they were princesses and perhaps they were, although I harboured my doubts. Princesses don't travel by train, especially in a second-class carriage. But they were fun to be with, sharing their wonderful home-cooked food and the five of us chatted like old friends the whole way, till we finally arrived at Howrah station.

This Godzilla of a railway station dwarfed anything we guys had ever seen before. When we stepped out of it, we were met by a seething mass of humanity and a crescendo of sound. Car horns blared, rickshaw drivers trilled their bells and people were everywhere. It seemed every spare inch of pavement was occupied by the trample of feet. It was hot, humid, grimy and chaotic. It was also very alive.

We were met by jockey Alford who greeted me like a long-lost buddy and took us to his home, where we were going to stay the night.

'Ma, this is Bidz, Skinny and Ken and they are the Trojans,' he told his mother when we entered his house. He made it sound so matter-of-fact, like we were household names everyone should know. 'They'll be staying with us for a couple of days, till I find them a place.'

It was as simple as that. Three strangers made totally welcome. We could have been fugitives from a mental asylum for all his mother knew.

The three of us shared the spare room and once we had unpacked and had a few minutes to ourselves, I decided to do a money count. Ken had Rs 90 left after the journey, Skinny had Rs 75 and I, with the halo, had Rs 110 to my name. That made up a total of Rs 275 between the three of us. Whichever way one cut it, the sum was derisory. Pitiful really.

'What do we do, Bidz?' Skinny sounded alarmed.

'I don't know,' I answered and frankly I didn't know what to do. 'We're on shit street boys,' I added, resorting to rare crudity.

Later that evening, jockey Alford was taking us into the main part of the city, the part that buzzed with five nightclubs, restaurants and bars, making Calcutta the most exciting, electrifying and pulsating part of prosaic India.

'I'm taking you guys to Trinca's on Park Street,' he said casually.

'What's that?' I asked.

'Only one of the best places in Cal for music and dancing,' he replied with a certain air of nonchalance. 'They don't have a floor show like the others, but they have a great jazz band there. You guys will love it. Be ready in twenty minutes.'

We decided to wear our Beatles outfit; you know, the bleeding Madras jackets, the sprayed-on black trousers so tight you could almost tell which religion we belonged to, and the black Cuban boots. Frankly, we did not have much else in our wardrobe.

We hit the heart of Calcutta, and our eyes popped out like 38DD breasts in a 34B cup: girls everywhere. Miniskirts and high heels for the young and the older woman were in saris and cholis so brief that, had this been Saudi Arabia, they would have been stoned to death. Crazy neon signs displaying Trinca's, Mocambo's, Blue Fox and a host of other eateries and clubs lit up the late evening gloom. It was all too much for us small- town boys.

We got down from the car and walked up the steps of Trinca's as the doorman dutifully opened the door. The rush of cold air from the air conditioning hit us with a welcome relief. We walked in and another cameo of adult life revealed itself. The place was big and crowded with diners. Tables of four, six and eight were scattered around the room, set with flowers and candles on tables encased in glass. There was a sunken dance floor on which couples moved to the music, some embracing while others twirled their partners in a form of cha cha cha or beguine. And just beyond the floor was a slightly raised stage on which a crooner with an hourglass figure and in a figure- hugging dress caressed the microphone while the piano player leaned over his ivories, his eyes closed in concentration as he teased the notes out from the keys. A bass player in dark glasses plucked his double bass, cool as a frozen daiquiri, as a guitarist slinked some smooth chords and the drummer at the back of the stage splayed his brushes on the snare with one hand, while the other hand syncopated a delicate tattoo on the riding cymbal. A saxophonist waited to blow some notes and the crowd away. The room was covered in burgundy-velvet wallpaper and chandeliers hung precariously from the ceiling. It seemed like everyone held a cigarette between his fingers. It was smoky, sexy and hedonistic, like another world, another period. This was Chicago and the year was 1940, and for a few hours the open drains, the wiry rickshawallahs plying their inhuman trade and the squalor of Calcutta did not exist.

While we were struck dumb by this melange of sound and colour, the crowd in the room was eyeing us like we had come in from outer space. Remember, the three of us were dressed like the Beatles, and jockey Alford in his sharply cut suit looked for all the world like an impresario. We were given a table, and the menu to peruse. Suffice it to say, the cheapest dish on the menu was too expensive for us. We finally settled on a Russian salad each, which was Rs 12 a bowl and a nimbu paani to sip on. A week of this high-living and we'd be on the streets with our begging bowls, living the life of sanyasis. All eyes were still on us, and then as if the gods were looking down and admiring our outfits, the owners of the restaurant – a Messrs Joshua and Puri – walked up to our table and asked us if we were an act.

'They're the Trojans,' jockey Alford said, puffing his chest.

'We sing,' I replied, trying to add some detail to the conversation.

'Then, will you boys sing tonight?' Mr Joshua requested of us.

'People are asking about you young men.'

WE WALKED ON STAGE, TO THUNDEROUS APPLAUSE FROM THE HOUSE. Sometimes I think it's best to get the adulation over before they hear you. Ken picked up the guitar, while I asked the drummer to give us a back beat on the snare drum. After a brief introduction by the owner, we went into 'Please Please Me' and 'Love Me Do'. We shook our heads till the dance floor was covered in dandruff and we yelled, 'Yeah, yeah, yeah!' It was a bit amateurish but the crowd loved it. When we went back to our table, the clapping still ringing in our ears, the owners came over once again. This time with a proposition we couldn't refuse.

'We'd love you boys to play at the restaurant every night,' a smiling Mr Joshua said, looking at us boys with all the charm of a maître d'.

As per the offer we boys would get Rs 700 a month, plus one evening meal before the show and our spot would contain three songs, six evenings a week. Without doing the math, we grabbed it. No negotiations, no bargaining or horse-trading. We boys had been rightly seduced by the 'open sesame'-like charm of that door leading into the restaurant.

Later that night we did do the maths and realized that unless we got digs for about Rs 200 a month, we would be on a diet of water and biscuits for the last two weeks of each month. Luckily, we managed to find rooms in a part of Calcutta that had not been discovered by the East India Company. All right, I exaggerate a tad, but it was miles and miles from Trinca's and Park Street.

But we fell in love with Calcutta. It had a sort of vibrancy and spirit that cut through the pollution, dirt and gut-wrenching poverty of a city left behind when the British Raj vacated it for Delhi, the new capital.

SO BEGAN OUR STINT AT TRINCA'S AND IT WOULD LAST six months. We would wake up sometime around noon and head for the restaurant around 6 p.m.; the commute took almost an hour and included a change of buses. Once at the restaurant we would make sure we had our one meal on the house, get changed into our show clothes and be ready for our performance. Our show was usually at 9 p.m. and lasted half-an-hour. The house band had learnt our repertoire so our backing was augmented with some decent sound. The crowds seemed to go for this in a big way. This was new and, in a way, avant-garde. People had heard of the Beatles of course – after all, this was January '1964 – but here in Trinca's they were getting their own cheaper, desi, Indian version. So within a few weeks, word was out about the Trojans and we became minor celebrities. Big fish in this little pond. We just had to make sure we didn't drink the pond dry.

We soon made friends with a whole crowd of people. Jockey Alford popped in to catch our act whenever he was not racing. The five or six nightclubs had bands and cabaret artistes who formed a subterranean and nocturnal way of life, when most sane people were already tucked up in bed. Some of the boys in various bands, plus the three of us, and a bunch of singers like Pam, Betty, and Kitty, plus cabaret artistes like Shirley, Veronica and Lola would meet up around midnight at the club whose floor show ended last. Then a whole phalanx of us would go to an all-nighter called Nizam's for delicious hot kebabs in freshly baked naan. This café was in a poor part of town, where truck drivers, hoodlums and low life hung around, an undercurrent of menace always fanning the air. There must have been a frisson of excitement for those men, as most nights our crowd would turn up to taste the mouth-watering cuisine from the cafe, with the girls in their slinky outfits, their laughter and chatter tinkling like fragile glass, inviting leering stares while some of us guys, still in our stage gear, looked like peacocks on parade.

Skinny had by this time got friendly with Pam, who sang at the Blue Fox. This in itself was not a bad thing, but Skinny was eighteen years old while Pam was closer to thirty-four and, more important, married. I gave the illicit affair all of two weeks. To add toxin to the mix, her husband, an Englishman, worked with a major British company. The job came with a huge house, car and driver. Perhaps the marriage was on the rocks, we never found out, but

Pam's generosity and house became the de facto party pad after our stopover at Nizam's. Every night, about thirty of us would meet at her place, the adrenalin still cruising through our bodies after our cabaret performances and we'd dance to loud rock and jazz, the conversation (always fuelled by whiskey and beer, and, in my case, being a teetotaller, a cola) often louder than the music. During our first year at Trinca's we never got back to our hovel before 6 a.m., when the early morning sun was just beginning to make its benign appearance on Calcutta's consciousness. The streets would not yet be filled with the rowdy cacophony of a city come alive, but just with desperate souls who lived on the pavements doing their rather public morning ablutions as the women stirred their cooking pots, wisps of smoke disappearing into the air. Within this tapestry of life you would find the three of us at a bus stop, waiting for the Number 23 to take us back to our unwelcome apartment. Oh, the glamour of it all!

6

GO WEST YOUNG MAN!

WE HAD BEEN IN CALCUTTA FOR NEARLY FOUR MONTHS and time I was in during this touch with my mom. In fact, I had called her within two weeks of my coming to Calcutta, and apologized, in a matter of speaking, for not telling her I wasn't returning to Bangalore. I wrote to her every two months after that – letters that had a great economy of truth in them, telling her I was fine, everything was hunky-dory and how we had a beautiful apartment to live in. It gave her some peace of mind and she would write back long letters full of love that only a mother could feel and express.

We had settled into a routine of work and play. Skinny was still going out with Pam. They were closer than sardines in a tin, so I gave up trying to work out when this dangerous liaison would end. Ken was more restrained in his choice of a girlfriend, settling for Veronica, a dancer. For my sins I dated a girl called Kim who was a go-go dancer. She was an exceedingly pretty but jealous young woman who cried copious tears and constantly accused me of flirting and looking at other women. Having just reached my nineteenth birthday, this was all a bit too much for me, trying to live under her restraining orders. I could take it no more, so three months after meeting her, Miss Go-Go went-went, while I migrated to less tearful pastures. Fortunately, I met an English girl called Carol, a coltish eighteen-year-old not given to a propensity for tears. Her father had been posted to Calcutta from London, and Carol was trying to pick her way through something of interest to occupy her time in India. She came to Trinca's, saw the Trojans, and the rest, as they say, is pure exaggeration!

I was now beginning to sense the need for fresh pastures and new horizons for the group, lest the daily routine of our show lose its lustre of inimitability and a veneer of staleness begin to creep in. The obvious next move was to Bombay, and fortunately Mr Joshua had a Greek gentleman friend called Jack who owned the Ambassador Hotel at Churchgate. It was in the heart of the metropolis. This Mr Jack wanted us to come over to Bombay and play at the restaurant in his hotel, so we grabbed the opportunity. Once again a deal was worked out and – once more like monkeys – we were playing for peanuts.

WITH FINAL FAREWELLS, BROKEN HEARTS AND PROMISES TO BE BACK, we boarded the train for Bombay, a journey of 2000 km running across the baked plains of India, from the east coast to the west. The journey was three nights long and no bed of roses. We were travelling third class, which was two classes below how God had intended us to travel. It was hot, gruelling and smelly, and to add to our discomfort, the carriage was overcrowded with the jetsam and flotsam of life. Whole families with grannies, children and the ubiquitous crying babies in their mother's arms kept up a continuous wail and nothing would shut the little buggers up.

Add to this Ken and Skinny's mutterings of discontent.

'You should have asked for first-class tickets, or air fares,' Skinny mumbled his grievance.

'Yeah! We woulda got to Bombay in less time. Now look at us?' Ken said, looking around. 'We're bloody shattered.'

'I'm sorry guys,' I said, metaphorically going down on my knees, while throwing in an ounce of sarcasm. 'Maybe we should get Brian Epstein to manage us.'

'Is he available?' Skinny replied without too much bother.

Finally we reached the outskirts of Bombay city and sensed the culmination of our arduous journey. With our life force gradually restored, we disembarked at Victoria Terminus, a building of great architectural magnificence. It was June 1964.

BOMBAY WAS A REAL EYE-OPENER FOR US AND WE GAWPED like little children at the high-rise apartments and buildings that were clustered across south Bombay. It was a city infinitely cleaner and flashier than Calcutta. A never-ending sun browbeat the city as we approached Marine Drive, a scimitar-like sweep of road built for six-lane traffic with uniform buildings lined on one side and the sea on the other, and across the water you noticed the silhouettes of other tall stalagmite-like buildings through the faint haze of pollution. Then as we came towards the end of Marine Drive, we turned left into Churchgate and right there on the left side of the road was the Ambassador Hotel, a small but prestigious four-star establishment.

We were greeted by the owner. Jack was a bear of a man, as wide as he was tall, with a handshake as firm as clamping irons and a voice that rasped like sandpaper.

'Welcome. You play here,' he said in his guttural English, taking us into a little room, plush with velvet curtains and tables for two and four with light-pink tablecloths and lilac walls. It was cosy, it was romantic, it was expensive but it wasn't us. That was the downside. The upside was we were given rooms two buildings away from the hotel. So at least we were staying in the best area, unlike in Calcutta where the building could have done with a long stick of dynamite and a short fuse.

The shows in The Other Room, as the restaurant was called, weren't particularly satisfying. In fact they were slightly demoralizing. We were used to the big, lively crowds of Trinca's where there was an electrifying vibe. Here, it was hard to get a customer and his mistress all jumped up to 'Can't Buy Me Love' and 'I Saw Her Standing There'. The restaurant being small (there were only ten tables), the amplification of the music had to be turned down accordingly. The response was subdued, too. But like true pros we got on with the job.

I met up with Suresh and Ashok, the two boys who used to come to Bangalore for their vacations. They had now majored to wearing long trousers. In fact Suresh lived on Marine Drive, about two hundred metres away from the hotel, so the two of us would hook up regularly. He was just forming a band with some of his school chums, with Ashok as their manager. They called themselves 'The Jets'.

When I told Skinny and Ken about it, they looked at me with amazement. Their first reaction was, 'So they have a manager already?'

'Maybe we should get a manager?' Skinny furthered the thought.

'Sure. I don't mind,' I replied, but minding it all the same. I felt it was a slight on the unpaid job I was doing. 'When we find a guy we know and we can trust, I'm all for it. Don't forget he's going to take 20 per cent for his efforts.'

'Ya, but if he can get us a deal that's 30 per cent better, then he's worth it,' Ken replied pragmatically.

This was the second grumble we had had in three weeks and like most married couples it was about money, or the lack of it. That trustworthy manager we were looking for was elusive, because we never found one and so we had to make do with my inferior bargaining powers.

Mercifully, our spell at the Ambassador was for three months only, and although we enjoyed Bombay and loved going to Juhu to spend our day off at the beach, made new friends and got invited to a few parties, we missed the pulse of Park Street, where we had felt we were at the epicentre of things.

So once again we were back on that train, on the nightmarish ride to Calcutta, but at least the anticipation of getting there kept us going. It was the middle of September 1964 and as the train lumbered into Howrah station, the skies opened up and the rains ganged up on us. The city was caught in a torrential downpour. It was a damp homecoming, not quite the reception we expected.

Trinca's, however, greeted us like long-lost lovers and soon we were in the midst of its welcoming arms, packing the crowds and reliving the habit of going to Nizam's for our kebabs and then onto Pam's house to party.

One night we went to Nizam's in a taxi, and while the taxi engine idled discreetly by the kerb, Skinny got out to order some food. He walked past the paanwallah's tiny kiosk towards the entrance of the restaurant. I noticed a small exchange of words between Skinny and one of the men standing by the kiosk, but nothing to deflect the mood of flippancy in the taxi. Two minutes later he was back with the piping hot kebabs and naans wrapped in last week's papers. He got in next to me in the front of the cab, and as he was about to handover the parcel of food, a huge dagger whizzed through the open car window like an exocet and embedded itself into the backrest of our seat, inches between Skinny and me. Most of the blade was lost in the upholstery itself but the handle that was sticking out with a slight tremor was a good eight inches long. I saw some men at the paanwallah's stall laughing and running their tongues lasciviously across their lips. One spat out the venomous red betel juice which bloodstained the earth near his feet. It was all good fun I'm sure and probably broke up the tedium of their lives, but we failed to see the humour in death by dagger. It was only when they started to move in our direction that I awoke to the very imminent danger.

'Run,' I shouted to the taxi driver. Although what I had meant to scream was, 'Drive!'

Fortunately, the driver held his nerve enough to disregard my error of command and put the taxi into gear, hitting the accelerator at the same time, and we sped away almost as fast as our heartbeats.

'That was a close shave,' I said, stating the obvious when we had gone some distance.

Ken's girlfriend who was the only female in the taxi broke into tears, hyperventilating and clutching her bosom, while Ken consoled her by pulling out a handkerchief from his pocket. Skinny wrenched the knife out and the two of us gave it a cursory examination. The blade was at least ten inches long.

'Did your whole life zoom past you, Bidz?' Skinny asked me, trying to appear nonchalant about the whole frightening episode.

'Not really. Only this bloody dagger. Another inch either way and it would have been net curtains for one of us,' I replied, rather shaken by it all. It could have been the tension of a minute ago, but for some reason we all found that weak stab of humour unduly funny.

'This is for you,' Skinny said to the driver, who accepted the dagger gratefully. In India you never refuse anything that's free.

7

A Musical Divorce: No Alimony

We played at Trinca's for the next three months. The owners had decided that we would play on till Christmas Eve and then, on Christmas Day, go back to the Ambassador in Bombay for the New Year's Eve bash and stay there for three months. The rest was lost in the mists of uncertainty. That was the arrangement the big boys had worked out between themselves. It was quite obvious that slavery was still operating in India at that time.

Skinny was still tight with Pam and did not really want to leave her.

Ken was also quite ambivalent about going all the way back to Bombay. But we needed to remain fresh as a group and something had to be done to quell the risings of a mutiny within. If we stayed on at Trinca's ad infinitum we would become part of the wallpaper, and I got the impression the owners wanted us only in three-month stints, or as an estate agent would declare, on short lets only. New groups were making the scene in Calcutta; in particular, one called 'The Hellion' was almost as good as the Rolling Stones, and had a similar line-up. What those boys lacked in looks and charisma they more than made by sheer musical talent. So I used whatever persuasive powers I had to convince the boys that we had to go to Bombay. We really had no choice.

On Christmas Eve, Trinca's was decorated to the pins with buntings, fairy lights, crackers and balloons festooned all over. The place was raucous and heaving with the expectancy of a great party. And it was. Four hundred people thronged the restaurant and the dance floor was more crowded than the infamous Black Hole of Calcutta.

We got back to our apartment at 5 a.m., bleary-eyed and our adrenalin all spent, to pack and catch the 8:45 a.m. train to Bombay. We made it to the station with minutes to spare. This time, thanks to my great negotiating skills, we were going second class. One day, first class would beckon. We got into the carriage, placed our cases on the top shelf, rolled up towel as pillows, stretched ourselves out on the narrow wooden benches and slept as only young people can, for ten straight hours, dead to the world.

New Year's Eve came and went, as did January and February of 1965, in a monotone of performances that we executed with our eyes closed. The Other Room was not the place for three youngsters to shake their heads and go 'Yeah! Yeah! Yeah!' It was more of a 'Moon River' and 'Fly Me to the Moon' kind of place. There were other areas of concern as well. Although we had the trappings of luxury, we did not have the money to go with it, and in the fifteen months as professionals we hadn't saved a dime. The learning of new songs also became an issue, and Skinny was missing his paramour in Calcutta. In this brew of dissension, arguments became more frequent. Perhaps because of the estrangement, I was spending more time at Suresh's place and with a bunch of new Bombay buddies like Hash and Alwyn.

It was bound to happen. After our three months at the Ambassador, the group broke up with no great fuss or animosity. We had just approached the end of this particular journey. No alimony was involved and it was a painless divorce. The dream had come to an abrupt end and world domination ceased at Churchgate in Bombay.

Skinny went back to Calcutta and Pam, Ken went home to Bangalore, and I went into a small depression. The Trojans were no more.

The hotel was kind enough to allow me to stay at the apartment for another week while I sorted out my life and living conditions. I did not know what to do. One thing was for sure – I could not go back to Bangalore. I had nothing happening in that town on the career front, and though I knew it would keep my mom happy, it was a step back that I just could not take. It was during this period of pessimism that another of life's seminal moments occurred.

I WAS WALKING DOWN CHURCHGATE, HANDS IN MY POCKETS AND a slight hangdog look on my face, when I bumped into a chap who recognized me. I wouldn't say he was a fan, but he knew who I was, as he lived a few buildings away from the Ambassador. He introduced himself to me. Regrettably, his name escapes me after all these years. Anyway, we got talking, and he asked me if I would like to come up for tea and lemon cake. I kid you not. In India, an invitation to tea is not a strange proposition. Well, it certainly wasn't in the 1960s. He wasn't making a pass or anything like that. He probably wanted to hang out with an ex-Trojan! Ha! Ha! Since I had time on my hands and a weakness for cake, I said okay. We went up to his apartment, and he introduced me to his mom, who went into the kitchen to make the tea.

'Do you listen to a lot of music?' he asked, eager as an Easter bunny.

'Not really,' I replied laconically and secretly wished I hadn't bothered to come up.

'I love music,' he rattled on. 'My uncle sent me this album from the States. Have you heard it?' He shoved the record in front of me.

I looked at the cover and asked, by way of conversation, 'Trini Lopez? Who is he?'

'I don't really know. But it's not bad. It's okay,' he said, shaking his head from side to side like a Bharatanatyam dancer. 'Want to listen?' the eager beaver asked.

'Mmm.' I hesitated.

'Come on, let's listen to it, ya,' my keen-as-mustard friend decided, and placed the vinyl on his gramophone.

That was the moment which changed my destiny in Bombay. The music of Trini Lopez was as infectious as dengue fever. Catchy, sing-along stuff. We played the album once, then I asked if I could hear it again. There was something about the music that got me thinking. Not too profound a thought but thinking all the same. I noticed Trini Lopez was a solo singer, just a guitar and a small three-piece band to back him, with a lot of audience participation. I could do something like that, I decided. We played the record again and again.

Over several pieces of lemon cake dipped in numerous cups of tea, I began writing down the lyrics of the songs I wanted to sing and learning the melodies. Songs like 'If I Had a Hammer', 'La Bamba', 'Lemon Tree', 'This Land Is Your Land' and many others. I visited this nameless friend again and within two days I had a repertoire of nine or ten songs. I sat in my little room and rehearsed the songs on my guitar, till they felt as comfortable as a second skin. I had my act. Next I needed a name. I decided to call myself the Lone Trojan, hoping to benefit from a residue of goodwill. Believe me, at that time the name didn't sound so ridiculous. Some people thought my first name was Lone, which was cool in its own way. Finally, I needed a residency at a club or restaurant. I was down to my last eighty rupees, and the nagging stench of penury was within sniffing distance. I had three days left at the apartment rented by the Ambassador, and after that it would be life as a pavement dweller.

I spoke to my friends about it. Hash thought I should try a few of the restaurants near Flora Fountain, a mile down the road. On impulse I went to a hotel called The Astoria, at the end of Churchgate. (Why travel a mile when a few metres will do?) I noticed the hotel had a restaurant called Venice, which faced the road. So I walked into the hotel and asked if the owner was around. He happened to be standing next to the cashier's desk. A clever place to be positioned, if you want to keep your eye on the takings.

'Yes?' he said, looking at me as if I was something the tide had just washed up.

'Sir, I am a singer,' I replied, pandering with overblown courtesy. 'I was wondering if you are looking for a singer for your restaurant.'

'So you sing?' his reply was prescient.

'Yes, sir, I'm a singer,' I replied.

'I see,' he said, nodding his head with Solomon-like gravitas.

Things were moving far too fast for me! I felt I was wasting my time with the man, when suddenly he said, 'Come back later this evening at seven and sing when the band is here. I'll listen to you then.'

It was a start. I could always go to Flora Fountain the next day if this audition didn't work out.

I RETURNED TO THE ASTORIA AT 6:45 P.M.; THE BAND members were already inside Venice getting ready for the evening's performance. Once again, it was a jazz quintet, with a female crooner. I had twenty minutes to rehearse and do two songs to impress the owner before the crowds began to fill the place, usually after about 8:30 p.m.

I rehearsed 'If I Had a Hammer' and 'Lemon Tree' a couple of times with the band. The pianist, Neville, was a jovial chap who followed my guitar chords, while the bassist, a nattily dressed dude called Balsara thumped his voluminous instrument with agile, flying fingers, and the drummer Vinci tattooed a solid groove. The band leader was a saxophonist by the name of Bras, who played with a velvet touch and the fluidity of mercury, while the fifth member, a singer called Sweet Lorraine, stretched her feline body on a chair, to see what this young upstart would deliver. (For the uninitiated, you will notice that, like in Calcutta, almost all the musicians had Christian names. That's because most Indians in clubland were either Anglo-Indians or Goans, with the occasional Hindu thrown in for good measure.)

When we had finished rehearsing, the waiter went across the hallway towards the hotel to call the boss. I did my two numbers for the pleasure of the boss man and the languid Lorraine.

'Okay. When can you start?' he asked without any great ceremony.

Without looking in my diary I knew there was a window of opportunity open every second of every day of my life. 'What about day after tomorrow,' I replied, not wanting to sound too eager.

'Fine,' he replied. Then he took me aside and like conspirators in some Machiavellian plot he whispered that I would get Rs 500 a month, a single room in the hotel and two meals a day – breakfast and dinner. So grateful was I at this cornucopia of goodies being tendered that I didn't bother haggling for a better deal. It was a facsimile of my pride that prevented me from bending down to touch his feet in reverence and gratitude. But Rs 500 for one person with board and lodge was a darn sight better than Rs 700 for three guys. It was a no-brainer. In my mind I was Croesus-rich. I now had a venue to play in. My new incarnation as the Lone Trojan was about to begin. It was April 1965.

8

JAM SESSIONS IN THE TIME OF WAR

I GRADUALLY GOT INTO THE GROOVE OF SINGING SOLO, although the resident band accompanied me and gave some width to the music. But there was no one else on the front line to share my vocals with, and no nervous sideways glances to throw at a compatriot. No arguments after the show, about who fluffed their harmonies or played a duff chord, but also no camaraderie between mates either onstage or off it. I was on my own. It was Bangalore and the Catholic Club all over again. My two Beatles suits lay at the bottom of my suitcase. I still wore my hair long, but now I preferred shirts with ruffles and, sometimes, a waistcoat and hip-hugging trousers: low on talent, maybe, but high on style. I played six nights a week around 9:30, when the place was full and flying. I would come on and do five songs, often throwing a couple of tambourines into the crowd, so they could bang away.

'Clap your hands,' I would shout like a sergeant major, as I launched my rhythm guitar into a flurry of chords, and like a bunch of dutiful cadets, everyone in the audience would clap along. The sound of eighty people clapping and whooping in a room with the band pumping away was adrenalin inducing. It was no big deal but it was probably the first time in India that an audience participated with the singer on stage. Although I was playing to an older crowd, my act was going down well and I was beginning to enjoy Bombay and the freedom of singing on my own. Every night after my show, there would be a bottle of whiskey, gin or rum left outside my door by people who had come to see the act. This was their unique way of saying thanks for a good time. They must have thought I was a real dipsomaniac. It reminded me of this joke:

> 'Do you drink too much?'
> 'Let's just say I wouldn't go into rehab unless they were serving alcohol.'

I would give the booze away to the staff in the hotel.

My friends mushroomed. A new close friend was a guy called Anil, who was a couple of years elder to me. He lived a block away from the Astoria, and his father was an actor and rather well known. His name was I.S. Johar. In fact, he was the only actor at that time to star in English films, like Bhowani Junction and Harry Black and the Tiger. I used to spend a lot of my afternoons hanging out at his place. On Sundays, I would often go to Juhu Beach with Suresh, and a bunch of guys, as Suresh's mom and dad had a beach shack. We'd drive down to Juhu and spend the day swimming in the sea, while his cook made a mountain of food for us hungry mouths.

I WAS ENJOYING MYSELF AND THE MONTHS FLEW BY. THEN, out of the blue in September, the good times came to a sudden and dramatic end. India and Pakistan went to war, and a shutter-like curfew descended on Bombay and other major cities of India. No one was allowed out on the streets after 8 p.m. No street lights or house lights were allowed to be on display after that witching hour, in case enemy aircraft could see the telltale signs of life and the city. Blackout curtains had to be fitted on windows if we had a light on inside. At night the wail of sirens filled the air. It was an eerie, ghostly feeling as searchlights roamed the skies looking for enemy planes. This city of ten million people, which throbbed in the daytime with unbridled chaos and the madness of life, came to an abrupt silence as dusk fell. Nothing moved save for police and army jeeps; no cars, trains or planes. All evening work was suspended. No restaurant, bar or club was allowed to remain open. Business came to a standstill and I was on a sabbatical. No work, but still being paid. The evenings became dull and boring as we could not go out to visit friends or meet people. So I sat alone in my hotel room, with just a small table lamp to illuminate the darkness all around. Remember, there was no television in India and just the one government radio station that was now playing patriotic songs. This went on for over a week.

Can you imagine what was going through the hotel owner's mind, apoplectic at the thought of having to pay while I wasn't playing?

So one day he came to me and said, 'I want you to start playing every morning.'

'Every morning?' I replied incredulously, my tone rising an octave and my eyebrows arched in a crescent.

'Yes. Every morning,' he reiterated. 'I will ask the band to come in at eleven and we will have a morning session. You can sing at noon. Since we cannot open the restaurant at night, you will all play in the day. No problem.'

To him it was simple logic.

'But, sir, who will come in the morning, tell me? We'll be playing and singing to an empty room,' I tried to reason.

'I am sorry, but I am paying good money for nothing. You think money is growing on trees?' he went on about that old chestnut. 'So either you and the band play or I withhold all your wages till this bloody war is over. It's up to you people.'

He had thrown the ball in my court. We had no idea how long this war would last. The Second World War, I remembered, lasted almost seven years. We definitely couldn't wait that long.

I spoke to my friends Hash and Anil about it. 'Can you guys come to the morning show and fill up a table?'

So two days later, the morning sessions began, the band played and I sang to a crowd of seven people. Hash had brought a friend called Kika, while Anil brought along a dude whose name lies forgotten in the archives of my mind. I think Ashok, manager of the Jets, was there. Two passing strangers made up guests number six and seven. Talk about downers. From playing to a crowd of at least eighty to a hundred every night we now played to seven people and four waiters. At least we had hit double figures if you included the staff. So, no cause for complaint. I sang my five songs to rapturous applause that rang only in my head.

Day two was slightly better. A few more friends turned up to cheer me on. They should have worn black armbands; it would have been more appropriate. There were fifteen people in the room. This was progress. By day four it had grown to fifty, a veritable tsunami of a crowd. The owner in a moment of largesse put a board outside the restaurant that read: 'Jam Session Every Morning from 11:00 a.m. Featuring the Lone Trojan.'

BY THE END OF THE WEEK THE PLACE WAS PACKED. Almost a hundred college-going boys and girls began to congregate daily at the Venice jam sessions. It soon became the place to meet and be seen. Over the months the crowds grew larger and larger. Soon there were nearly two hundred people crammed together and huddled over their colas and chips. The more affluent ones would dig into their hamburgers. The modern youngsters in Bombay were going through a renaissance, a revolution in their lives. They were throwing off the yoke of their frustrations. Aware of the freedom afforded to Western kids they read about in magazines and saw in films, they now wanted to ape their counterparts. Hindi film songs had yet to make their omnipresence felt and though the music had a market, these college kids wanted the sound of young America and young Britain, which was reverberating through the major cities of India.

The students would turn up at Venice around 10 a.m. and wait for the doors to open at eleven. They were majoring in their new-found freedom and lived it through the music at Venice, while their unwitting parents thought their children were at college studying for their degrees. Boys met girls at the jam sessions. They dated, fell in love and then broke up. They bunked college to spend time at this watering hole.

THE WAR WITH PAKISTAN ENDED SOON. NO ONE REALLY NOTICED when the end came. We were too busy with the music. The owner of the Astoria decided to keep the jam sessions going, along with the evening performances. If you can get two litres of milk from a cow, why stop at one? I got paid an extra Rs 300 a month and I accepted it without debate. A manager like Ashok of the Jets, who was sharp as a pinprick, would not have settled for less than Rs 1000. Brian Epstein, who was the Einstein of managers, would have asked for even more.

I would come on at 11:30 a.m., and do my five songs to wild cheers and whoops from the students. Gradually, the five songs became four as I chatted to the crowd and joked with them. Till eventually the four songs became three, as the talk usurped the singing. The three songs and chat then became my standard routine and they were often accompanied by the karaoke-like effect of two hundred kids singing along, clapping or banging a tambourine. By now they knew most of the songs by rote. Future film stars were in the audience, budding young entrepreneurs and potential corporate heads had skipped classes to be seen at 'the scene'. I began getting letters from colleges, asking me to stop performing in the mornings, as it was disruptive to the classes. 'What are you saying?' the owner laughed when I told him about the irate letters. 'THEY are studying at the University of Venice. THE professors should be damn bloody grateful the students are bunking classes.'

SO THE SHOWS WENT ON.

In between my shows I began to spend a lot of time with my new friend Anil. You know the one who lived two blocks away and whose father was a top-drawer actor. Anil was a real charming guy with a laid-back sense of humour. I'd often have lunch at his place and I would pump him for information about England in general, and London in particular. He had been there a few years previously, and in my eyes that was enough to put him on a pedestal.

'Tell me all about London,' I would ask.

'What's to tell ya?' he would reply in a cavalier fashion. 'London is London. Babes, shops and Hyde Park. You'll love the babes.'

He flashed a smile that spread slowly like butter on oven-fresh ciabatta.

'There's got to be more than that,' I'd reply, expecting him to tell me the streets were paved with gold, everyone spoke with a plum in their mouth and the Queen drove by Oxford Street every day, waving regally to her subjects. Oh, and the Beatles, the Stones and Cliff Richards hung around coffee bars in London's Denmark Street, eagerly awaiting my arrival.

YOU PROBABLY WANT TO KNOW IF I HAD TAKEN A vow of chastity or celibacy during this period of my career. It's obvious I hadn't spent time in a monastery. Was I so immersed in my sing-along marathons that the fairer sex eluded me? Did no one really excite or tickle my fancy? Erectile dysfunction perhaps? Well I won't deny there were one or two maidens testing my libido and my patience. One, a rather attractive dusky damsel called Sherry, was short on intellect but long on shape. She decided after a month of dating she would like me to meet her mother. So she organized a hairdresser to come to my hotel room and trim my locks a day before the tête-à-tête.

'I don't want Mummy to see you with such long hair,' she cooed like a pigeon. 'I love it, but Mummy's a little old-fashioned, you know.'

I could not believe what she was saying. I was hardcore annoyed. It's one thing her wanting me to dab some cologne or wash behind the ears to meet her mom, but this? Nay, this was a bit much.

'No way, Sherry baby,' I protested.

'Just a few inches off the length, that's all,' Delilah pleaded. A scissor to my hair was like kryptonite to Superman. I knew I'd have to get rid of the dominatrix, beautiful as she was. My infactuation was melting like ice cream on a summer's day.

Soon it would be no blue jeans: 'Mummy frowns upon denim, you know?'

'I'm afraid I can't cut my hair, Sherry. Not for your mom, my mom or anyone,' I said sounding exceptionally determined. 'Quite frankly I'd rather have my willy cut off.'

She looked aghast. I know you, dear reader, might think this rather drastic and extreme. But her wish required a swingeing reply.

On stage, a singer's hair is his crowning glory. No one cares about his penis, except only offstage. And needless to say, lovely Sherry was consigned to my extremely slender book of conquests.

9

TICKET TO NOWHERE

IT WAS TOWARDS THE TAIL END OF 1965 THAT a minor phenomenon began to take shape in Bombay. One or two enterprising college students with a weakness for money, like my buddy Hash, decided to put on shows during the weekends.

A bunch of them would hire a hall that seated, say, a thousand people. Then they would book four or five beat groups plus the Lone Trojan and put together a concert or a beat show, as these sessions came to be known. They would sell out the concert hall at Rs 10 or Rs 15 a ticket, make a brochure or programme with paid advertisements from their friends' fathers who had shops and businesses. The combined sales of ticket and programmes would fetch them close to Rs 100,000. The cost of hiring the hall, payment to the various acts, printing of the brochure plus ancillary expenses would come to approximately Rs 50,000, which left these young entrepreneurs with a tidy profit. Not quite oligarch status, but enough money to flash around for college-going dudes.

So almost every fortnight, a concert would take place somewhere in Bombay, and luckily I got asked to play in quite a few of them. A thousand or more young people in an auditorium, a rumble of heightened excitement as the MC announced each act, his introduction carried by the echo of the cavernous hall. Then the band would appear on stage. The opening crunch of an electric guitar, the sharp roll of a snare, and the low growl of a bass guitar – the youngsters found it irresistible. In many ways, music-wise, Bombay was replicating London with shows like 'A Bit of Liverpool', 'Thunderball' and 'Walk Don't Run'. Now, with my salary from Venice and these additional shows, I was building up a nice little nest egg for that trip to London. The dream was beginning to take shape. It was an open secret that I was dying to go West. It was only a matter of time.

That time came when I was performing at one of those beat shows. A young man approached me backstage and introduced himself. 'My name is Narain,' he said, shaking my hand. 'I'm a travel agent, and I'm a big fan of yours.'

My ears pricked up like a rabbit's. A travel agent and a fan! I ignored his Hitler-like toothbrush moustache and mousey demeanour.

'I hear you want to go abroad? I can help you.' His words were like honey to a bear.

He became my best friend instantly. God, how I wanted to go abroad! Did this guy not know that I had run away so many times that they would want me as technical director on The Great Escape?

'Sit down,' I said, offering him a chair. 'How do we go about it?'

'Getting out of India is very difficult, as you know,' he eyeballed me, in that honest and sincere manner.

I shook my head like a wise old owl and whispered, 'True, true.'

'Unless you have a degree and you've received a job offer from abroad, or you are going to a university on a scholarship, it can be most difficult. It is almost impossible.'

I felt a depression coming on, and it wasn't in the Bay of Bengal.

'But don't worry,' he said, noticing my look of disappointment. 'I'll get you everything you need to go abroad.'

'That's fantastic,' I replied. 'Are you sure?' 'Yah, yah,' he assured me.

'What do you need?' I asked with a degree of excitement. 'First and foremost, I need your birth certificate.'

'Okay,' I replied. 'That's in Bangalore, but I can get it.'

'Then I need all your details, passport pictures, money for the passport, tickets and black money. That's if you want black money. Otherwise if you're happy with the three-pound allowance, forget the black.'

'Three pounds?' I queried disbelievingly.

'Sterling, of course,' he replied matter-of-factly. 'That's the government allowance for a foreign trip.'

'I'll need the black,' I answered.

'No problem,' he replied with a wobble of his head. 'I can get you as much as you want.'

We agreed to meet the following day and take this conversation further. This we did and it was agreed that I'd go to Bangalore and pick up my birth certificate. Once he had the documents and money, it would take him six weeks to get the passport. The plane ticket and black money would follow a few days later.

SMASHING! I NEEDED TO TAKE A BREAK FROM MY SHOWS anyway; doing two shows a day, five days a week, plus the occasional weekend concerts was very demanding and I needed a breather to keep the freshness in my act and keep the public wanting not waning. It was Shakespeare who said, 'Enough, no more, 'tis not so sweet as it was before.' And if I may add my own two cents worth: 'Tis best to go while you'll be missed, don't hang around lest they get miffed.

So I felt it would be a good idea to go to Bangalore and spend some time with my mother and also bring back the documents for acquiring a passport. The trip would help erase some of the guilt I carried regarding my previous departure from home. But it wasn't a totally unselfish gesture, more like a career move. I was given a month off work by my reluctant boss, and another long train journey began.

I was welcomed back home like the prodigal son and made a fuss of by my mom. The bungalow looked smaller than I remembered it. Perhaps I had grown. I also got to spend time with my sister, who was seeing a fellow tennis player. Every day they played for two hours during the hottest part of the afternoon, around two o' clock, at the Bangalore Club. I'm sure all that sun must have affected them, because one day they would get married, and to each other. A real love match. As for my brother, he was still working at a tea estate.

To keep myself occupied I would sometimes go to the Bowring Institute, that old haunt of mine, to spend an hour or two in the huge reading room, where they had several English newspapers. These newspapers were thickly bound, once-a-month editions, carrying, I would imagine, approximately thirty days' worth of news in each edition. I would glean The Daily Sketch and The Mirror for any titbits on the Beatles, the Rolling Stones or even Cliff Richard. I remember reading an article which said the Stones had been arrested for urinating by the wall of a petrol station. It took up yards of newsprint. The Archbishop of Canterbury or London (I forget which) got in the act and condemned these renegades. He thought their public urinating was the ruin of the nation, and the country was in steep moral decline, etc. The Archbishop had obviously never been to India, where urinating and defecating by the roadside was the customary form of ablution for the poor.

I read a small piece about the Walker Brothers, a three-piece vocal group with a lead singer whose voice could soothe an erupting volcano into quiescence. His name was Scott Walker and I was a big fan of his. The piece mentioned that Scott was planning to do some solo recordings. I filed this article in the receptacle of my mind for posterity.

A month is forever when you're a prisoner in your own mind. I was missing the action at Venice, not to say the adulation, and was, once again, caught up in the extravagance of youthful self-obsession. However, I knew I would not see my mother again for a long, long time, so I made it to the end of the month determined to spend precious time with her, till finally another teary farewell beckoned.

She did not want me to go. I was the youngest in the family and, in many ways, her favourite. My leaving was like a piercing of her heart, but she would not stop me. Neither would she mention it. When you truly love somebody set him free, the saying goes. That mantra never had a truer ring than when I was leaving home that day for good.

'Don't forget to write when you get to England,' she begged. 'I'll miss you, son.'

'I promise I'll write, ma,' I told her and it was a promise I would keep for the next twenty years. I would write to her every six weeks, while she would reply immediately giving me all the news on the home front, plus which aunt or uncle had fallen seriously ill or passed away. This last bit of information usually went over my head. Bereavement, I realized, was a topic of conversation in India, just like the weather was to the people in Britain. I finally stopped writing to my mother twenty years later when phone lines improved between London and Bangalore. I preferred the intimacy of talking and hearing her voice.

In the habit of the times, I got on a train back to Bombay and promised myself this would be the last bloody time I would travel by locomotive anywhere in India. I have yet to break that promise. During those two years my derriere had spent more hours sitting on hard wooden benches belonging to the Indian Railways than I care to remember.

Within a day the crowds came back to Venice, tumbling into the room in an avalanche of youthful energy.

'We missed you,' some in the crowd yelled on that first morning.

'I never really went away. I was always with you,' I whispered solemnly into the microphone, sounding dreadfully wise and sagacious.

'Then hit the groove, guruji,' I heard a girl yell as her table broke up in squeals of laughter.

I flashed a smile and hit the opening three chords of C, F and G to 'La Bamba' and we were off. The jam session was in full swing; Vinci the drummer was hitting the skins with added venom, the tambourines in the crowd were being smacked against bottoms with rebellious satisfaction and the noise level upped another twenty decibels. This time it really was like I had never gone away.

THE NEXT MORNING I MET UP WITH NARAIN, THE TRAVEL agent and my new best friend.

'I only need this,' he said, taking the birth certificate. 'These school credentials mean bugger all. You can buy them anywhere. How many do you want?' Laughter erupted from within him.

Then I handed him all the money I had, except for Rs 400, which I thought I might need for emergencies.

'Sixteen thousand rupees,' he said, counting the money with the speed of light.

That's when it was around Rs 14 to the pound. It would take care of the airline ticket, which cost about Rs 6000, and even after expenses for the passport and any palms he may have to grease in getting the document, it would still leave me a decent sum of black money for, say, three months in London. In my mind I assumed I would need two weeks to conquer the music scene; the worst-case scenario was twenty-one days.

We shook hands and while Narain went away to organize my dream, I planned to announce my departure for London, and accordingly made arrangements for my farewell show. I went to see the owner of Venice and had a chat with him.

'I'm going to London,' I told him.

'Why? You don't like it here?' he sounded surprised.

'No sir,' I replied. 'What I mean is I like it here, but it's my dream to go to London.'

'You know it is cold over there.'

I almost sensed a shiver in his voice. He just could not fathom why someone doing rather well in Bombay with its abundance of sunshine and lovely curries would want to go to cold and miserable London. Ambition was too long a word for him to comprehend.

'You know the food is also bloody rotten. You'll come running back,' he added grist to his confused argument.

I smiled, but told him that I would be terminating my shows in four weeks' time.

I was interviewed by the Bombay press and I announced my farewell concert for the last day in September at the Shanmukhananda Hall – a 3000-seater that I thought would be an appropriate venue for a send-off for Mr Lone Trojan. I could not believe I was finally realizing my dream. No dodgy railway stations, hiding behind pillars and girders like an illegal immigrant, trying to make a furtive escape. This time it would be on Air India and for all to see, being attended by an airhostess or purser (my cousin, perhaps) asking me if I would like a tomato juice and peanuts. The excitement was too much to contain. If bliss had a face, I was wearing it.

I FINISHED MY SHOWS AT VENICE AND SUBSEQUENTLY HAD TO move out and into the Airline Hotel for a few days, while awaiting my passport. This hotel was across the road from the Astoria, and moderately priced. Since I was now footing all my bills I decided the cheaper establishment was infinitely more accommodating. Anyway, it was only for a week or two before I made that trip to the airport.

On the day of the concert, I imagined I would be performing for the last time in India. My drummer, Vinci, was, as always, backing me with the power of Thor, the God of Thunder. It was a full house and I went on stage as the final act and spoke about my forthcoming trip to London, how I would miss Bombay and how much I loved everybody. I just missed out saying I was praying for world peace and would work with the poor during my spare time. It was a tad maudlin, so to change the vibe I gave them a final piece of advice.

'Remember one thing, my friends,' I said in that fake esoteric tone I often used when dispensing my homespun philosophy. There was an expectant hush in the auditorium. 'When you borrow money, always borrow from a pessimist. He won't expect it back.'

The crowd roared with laughter, and I smashed into the opening riff of 'If I Had a Hammer'. The show went down a storm and when I took my final bow it was a touching moment. The next time I sang and performed, the safety net of my friends and the warmth of the Bombay crowd would not be there. In fact, my guitar and amplifier would not be there either. Because, in a flagrant display of breathtaking stupidity, I lost both of them in a card game the following day. Let me illuminate you on my folly.

THE DAY AFTER MY LAST CONCERT PERFORMANCE, I WAS ON a liberated high (not on an inebriated high though!). After all, in two weeks' time, I would be flying, literally. It was not uncommon for a few of us musicians and buddies to often have a card game at my friend Allwyn's apartment on Marine Drive. The game we usually played was three cards flush, which is extremely popular in India. The top hand was three of a kind, with three aces as the highest, followed by a run in the same colour called a run and flush; the lowest decent hand was a pair of twos. On this day, I was on a losing streak and down to just a few rupees. Then on one particular deal, one of the guys raised his bid to Rs 100. I didn't have that kind of money on me at that moment. I could either fold or raise him, so I suggested my guitar in lieu of the money. This was accepted. The opponent raised his bid once again, and I tried to bluff him by raising my bid, so I threw in my amplifier as collateral. When we finally did a show of cards he had three kings while I had a pair of tens. He won hands down and this guy who was the manager of a beat group actually took the guitar and amplifier as his winnings. I realized when you look around the table and you can't see a mug, that's because it's you. It was a salutary lesson but I only had myself to blame.

Back in my hotel room, I decided to call Narain. It was exactly six weeks to the day of his promised delivery. I tried his number a few times but got no reply. There was no panic in me, because in India, time is inconsequential. A date is just an approximation and tomorrow can mean any day in the near future. I also tried not to dwell on the loss of my guitar and amplifier, although I was annoyed at my wanton recklessness. I could have sold the equipment to a budding musician for around Rs 400. Ah well! C'est la vie, as the French would say.

Two days later my friend Hash popped round to see me. 'Have you heard from your guy?' he asked.

I knew whom he was talking about.

'No,' I replied. 'I've been calling his office the last couple of days but there's no reply. Do you think he's ill?'

'Could be,' Hash didn't sound too worried by this. 'But if you don't hear from him in two days, we should go round to his office and find out what's the bloody delay.'

THREE DAYS LATER, HASH, ANIL AND I WENT TO SEE the agent. I had tried calling him for the last forty-eight hours but his phone had kept ringing out, with no one answering it. Did he have a secretary? Did he have a partner? I didn't know a dickie bird about the guy and I'd never been to his office either. All I had from him was his calling card. He could be dead from a heart attack for all I knew, or run over by a bus. If he was still alive, the idea was for the three of us to use some muscle and lean on him, if you get my drift. American movies obviously had an exponential influence on our lives.

When we arrived at the office, we found it was closed and the iron grill had been drawn shut and padlocked. This worried me a modicum, but given the simplicity of the times, I didn't think the worst.

'Where is the man from the travel agency?' I asked a lady behind a typewriter in the next office.

She looked up as my eyes darted to the next office as an indication.

'Who? Narain?'

'Yes, Narain, the travel agent,' I said raising my voice, palpably agitated by her slow reaction. My heartbeat was just starting to go into a canter.

'Oh! He has emigrated. He went to Canada two weeks ago,' she replied cheerily, glad to be the bearer of good tidings.

'Are you sure?' I asked incredulously, hoping the woman might have made a mistake.

' Yah, most definitely,' she replied, quite unaware she was the harbinger of my misfortune.

We guys looked at one another in shock. I felt a sinking feeling in the pit of my stomach. My throat went dry and I couldn't speak, stunned into silence by this revelation. I didn't know what to say or do as my mind soared into a thousand caves of doom. Hash and Anil were now speaking to the lady, but I didn't hear what they were saying. I cursed a hundred damnations on that man, but did it matter? The agent had taken my money and done a runner to Canada. He must have thought I was a pessimist and wouldn't want the money back. The joke had come back to taunt me.

I was down to my last Rs 200 and with no guitar or amplifier, that gambling loss now began to haunt me as well. I sat alone in my hotel room and felt the rage build within me, till my anger turned to frustration and the frustration turned to tears and I cried silently. As the tears streamed down, I felt lonely and abandoned, for the first time in my life. I had let my modest achievements lull and cocoon me into a false sense of security, oblivious to the fact that in the real world, anything or anyone could hijack your dreams. For the last year I had been riding on the crest of a wave, and I hadn't considered the possibility that at some time that wave of success would have to crash against the shore. For what he had done to me, the bastard agent deserved to be burned at the stake.

10

More Farewell Shows than Sinatra

I was pulled out from the well of my despair and humiliation by Anil, who suggested I come and stay at his place. It was an offer I could not refuse. His home was infinitely more comfortable than the thought of the pavement or of going back to Bangalore (an option I did not even bother to entertain). Plan A had come crashing to the ground and, once again, like those early escapades during my schooldays, I had no plan B. It was obvious I had to get back to singing and make some money for another ticket to the West. Venice now had a beat group playing the morning jam sessions, so that was out. There were still concerts being held at weekends so this was an avenue I would have to revisit.

Staying with Anil was a big help as my living costs came down to almost zero. His father was an extremely humorous man and we got on like father and stepson. Apart from being a major star, he also wrote an agony column for a movie magazine called Filmfare. He'd be lying there on his bed, working out extremely humorous answers to people's questions and dilemmas. Often Anil and I would join him, plonking ourselves on his bed while he worked out funny one-liners, aiding, abetting and occasionally impeding him.

My buddy Suresh, who had disbanded his group, the Jets, agreed to lend me his guitar and amplifier in a gesture of friendship and benevolence and I set about doing those weekend shows. Most of them were billed as 'The Lone Trojan's Farewell Concert', 'The Ultimate Farewell Concert' or 'Last and Final Show' and 'Definitely the Last and Final Show'. Some people doubted if I would ever leave India. I was like those stores offering 60 per cent discounts with banners that read 'Closing Down Sale … Last and Final Days', and yet year after year, those same shops remain open. In fact, I did more farewell concerts than Frank Sinatra and I thought surely the citizens of Bombay will eventually take up a collection on my behalf just to see the back of me.

Suresh and Ashok decided to join forces with me as a threesome called High Society and we played a run of gigs in the Crystal Room at the iconic Taj Mahal Hotel. Ashok was on drums while Suresh and I handled vocals and guitars. Thus, gradually the money started to filter in and my savings grew towards that eventual flight to London.

THEN ONE DAY, TOWARDS THE END OF NOVEMBER, I WAS performing at a weekend concert when once again, a man came backstage and introduced himself to me.

'My name is Harish and I'm a travel agent,' he said, and before I could tell him to take a long walk off a short pier, he interjected, 'I know what happened to you with a fellow agent, so I want to help you.'

'Help me?' I said angrily. 'How are you going to help me? Are you going to get me my money back?'

'Listen,' he pleaded. 'I can understand your anger and all that. That bugger has given us travel agents a bad name. But I can get you a ticket and passport and get you out of the country. That's the very least I can do.'

'How the hell are you going to do that?' I asked, as the irritation rose in my voice. 'I don't even have a bloody birth certificate.'

'Don't worry,' he replied calmly. 'I will get you a passport. I promise. You just have to trust me.'

Ha! Trust! That most unreliable of friends. I had two choices—either tell him to take a hike or have some faith in the guy and see what he could do.

'I don't have much money,' I said with a modicum of humility.

'Whatever you have, just give me. I will do the rest,' he said reassuringly.

I had about Rs 3000 or approximately £220 (at 1967's exchange rate), which was not enough for all the things necessary for my trip. No black money would be forthcoming for sure. I made sure I had witnesses to see the handover of money to Harish, with a subtle warning that I had other friends who were capable of creating trouble for him.

'Here's my number,' he said, giving me his telephone number on a piece of paper. 'Call me anytime. Give me three weeks. I'll have your passport and passage.' He looked at me with the doleful eyes of a dog. 'Trust me,' he added, walking out into the blinding Bombay sunshine.

AT THIS POINT YOU'RE PROBABLY THINKING THE AUTHOR IS A few bricks short of a full house. He has somehow failed to make the evolutionary shift from chimp to human. How many times is he going to get taken for a ride? How long will he remain a gullible fool? Can he not see a butterfly when it sits on his nose? Well, three weeks later, Harish appeared with a shiny blue-black passport bearing the emblem of the Indian government with the gold embossed words REPUBLIC OF INDIA on the front and my picture and details on the inside pages.

'Here it is as promised,' he said, beaming broadly.

I handled the passport gently, almost nervously, feeling the newness and crispness of its pages with the smell of the printing still vaguely detectable. I wasn't too happy with my photograph, but I couldn't blame Harish for that. There was a page that read 'Countries for which this passport is valid', and a whole host of countries listed below. It was a mini geography lesson. I noticed the one country not on that list was Israel. Anyway, I was finally holding in my hands my get-out-of-jail card. The passport was absolutely genuine or kosher as they say in the country I was not allowed to visit.

'How did you do it?' I asked, delighted, elated and curious. 'It's part of my job,' he answered modestly. 'Here is your ticket.'

He gave me something that did not resemble an airline ticket. 'What is this?' I asked slightly worried.

'It's a ticket to Basra,' he replied.

'Basra? Where's that?' I said mystified and confused, while a worm of a frown formed on my forehead. 'I thought I was going to London.'

'The only way I could get you out of India is to tell the authorities you wanted to go to Mecca on Hajj. The boat goes to Basra.'

Basra, Mecca, Hajj, boat – the words were not common in my lexicon.

'But Harish, I'm not a Muslim. I'm not even circumcised!' I said, getting worried and not without reason. I was seeing my dream slip away once more.

'I know that,' he replied, rolling his eyeballs in exasperation. 'But don't worry, no one will bother you. I guarantee that. The airfare to London is much more than what you gave me. Most of the money went on getting you a passport and P Form (the precursor to visas). This was the only fare available with the rest of the money. The Hajj pilgrimage is partly government-funded. You're lucky to have this, so get to Basra and then make your way onto London. No problem.'

No problem indeed! I didn't know what to say. I now had a passport but I wasn't leaving by the front door; more like the tradesman's exit, going by boat to Basra, which I found out later was a port in a place called Iraq, wherever that was. I paused for a moment trying to gather my thoughts. I could throw a tantrum or I could get real.

'What kind of a boat?' I asked Harish who was beginning to go down in my estimation.

'One of those cargo boats I think. You'll catch it from Ballard Pier. It only takes six days to reach Basra, so relax,' he said reassuringly. 'And here's three pounds for you.'

He handed me the money, which I put in a pouch along with my passport and ticket. I should have been grateful for what the man had done, but somehow the patina of excitement had faded. Anyway,

I thanked him for everything and reconciled myself to the journey by boat.

When I told Anil about it, all he said was, 'Trains, boats, planes, who gives a damn, dammit. Just so long as you get there.'

That made me feel a lot better. I was leaving in ten days' time and Anil also wanted to come to London. So he spoke to his father about it.

'I don't mind you going to London if Biddu is going to be there,' the father told him. Clearly he thought me a responsible young man, who could be depended on to keep an eye on his son.

Later that evening, Anil decided we both should meet up in Beirut. Fortunately, I had heard of Beirut.

'When you get there, call me and I'll fly to Beirut and we can do the London leg together.'

I thought this a capital idea. At least I would be going to London with a friend, and one who had been there before. My spirits started to perk up. The idea of the boat trip now didn't seem that radical or extreme.

The following day we walked down the road to the Moka Coffee Bar a block away from Anil's apartment, and relaxed with a few friends over cold coffee with ice cream. We sat at a covered courtyard surrounded by potted plants while a fan gently plied overhead. At a table nearby was a group of foreigners, boisterous in their chatter. We found out from the waiter they were Greek sailors who had come ashore to stretch their legs. I noticed one of the men had a guitar on his lap. It was an acoustic one and smaller than a regular-size guitar. As often happens in an informal setting, we got into a conversation with them. They wanted to know where and what to visit in Bombay.

'Chor Bazaar,' we replied. 'It's the thieves market, you'll get all kinds of antiques and there's also the Gateway of India.'

We told them where the two places were and they made a note of it.

'Anything else?' they wanted to know.

'Not really,' one of us answered, which brought a juvenile chuckle at our table.

'Can I see your guitar please?' I asked the gentleman whose guitar lay on his lap like a Shih-Tzu.

He passed it to me without saying a word and I strummed a chord. The guitar felt light, its tone mellow and rich.

Will you sell it to me?' I asked.

He laughed and said, 'How much?'

'Not much,' I replied. 'We are a poor country.'

'But many rich people, eh?' he said, shrugging his shoulders and with a voice as embracing as a warm sea.

'Three hundred rupees,' I said as an opener.

'No, crazy,' he replied a few seconds later, doing the currency calculation in his head. 'One thousand rupees minimum.'

We haggled playfully like merchants in a Byzantine era and finally struck a deal. It was Rs 550 and I walked back to the apartment happy with my bargain.

THE WEEK PASSED LIKE THE TURN OF PAGES IN THE breeze, and finally it was the day of my departure. I put in a spare pair of blue jeans, a denim jacket as protection against the cold, a shirt, a second T-shirt, some underwear and socks and toiletries into a rucksack. Past experience had taught me to travel light. I would be wearing a pair of jeans, T-shirt, boots and a cowboy hat. Oh, and the guitar I had bought the previous week from the Greek sailor.

My friends came to wish me goodbye or conceivably to make sure I was leaving.

'Bon voyage,' they shouted, as I climbed into the cab. 'Come back soon.'

'I'll be back in forty years,' I replied, laughing.

'Thank God!' They let out a collective sigh of relief as fake as a Chinese Rembrandt.

As my cab slowly drove away, I turned round for one last time. I saw Anil, Ashok, Hash and Suresh and a couple of other friends waving like worshippers cheering the Pope on his balcony. Then they stopped waving and turned away, immersed in their own lives, and I looked at my watch. It was nearly 4 p.m. I turned towards the driver and nervously told him, 'Ballard Pier, bhai.' My taxi stopped outside the Bombay Port Trust and I walked through its gates amidst the rush of travellers lost in the labyrinth of a different world, in a strange jamboree of life, looking for their respective boats or ships and walking in haste behind coolies carrying their cases. Men unloading containers from trucks, overseers yelling their orders to the workers, officers in uniform walking with an air of purpose and importance, while some workers – perhaps on their break – stood idly near the dockside, chatting and smoking their beedis.

I asked someone the way to Ballard Pier; he pointed his finger and with a tilt of his head gave a mute indication of where it was. When I reached the pier, I saw my boat berthed by the dockside. It was big but not as big as my imagination had made it out to be. On first impression, it was like Noah's Ark, only less modern! There was a walkway of slated steps leading up to it. At the base of the stairs was a dilapidated and paint-weary white table and chair with a uniformed gentleman sitting behind it. He examined my ticket thoroughly, gave me a cursory look and with a nudge of the head ushered me up the walkway. With all the ensuing noise and babble around me, I had made it from the port entrance to the boat without a word being said to me.

I walked up slowly, holding the railings for support, my boots finding their grip on the shaky stairs. I had my guitar slung over my shoulder, my cowboy hat shading me from the evening sun, the ends of my long hair poking through from the nape, and my rucksack firmly in my grip. At the top of the stairs was another officer, once again to check the ticket and probably show me to my cabin and offer me a long cool drink. As I reached the deck, it hit me. My jaw dropped in disbelief.

11

Give Me the Titanic any day

I was greeted by an army in White: almost 400 men draped in white robes and with shaven heads; some had beads in their hands, mouthing silent prayers, parading on the deck like holy warriors awaiting god or his nemesis. They were pilgrims on their way to Hajj. I looked at them, stunned into a momentary silence. The visual was dramatic and surreal, like egg-white stalagmites against an endless blue sky on a bobbing ocean. They, in return, observed me with subtle confusion. A cowboy hat, boots, a guitar and hair like a woman's. What kind of apparition was this? The devil incarnate? I felt as welcome as swine flu.

I walked nervously through the multitude as they peacefully parted to receive this newcomer, and made my way to the sleeping quarters below deck. I thought it best to pick out my cabin and unpack my meagre belongings and set my territory; hang up my guitar and hat on a hook, close the door behind me, kick off my boots and relax. I walked down the stairs and came across a miniature stadium of row upon row of wooden slatted slabs. Most of them had bedrolls unfurled over them. I looked around. There were no cabins in sight. It dawned on me these were my sleeping quarters. It was another jaw-dropping moment.

'Okay,' I thought, 'I can handle this. But first, the bathrooms.'

I must tell you I have a thing about bathrooms. Call it a fetish, but they must be pristine, clean and modern. So I strolled towards the toilet zone and peeked through the swing doors. There were six Indian-style squat-on-your-haunches-type toilets. I shuddered at the sight of these unseemly hole-in-the-ground jobs. I noticed six sinks for washing and shaving. Four hundred of us were to share these facilities. My heart sank into my ankles. I would fight them in the trenches, I would fight them on the shore, but I could not fight them in the rush to an Indian-style kazi.

I sat on a wooden slab for a while, thinking up Plan B. Suddenly I felt a jolt as the boat came to life. I could hear the drone of an engine and the ungainly movement as the vessel lurched forward clumsily and we were on our way. This I could not miss. So I scrambled back up, onto the deck and looked at the city I was leaving behind. It was nearing sunset and against a blood-red sky, the Gateway of India and the Taj Mahal Hotel steadily decreased in size as our boat cut through the frothy dark-emerald waters of the open sea. I stood there clutching my rucksack, that little suitcase full of dreams, till the shoreline disappeared.

GRADUALLY, THE EVENING SUN WENT DOWN AS DARKNESS CLOSED THE door on light. I put my rucksack to a side, gently placed my guitar next to it and sat down. Sleep would not come easy this night. I looked up as a thousand stars put on a show, flickering like fireflies against a black velvet sky and a warm breeze gently followed us. One star in particular was bigger than the others and shone twice as bright. It twinkled and winked at me, making me smile. It was my Eastern Star.

The pilgrims were downstairs, probably resting on their bedrolls and having a right old gossip. I had finally left India behind, as I had always wanted to. Like I always dreamed I would. But fear began to envelop me like the surrounding darkness. Every part of me had wanted to leave, and yet at that moment, a part of me – a tiny, infinitesimal part of me – longed to stay. I hoped the feeling would pass.

As I lay there on the deck, I could hear the water slapping against the sides of the boat, maintaining a hypnotic tempo. Eventually I fell asleep, resting my head on my bag, one hand clutching my guitar, just in case one of the pilgrims should want to steal it!

I AWOKE IN THE DIM LIGHT OF DAWN, TO THE placid rise and fall of the boat, as a veil of mist made the world opaque and mysterious. I stretched my stiffened bones and decided to use the bathroom before the morning sun could announce itself and well before the queues for the washroom began. I went downstairs, to find the lower deck busier than Times Square on New Year's Eve. Obviously, every pilgrim had the same idea about their morning ablutions, especially before prayers. I stood in line, determined to carry diapers the next time. I clenched my buttocks, pinched my nose, held my breath and waited my turn. Thank God for yoga.

Later that morning I made my way to see the captain of this vessel.

'Captain,' I said, showing respect for his uniform if not for the man himself. 'My name is Biddu. I am not a pilgrim but I'm also going to Basra, on my way to London.'

He shook his head gently but without any great response. 'You see, I am a singer and rather well known in India.'

'I see,' he replied, with a smidge of enthusiasm.

'The point is, I'm not used to sleeping on wooden slats and using Indian-style toilets. I hope you understand.'

He looked sympathetically at this moaner and said, 'What to do, sir? This boat is for plying pilgrims and some cargo only. It is not a passenger boat. So sorry.' He seemed to be on the verge of tears while tendering his apology.

'Captain, do you have a spare cabin for me?' I pleaded with some deference. 'I will pay you.' I wanted to use the word 'handsomely', but I did not think three pounds demanded or necessitated the term 'handsomely'.

'I am very sorry, sir,' he apologized. 'But there are only three cabins on this boat. One, I am afraid, is mine, and the other two are occupied.'

FROM HERE ON, THE STORY TAKES A TURN THAT WOULD only come under the heading, 'Believe it or not'. But believe me, dear reader, what happened is true.

'But captain,' I implored passionately, 'you have to help me here. I cannot last another five days using those toilets and sleeping with 400 pilgrims. They are in a state of godliness, while I am in a right state. Last night I slept in the open. I cannot do that every night.'

'What to do?' he reiterated. 'Unless you want to speak to the two brothers who are occupying the other two cabins.'

'No problem,' I answered, sounding like a native.

'They are married to two sisters and each couple is using a cabin. So you see there is a slight problem.'

That did put a damper on things. But I was desperate. There was no other word for it.

'Can I see these two couples?' I asked the captain.

So we toddled off in the direction of the two cabins and the captain knocked on the doors of both of them. A man emerged from each one.

'This young man would like to talk to you both,' the captain announced cryptically.

Then followed this brief conversation.

'Gentlemen,' I said, looking at the two brothers and noticing how similar they were in appearance. 'My name is Biddu, and I am a well-known singer in Bombay.'

They wore a look of curiosity or apathy, depending on the interpretation. Perhaps they were not from Bombay.

'You see,' I began and continued with my rant about not being used to sharing sleeping accommodation with 400 room-mates or using Indian-style toilets.

'I see,' they replied, having heard my diatribe.

'So, if you gentleman and your wives would move into one cabin, your generosity would allow me the use of the other cabin. I shall pay you for the slight inconvenience. I would not normally ask you this favour but I am doing it as a last resort. Please take this.'

I held out two pounds as the carrot.

'We will have to talk to our wives,' one of them said meekly. 'It's up to them. We must get their permission first.'

They did not seem to be unduly bothered by my bizarre request. Ten minutes later they met with me.

'All right,' said one of them, shaking his head and letting slip a hint of a smile. 'Our wives have agreed, but on one condition.' 'What's that?' I enquired. Fearing Indian men as monetary predators, I had held back a pound, in case I had to up the stake.

'You said you are a singer,' one of the men replied self-consciously. 'But please to beg your pardon, we have not heard of you. Our wives are requesting that in return for the cabin you please sing one or two songs for us.'

So, by the time the boat had docked for its brief stop at Karachi, I had acquired a cabin for myself in return for two pounds and an Italian version of 'Hello Dolly' called 'Hola Chica' and a rendition of 'This Land Is Your Land' in the original English.

I COULD NOT BELIEVE HOW KIND AND POLITE THESE PEOPLE had been. It was simply amazing. No further persuasion was required after my initial request. It seemed the most natural thing for them to do, passing up their own privacy and comfort for a total stranger. The cynic in me thought the money may have helped. I thanked them profusely and told them that at any time during the trip if they wanted me to sing for them, all they had to do was ask, and I would gratefully burst into song.

They never made a request during the whole journey.

The cabin had two beds, so I can only assume the couples were having a few risqué nights thanks to a 'well-known singer in Bombay'. As for me, the rest of the voyage was in relative luxury, even though the food was largely inedible and rats jumped ship rather than eat our leftovers. For the most part, I was oblivious to the praying mantis-like drone of the boat and pilgrims in prayer, and five days later we came up the Persian Gulf to its final destination, the seaport of Basra.

12

'Bee-taal' in Basra

THE FIRST IMPRESSION THAT STAMPED ITSELF ON ME WAS the relative peace and quiet of Basra. It may have been considered a bustling port city by Iraqi standards, but compared to Bombay and Calcutta, the place was meditatively calm.

I walked to the main square, admiring the ubiquitous minarets that are such a part of the landscape of the Middle East, clutching my belongings, smiling nervously and fully aware I was the object of people's fascination or derision. Men passed remarks in Arabic, clearly poking harmless fun at my expense. No doubt the strange garb of this man/woman was a talking point. I looked around and noticed a certain greyness of hue. Although the city looked clean and fairly prosperous, there was a dearth of colour in the surroundings. I felt the striking lack of women on the streets – and those present were covered by the burqa – and the colour and vibrancy that they often bring with their clothes and jewellery. Things were more muted, even drab, compared to the brilliance of the street markets back home. The mosaic of colour so evident in Indian life was missing.

But there was an air of pious friendliness in the air and not for a moment did I fear or worry for my safety. To most people at the time, India and places further east had a mystical value; there was a spiritual resonance about Varanasi, Kathmandu and Rangoon while the Middle East was an inexplicable mystery- unknown and largely unexplained.

In the square I noticed the narrow streets leading away from it. I walked under the covered bazaars, as merchants tried to sell their wares. I saw piles of woven silk throws, boxes with inlaid mother-of-pearl, jewellery, brass artefacts and heaps of cheap, rather badly made leather handbags. Some of the stalls sold aromatic herbs and the covered stalls were redolent with the fragrance of spices and attar. The smells from the bakery churned the emptiness in my stomach and reminded me I was famished. As the rays of the sun filtered through the awnings, I could hear the chatter of voices (mostly of women) from the balconies above, their wonderful wooden-fronted facades filled with intricate work. I was walking back in history.

'BEE-TAAL, BEE-TAAL,' A MAN CRIED OUT AS HE BECKONED ME. He wanted me to try some of the street food he was cooking. It was lamb on a spit and what looked like naan bread. He scooped some meat into a roll of bread and gave it to me.

'Akl,' he said through a wisp of a white moustache and beard. (I learnt later that it was the word for food.) His gnarled face was burnt by the sun into a lovely nutmeg-brown.

'Bee-taal,' he continued, grasping my elbow and thrusting the lamb roll at me. I understood his persistence and took it.

'Shokran,' I replied gratefully, thanking him. I was hungry and close to dying of starvation, not having eaten for about six hours, so this food was welcome indeed. The herb-flavoured meat, still moist from the spit, tasted delicious. I ate voraciously, and then offered him the pound I still had in my pocket.

'La-ah! No!' he protested. 'You Bee-taal.'

Perhaps he thought I was one of the Fab Four or he just wanted to show his generosity to someone who looked like a tourist in a city not visited by many.

IN MOST OF US INDIANS, THERE EXISTED AN INNOCENCE ABOUT the outside world, especially the Middle East. It was not in our scope of concern and we had a vague idea where it was on a map. Probably the only country that invited a flicker of recognition was Iran, as the Parsee community fled from its religious persecution and came to India in the eleventh century. Otherwise, it was unknown territory. Jordan was a person's name, not a country. Oil had yet to become the commodity of importance it is today, and the image of the Middle East was one of endless sand and Bedouins on camels. Foolishly, I was not carrying a map on me, so I had no idea where I was headed, neither did I seem particularly worried by this lack of prep. Why change the habit of a lifetime by carrying a map or a compass? The caged bird was free and that's all that mattered.

I had a destination – Beirut. That was good enough. I had a thumb, which would help me hitch a ride to my eventual destination. And I still had that pound.

I SPENT THE EVENING IN THE MAIN SQUARE NEAR A fountain. Towards the far end, I saw a small mosque, men continuously going in or coming out of it. I remember hearing the muezzin calling the worshippers with his prayer to Allah. At sunset the lights from the pastry shops and cafes filled the night sky. I listened to the voices of men (it was always men) sitting on wooden chairs outside these cafes – tiny cups of tea or coffee on the tables along with a bowl of pistachio nuts – smoking hookahs and talking animatedly, some involved in spirited discussions that always ended in boorish laughter.

Then the old man who gave me the lamb roll, or shawarma, saw me and came towards the fountain. He was accompanied by a younger man who I later learnt was his son. Through a pantomime of gestures and one or two English words his son had picked up, they invited me to spend the night at their home. Through a form of sign language and exaggerated gestures of the eyes and mouth, I told them I was quite happy to sleep in the square. They would have none of this. In a wave of arms more dramatic than a Shakespearean actor, the old man insisted I come home with them. So began my journey through the sands of time.

During my whole journey through the Middle East, never once did I go really hungry and very rarely did I have to sleep in the open air. Maybe an angel or deity was looking after me; perhaps it was a period in time when the world was less in turmoil and more at peace with itself, or people just had time for one another. Whatever the reason, the warmth and friendliness of the people carried me through those days. I ate wonderful meals in humble homes of peasants whose generosity exceeded their wealth. Ironically, it was those with the least who offered the most.

THE NEXT DAY, AFTER A FITFUL NIGHT'S SLEEP AND A breakfast of sweetened tea, biscuits and dates, I walked towards the main road near the port. My host told me it was the best place to get a ride. I stood for about half-an-hour near a big sign with Arabic writing on it, sticking my hand out whenever a truck or car passed by. Eventually a truck laden with goods and covered in canvas, slowed down. The driver, who had a loose turban woven round his head, stopped and opened the side door, beaming.

I got in without the fear of being mugged, kidnapped, murdered or any of those modern-day afflictions.

'Beirut?' I asked, hesitantly. He smiled, revealing a row of yellow-brown teeth, and shook his head. That was good enough for me. I piled my rucksack and guitar and we were off. We tried to make conversation for the first ten minutes, but gave up with the futility of two people not knowing a phrase or a handful of words to communicate with. I also wanted my turbaned friend to keep his eye on the road.

So we drove in near silence except for the occasional humming of a melody by my friend, who would then tilt his head, grin and look at me for approval. It was Indian Idol for the 1960s. We kept going for about two-and-a-half hours and came to a checkpoint. I had to show my passport, which was taken away for a couple of minutes. My driver friend had to show his various papers. The formalities hardly took more than ten minutes and we were sent on our way. The landscape was extremely flat, dull even, except for frequent oil installations that dotted the terrain like prehistoric animals. This was all new to me and mildly interesting. The only problem, I realized later in the day, was that we had entered Kuwait, which meant I was going in a southerly direction and away from Beirut. It wasn't a major catastrophe. At least I was on the move even if I was moving the wrong way.

KUWAIT WAS FLAT, DRY AND SANDY, BUT BENEATH THIS PARADISE of sand there was liquid gold; billions and billions of barrels worth of the stuff. Kuwait City, the capital, still in its embryonic stage, was clean, with rows of neat buildings, broad pavements and even broader roads and untold wealth within its grasp, but it was dull and as much fun as doing a postgraduate degree in cognitive behavioural therapy. Once again, I was confounded by the lack of people around. It seemed the world and all its brethren wanted to be born in India and, in particular, in Calcutta, while Kuwait was a great place for sand. Most afternoons, I wandered the city, once again the focus of people's guarded interest. The men wore long ankle-length garments, while the few women I saw wore those all-enveloping black shrouds called abayas.

I NEEDED MONEY AND BADLY, BUT THERE WAS NO POINT me taking out my guitar and trilling a few bars of 'La Bamba' on the street. For all I know, they could have had me beheaded or put away behind bars for creating a public nuisance or murdering a decent song. So in the glare of a thousand suns, I hit upon the idea of selling my blood – a perfect example of blood money. I had never done this before but I had heard stories of people selling their blood for all sorts of purposes. Starvation, I decided, was a good enough reason to do so. Just a pint, mind you, lest I fade into oblivion with no one to write my obituary. So as I walked those sun-baked streets, I found a rather splendid-looking hospital where I went in and sold a pint of my blood for twenty Kuwaiti dinars. This was a mini-fortune when I did a mental conversion of the amount into rupees. I was tempted to have my blood siphoned every day for the next week. If nothing else, I could have afforded the best funeral. Fortunately, wise heads (not mine) at the hospital prevailed.

My body may have been slightly depleted of fluids, but my pockets were jingling for the first time in recent weeks. I was ready to move on.

For reasons beyond my control, I kept heading south. It seems each time I picked a driver to give me a lift he was headed in the opposite direction to where I wanted to go. Whenever I said Beirut, the driver would smile and invite me in. I was also given a free ride on a bus that was filled with villagers and their chickens and goats. The scenery outside was generally bereft of any beauty, an unending expanse of sand. Occasionally, we passed villages of low-built houses and a few dozen people. The smell inside the bus was awful; in the stifling heat, one had to contend with the reek of goats clinging to your clothes and getting under your skin and into your nostrils. Quite often the goats would excrete a handful of black pellets on the floor of the bus and the owner would find this quite hilarious. But even worse than the stench of livestock was the Arabic music of the time. Through a tiny loudspeaker in the bus, you heard this tremble of a wail, a high-pitched violin and some Middle Eastern instrument like an oud being plucked at furiously to produce a discordant melody. This would go on throughout the journey and as a form of torture it rivalled the squeaky sound of fingernails scraping a blackboard or having your teeth pulled out without an anaesthetic.

Hour upon hour I had to endure the monotony of this jarring and unmusical sound, till finally we entered Manama, the capital and largest port city in Bahrain. The bus offloaded its grateful passengers after nearly six-and-a-half hours and approximately 430 km – a journey almost as excruciating as those Calcutta to Bombay train rides.

BAHRAIN WAS A FAIRLY UN-ISLAMIC COUNTRY. MANAMA HAD A SMALL frontier town vibe to it, nothing in it seemed of any consequence and it had no building of any merit. But, for some unfathomable reason, I liked it. Drinking alcohol was allowed and I noticed quite a few foreigners, mainly Americans who were probably working for the oil companies. It was the place I found most appealing, not that I had seen much of the Middle East by then.

I met an Indian gentleman called Srinivasan, who was an accountant for a multinational company and we got chatting. He told me about a place called Dubai which was in the Emirates and how it was being run by Indians. He mentioned a mutual friend of ours, a guy called Tony Jashanmal.

'Tony's family own most of the shops there. You know Sindhis? Sharp as bloody tacks when it comes to business. The Arabs are no match for them. They own half of Dubai.'

I thought it might be a good idea to go see Tony, even though it was taking me further away from Beirut. Srinivasan, or Sri, as I called him, put me up for the two nights I stayed in Manama. He had a one-bedroom apartment, so I slept in the lounge. And no, the thought of offering him my last pound in exchange for the bedroom did not cross my mind.

Sri suggested I take the boat to Dubai as it would be far quicker than a bus journey. To this extent he was decent and kind enough to buy me a ferry ticket.

'It was good to have your company and hear your music,' he said shyly. 'So please accept this as a parting gift of our friendship.' Educated south Indians often spoke with a certain formality which was quite endearing.

He saw me off at Manama port, having given me the address of Tony's department store.

13

A Paradise of sand

As we approached the creek, Dubai's landscape stretched out bleak and arid. For miles and miles I saw nothing but undulating sand dunes and beyond that, for good measure, more sand. Most of the buildings were just two or three storeys high and to my unpractised eye, they looked like unattractive breeze-block affairs. Only the minarets of the mosques rose above the crew-cut tops of the buildings. The place looked like any other Arab outpost, sleepy and mind-numbingly quiet, with no outward sign of the bullishness that was just around the corner. My boots trudged through the deep sand, each step inviting a thimbleful of it that slid into my boots and socks, making walking rather uncomfortable. Through a series of gestured directions and flicks of the head, I eventually found the department store.

'What the heck are you doing here?' Tony asked with a hug. Then pumped my hand furiously and seemed truly surprised and pleased to see me. The last time we had met was at one of my morning jam sessions at Venice in Bombay. There's nothing like an effusive greeting to make one feel at home.

'Srinivasan told me you were here, so I thought I'd take a detour,' I replied, smiling broadly and relieved to meet someone I knew. 'Oh!

By the way, Sri sends his best.'

We spent an hour talking about Bombay, mutual friends and Dubai.

'You know you can't go around in those,' Tony suddenly said, looking at my boots.

'Why? What's wrong with them?'

'You need desert boots, chum,' he replied. 'You'll wear those out in a jiffy. You can't walk in sand with them. Come with me.' A resigned grin on his face, he took me to the shoe department of the store and presented me with what I needed to become one part Lawrence of Arabia.

DUBAI WAS NO LOVE AFFAIR FOR ME. IT WAS A year before the building boom and before the wily rulers decided to make the Emirate a financial and real-estate hub by lowering taxes and increasing tourism. They planned more and more grandiose buildings and towers of vanity with the influx of foreign workers – mainly from India, Pakistan, the Philippines and Korea – who transformed this sandpit into the Fantasyland it is now. However, the treatment of these migrants by the sheikhs has been on par with slavery. The wages are incredibly low; eight men share a room; sanitation is terrible and the workers have absolutely no freedom of movement. Their treatment has been described by Human Rights Watch as '... less than human'. Sad, really, when you think of the immense wealth of the rulers.

I LEFT DUBAI THE NEXT EVENING, AS A BOAT WAS going to Basra. I had no ticket but it did not seem to matter. It may have been the ticket collector's day off. I made sure that when the boat came out of the harbour it turned left towards Iraq. A right turn would have meant it was going to Bombay. The vessel hugged the coastline of Iran and stopped near Khoramshah, probably to pick up passengers. Eventually, after nearly two days of chasing our shadow, we reached Basra. I had gone round in a circle, like a roulette wheel at a casino. I now resolved to continue in a north-westerly direction to Beirut and no messing around. To this end, I managed to find a map of the Middle East in English at the information desk in the port. Yes,

I know, I should have collected this the first time I visited Basra but apart from almost heading back to Bombay, my journey so far had been peaceful and largely uneventful.

With nothing to do in Basra, I went and sat near the fountain by the main square; when you have a lot of free time, people- watching is a good way to pass the hours. It was a warm evening and the sky was dotted with stars, sparking like embers in a flame. I played my guitar sitting there and some of the people around the cafes may have heard the strains of my music rise above the sound of the falling water. A few brave souls came up to me, smiled and spoke in rapid, indecipherable Arabic. I smiled back, shrugged my shoulders and kept playing. They listened intently. Soon, a Coca Cola was given to me, along with some sickly sweet dessert and other edibles. I had not begged, but sung for my supper. I still had a few dinars left from selling my blood in Kuwait, but I was saving them for a rainy day. Towards midnight the square emptied of people. I slept by the fountain, under a feast of stars and a lemon slice of a moon.

In the morning, a truck was going to Baghdad and the driver offered me a lift. But having checked my map I decided to get off at a place called Najaf, little more than 250 km south of the capital, and cadge another ride to Damascus in Syria, from where Beirut was a mere hop, skip and a jump away. As customary practice the driver shared his food with me, and we became best friends till he dropped me off by the roadside as we approached Najaf. I said my thanks, wishing him a safe journey and many sons. I looked around and in the distance, across the hump- backed sand dunes, I saw the minarets of the town of Najaf, seemingly not more than 2 km away.

The land looked harsh and unforgiving. It was austere and dusty and more biblical than where I had just come from. Along a dirt track, an Iraqi farmer with a stick in hand urged his small herd of goats and sheep towards pastures of withered greenery or, perhaps, the market. It was life or death for them, depending on the farmer's whim.

I had waited no more than twenty minutes, when a small open pickup truck, a little bigger than a Land Rover, came hurtling down the road, raising enough dust to cover me with a fine patina of sand. It stopped about thirty metres past me. Inside the truck were two men and sitting in the open back were another two; they looked a mixture of fierce and friendly, affable but daring. They wore black-and-white checked scarves, or kaffiyehs, thrown in a cavalier fashion over their shoulders. All four of them had Clint Eastwood-type facial hair.

One of the men looked out of the front cab and shouted, 'Amreekan!'

I looked anything but American. Although there was a phase in my youth, remember, when I did think I could pass off for Elvis and James Dean. I wore a cautious smile. If they wanted to think I was American, it was cool as far as I was concerned.

They reversed back towards me, smiling broadly, and again, shouted out, 'Amreekan!'

'Yes! American,' I said, my smile more open and friendly than the skies. We all shook hands, like GIs at a reunion.

'Band Aid,' one of the men said, as if smiling for a dental ad, and thumping his chest.

The rest of the men joined him in a cheerful chorus of 'Band Aid', their broken, uneven teeth not holding back their delight.

I had no first-aid kit on me, having only recently come by a map of the Middle East, for heaven's sake.

'Sorry, no Band Aid,' I replied meekly, but it didn't seem to matter to them.

'Damascus?' I asked. 'I want to go to Damascus.' I thought that might bring me better luck than saying Beirut.

They invited me into the back of the pickup and we drove off in the direction of Damascus, which seemed mercifully near. I noticed that the men carried belts with pouches and there were two rifles at the back. They were possibly hunters who had hurt themselves and perhaps needed some first aid. We bumped along the dirt road with fulsome grins and our bodies shaking on the uneven terrain like unsettled jelly.

'Amreekan good, Band Aid bad,' they said, laughing their heads off.

I realized humour changes with the culture and geography of the world. They probably wouldn't find the one about the rabbi, the priest and the call girl funny either.

WE DROVE FOR AN HOUR-AND-A-HALF AND THE OVERRIDING IMPRESSION THAT still stays with me was the plethora of mosques and towers of worship we saw in the distance as we passed small villages of little or no consequence. The sting of sand hurt my uncovered face and my throat felt parched and dry, making it difficult to swallow. We followed the signs for a town called Karbala, and headed down a mud road for a few kilometres towards a hamlet of huts. We passed through an alleyway, narrowly missing a few men by the proverbial coat of paint. Everyone found this wildly hilarious, including the near victims of this atrocious driving.

We came to a stop in front of a white house built of mud, cement and timber beams. The men got down from the pickup and I followed them past the walled courtyard and into the house. As we entered, the men barked some endearments and I noticed two women scuttle from the front room into the interior of the house, almost as if Satan himself had shown up.

TWO HOURS LATER, A WONDERFUL SPREAD OF LAMB, BREAD, RICE and vegetables appeared on a huge salver. We sat on rugs laid over a carpet and ate like pigs from the central dish, washing the meal down with mint tea. The men kept up a non-stop banter, often looking at me and smiling. The women did not eat with us, which was a shame, as I would have preferred female company for a change. Was it too much to ask? I think so.

Three of us slept in the room we ate in. The rugs and carpet provided enough softness and the cushions were good substitutes for pillows. I had taken a much needed bath, with water from a bucket and using a jug to rain the water over me, and slept in fits and starts, as the other two men snored and let out a symphony of wind at intervals. But heck, I was with a bunch of machos and this is how they did it.

The men were going to Samariyah to attend a family wedding. I checked my map and could not find it. But I was told through an assortment of gestures it was after Ar Ramadi, which I spotted. So it was decided I would get off at Ar Ramadi and head west towards Damascus. The next afternoon, around 5 p.m., when the sun had lost its severity, we once again boarded the pickup and left. During my twenty-four hours in that house, I managed to catch only three quick glimpses of the two women. They were not in burqa, but their heads were covered with a shawl that they often pulled across their face. Perhaps it was done because a stranger was in their midst. What a life, I thought to myself, but I wasn't about to argue women's rights with my hosts.

We drove hugging the Euphrates River on our right. I kept peering at the map to make sure we weren't heading for Basra. We soon arrived at the small town of Ar Ramadi and my rowdy companions took me to the bus station in the centre. They instructed me in Arabic on how to get to Damascus, which bus I should take, where I should change – all of which made no sense to me – and as they were leaving, one of the men gave me a five-dinar note to cover the fare. I tried to refuse, my pride going ahead of my needs. But the man was as determined that I should take the money. Not wanting him to lose face in front of his crew, I took it. Once again I had been bailed out by people's kindness. I thanked them, they hugged me and, like in the Wild West, they rode into the sunset on their snorting pickup.

'Why you friend with them?' a man asked me when my cowboys had disappeared. I turned round to see this dapper, educated-looking man. He was dressed in a jacket, shirt and tie - quite inappropriate for the place we were in. In fact he stood out as much as I did. Perhaps he was a doctor or professor; I assumed this because of his clothes and tenuous grasp of English, a tiddler of a tongue in a sea of Arabic.

'They are not my friends, but they have been very kind to me,' I replied, rather annoyed by this man's intrusive manner.

'They terrible people. Bad people,' he went on heatedly. 'They kill fellow brother Muslim. You understand. They are bandits, they not good Muslims.' (He mentioned the word Shia, but try as I might, I cannot remember the full extent of that reference.)

'Listen,' I said resignedly, 'they offered me a lift, and they did not kill anyone while I was with them.'

'You lucky they no kill you. They bandits. God is great,' he said.

'Inshaallah,' I said, going all native.

'Hameed,' he said, offering a smart handshake by way of introduction. 'Where you going, my friend?'

'I'm on a pilgrimage,' I replied tartly.

'Oh!' His eyes lit up. 'Pilgrimage? Very, very good. Where?'

'London.' I admit there was certain haughtiness in my tone. 'You not find god there,' he said with a shake of his head.

I wanted to tell him I wasn't looking for god, but kept the thought to myself.

WHILE WAITING FOR THE BUS MY WELL-DRESSED FRIEND TOLD ME the best route to Damascus was via Ar Rutbah as it had less stops. He himself was going to Damascus on business, so for once I had a fellow traveller with whom I could communicate. We had to wait for two hours as the bus was not leaving till 9:15 p.m.

The long journey was made marginally pleasant by the fact I had Hameed as a companion. He was forty-nine years old, but looked older and was in the business of printing religious books, holy scriptures, the Koran and suchlike. He told me his life story, which took an hour in the telling, but he had a captive audience and he knew it. The man had a devoted wife and Allah had blessed him with three dutiful and loving children, two girls and a boy. One of the girls was getting married in September. It would be a simple affair and I should come for the wedding, he insisted.

I told him I was a well-known singer in Bombay and let it go at that, because the subtle strains of his snoring drifted across to me. I, too, fell asleep as the pervading darkness outside the bus and the soft, violet lighting inside had a soporific effect on all the passengers, and soon, a collective snore filled the vehicle.

Eight-and-a-half hours later, we had made it to Damascus. It was close to 6 a.m. and the truculent light of dawn took over from the coal-black of night. We arrived at the terminal and already, that part of the city was bustling and alive. We saw buses coming and going; people were everywhere in the terminal cafe, some lying on the floor, resting, while waiting for their bus to arrive. One or two cafes were already open. After all, Damascus was a capital city.

I had slept for about five hours on the ride and done some thinking during the rest of the time. I thought about my mother and what she might be doing. I knew she would be worrying about me, but I did not want to dwell on that for too long so I let my mind drift to London. I was inching towards my Mecca. I thought about my friends back in Bombay, and about Skinny, my partner in the Trojans. Was he still with the singer Pam or had they broken up? Finally, I thought about the four men in the pickup who had been benevolent to me with food, shelter and the five dinars. Did they mean bandits and not Band Aid, I wondered. Had I misheard them, pronunciation and delivery not being their forte? They did have rifles, I remembered, when I hopped on at the back. If indeed they were bandits, as Hameed had accused them of being, I had indeed been lucky, although what could they have possibly done or wanted with me? Nevertheless, for a brief moment an icy shiver ran down my spine.

14

THE BOY WITH GOLD IN HIS HAIR

I GOT DOWN FROM THE BUS FEELING MORE TIRED THAN when I had started the journey; Hameed, though, seemed galvanized by his sleep.

'First, my friend, we wash, then I go pray, only then we eating. All right?'

It was more a command than a request.

'Fine,' I retorted. Hameed had been to Damascus many times, so who was I to argue.

He led me in the direction of an underground public wash and toilet facility. We surfaced from there twenty minutes later. I was feeling a lot perkier with the splash of cold water on my face. Hameed led me along the narrow streets of Old Damascus, its archways, hidden souks, restaurants and the ubiquitous bakeries that seemed to proliferate in all the Arab countries I had visited.

'Here the money is Syrian pound,' Hameed informed me. 'We can find money changer or use dinars, no problem.'

That really surprised me. Hands up, those who knew the currency in Syria was Syrian pound.

'Sit here, my friend,' he said, as we came to a pavement cafe. 'I must give my thanks. Fifteen minutes, I am being back.' And he dashed off in the direction of another street, which I gathered housed one of the 300 mosques that the city had.

I sat at the table, placing my rucksack and guitar on one of the chairs, and wondered if indeed he would come back. A waiter finally approached me for my order. My hands rumpled into my pockets. I could feel the shape of the various coins. With the subtlety of a magician I worked out I had at least four or five dinars.

'Coffee, bread and cheese,' I said, with the confidence of a wealthy traveller.

Ten minutes later he brought me some piping-hot bread, soft white cheese and Turkish coffee which I had never tasted before. I did not think I would like it, but was too nervous to send it back, lest it should offend him. Already I was picking up traits of the British.

I sat there, in the luxury of my breakfast, the morning sun beginning to warm things up; by mid-afternoon, the sun would rise to a point of dry discomfort. Ten minutes later, Hameed materialized from a warren of streets.

'Did you pray for me?' I asked in a jocular tone.

'For you and the world,' was Hameed's equally light-hearted response.

'Then I am saved,' I said, heaving an exaggerated sigh of relief.

Hameed also ordered some coffee and food and while we ate, traffic passed a few feet from us. Cars and lorries in equal numbers, the fumes from their exhausts adding to the flavour of my coffee. People walked deftly, sidestepping to avoid one another and the traffic. I saw women, many with their heads uncovered, buying oranges, cherries and watermelons from the fruit stall. I was told they were Syrian Christians. From one of the shops, a radio could be heard playing that familiar yet distinctive vocal refrain in praise of Allah, which filled the atmosphere; the whole place had an idiosyncratic Middle Eastern buzz.

'I must take you for see the Grand Mosque, my friend,' Hameed said between sips of his coffee. 'You know is biggest in the world. More bigger than in Saudi.'

'Sure,' I replied, quite happy to take in some culture.

As we chatted, a man came by our table and spoke to Hameed in

Arabic. He had dark piercing eyes with bushy eyebrows and a beard of some length. He wore an open grey cloak that hid his undergarments and had a turban on his head. He carried an old and battered leather bag across one shoulder. His face was lined and those lines contained his history.

'He is ask about you,' Hameed said looking away from the man and towards me.

'I see,' I replied, my curiosity not totally aroused.

'He is finding you of great interest and would like to read your future, he say.'

'Why not?' I said, sticking my hand out. 'He is read the Turkish coffee.'

The man pulled up a chair and sat down. Then he took my cup of finished coffee and looked at the dregs. He studied the pattern of the residue for a moment, mumbled to himself and twirled the cup round on its axis; then he spoke to Hameed at intervals.

'What's he saying? What does he see?' I badgered.

'He is seeing you for great future. Happy marriage and have many children, mostly sons.'

My enthusiasm diminished acutely. I had heard better stuff in Bangalore.

'You have job in England, Amreeka. He see much money. God's is showering blessing. You are boy with gold in your hair. People is liking you.'

'Fabulous,' I said not wanting to be a spoilsport. The man said a few things about my health, and asked me to remain pure in thought and to listen to my inner voice. He told me I would be a leader but stopped short of telling me that one day I would rule the world.

Frankly this was all ho-hum stuff and I'd heard variants of it on the streets of India; it was a harmless diversion and nothing more, although Hameed took it fairly seriously.

When I first see you, my friend, I also think you is special,' he said, turning soothsayer.

Surely, anyone dressed the way I was would look special in a land where men wore ankle-length robes and women dressed in ill-fitting tents!

The two men spoke in Arabic for a few minutes and then the stranger got up; as he was about to leave, I took out one dinar to give him. That was undoubtedly his game plan anyway: tourists, read coffee or tea leaves, make a few bob. QED.

'He say no,' Hameed replied for the man. 'He not want money.'

He bowed graciously, wished us farewell with a steely look and then said something to Hameed before walking away to find another sucker.

'He say you boy with gold in your hair.'

I wanted to find out about the bus to Beirut. Hameed had business to attend to so after an hour, we parted company. I was sorry to see him go. In many ways he was like an elderly uncle, a security blanket for me in Damascus. He gave me the address of a youth hostel in case I needed to stay the night.

'You come for daughter wedding, my friend,' he said as he left.

'I'll be there,' I replied. But we both knew it was only a pleasantry exchanged, one which would not be fulfilled.

I walked around the old part of town, looking at the mosques that seemed to crop up everywhere. Some of them were quite magnificent, with their onion-shaped domes and minarets; the floors of the main prayer halls were often covered in a fine mosaic of turquoise, mother-of-pearl or ceramic stones.

I did not have a camera, so I drank in the sight of these places of worship, swirled them in my head and hoped my memory would preserve them for posterity. I also noticed something I had not seen in the other Arab countries – beggars, who stood outside the places of worship, asking for alms, or baksheesh. It was not half as bad as in India, but the sudden visual reminder was unsettling.

I MADE MY WAY TO THE BUS STATION AROUND 11 a.m. and found there were frequent buses to Beirut, almost two or three a day. Also, taxis plied the route with a group of passengers. The bus fare was incredibly cheap, at around one Kuwaiti dinar for a journey of nearly 150 km. I bought myself a ticket for the bus leaving at two that afternoon. I still had about three dinars left, so I had a lunch of chicken shawarma, watermelon juice and ice cream, also at a ridiculous price. If things got any cheaper, my money would last into the next century. I was beginning to like Syria. It was my kinda price.

THE BUS RIDE WAS A THREE-HOUR, BONE-SHAKING JOURNEY ALONG WINDING roads badly in need of repair and then over stretches where the road ran straight as a plumb line. In the far distance, I remember seeing a mountain range, its snow-capped peaks glistening in the blazing afternoon sun. I knew we were now in Lebanon. As the bus drove through the outskirts of Beirut I peered out of the window. The roads were tree-lined and I realized I had hardly seen any trees in the cities I had visited so far. We came to a part of the town where there was an evidence of wealth. The bus came to a halt on this road, and some of the passengers alighted. So, like sheep that follow their shepherd, I got off as well. I looked at the relative prosperity all around. This area they told me was called the Hamra and it was the Oxford Street of Beirut.

I felt a certain lightness of being, standing by the bus stop. I had reached Beirut, the halfway point of my journey, without an ounce of difficulty. Money proved largely inconsequential because kindness had been my constant companion since I had left Ballard Pier in Bombay. Was I blessed or just a lucky fellow?

I walked along the Hamra, my rucksack and guitar providing a ballast in each hand. I was fascinated by the shops and the people, who almost to a man wore Western clothes. Shopkeepers urged me to come inside and buy their wares and I declined with a half-smile. For the first time, I heard Western music coming out of a music store. I stood outside on the pavement, listening to the song being played inside. The tune made the hair on my hand stand on end and I loved it. It was a group called the Four Tops and the song was 'Reach Out I'll be There'. The record was frighteningly good, the singing superb and I listened in awe like a kid mesmerized by the sight of Father Christmas. One listen only, but the song would have a generous influence on my career. It was the first time I had heard soul or black music or, for that matter, a black singer. In the words of another song, it 'Really Got a Hold on Me'.

I WALKED ALONG SOME MORE AND CAME TO A RESTAURANT that looked more fine-dine than an average eatery. It was not yet open for the evening, but two waiters in black waistcoats were laying the tables. I walked in and asked for the owner. A minute later, a dapper gentleman with a pencil-thin moustache came out from one of the back rooms and gave me a quizzical look.

'Hello,' he said, sizing me up and with enough of a smile so as not too appear rude. 'What can I do for you?'

'I am a singer,' I said with the cockiness of a choirboy. 'I was wondering if you were looking for someone to entertain your customers.'

'No. We don't have singers. It is not such a place,' he said curtly.

'Thank you for your time, sir,' I said and turned round to leave and hide my disappointment. I walked past the patio and towards the pavement, when he called out.

'Wait,' he said, quite unexpectedly.

I caught my breath in anticipation and turned to face him.

'Maybe...' he paused, 'you can sing going around the tables. I will not pay you, but you will get tips if you are good. Otherwise...' He shrugged his shoulders.

'Thank you,' I said, clutching at the straw.

'Do you know any slow, romantic songs? Most of my customers are men who come here, but not with their wives,' he said, with the slow, rancid smile of a snake-oil salesmen.

'I know quite a few love songs,' I replied. 'Like "Besame Mucho", "Granada", "Cuando Calienta El Sol", "Al Di Là" and a few others.'

'Very good. Very, very good. Are you Latin?" The owner seemed impressed.

'Brazilian. On my father's side,' I lied nonchalantly. Apart from Argentina, it was probably the only country I'd heard of in Latin America.

IN MY DEFENCE, THERE ARE TIMES WHEN A LIE IS as important as the truth. I needed that unpaid job, because I would make it pay and get me out of my financial plight. But my premonition told me that if I said I was Indian, he would lose interest unless he was looking for an accountant.

'Do you know any songs in French?'

'I know an English song with Paris in the title,' I replied. 'What's your name?' he asked, almost as an afterthought.

'Rafael,' I replied, with another sugar-coated fib. I was becoming quite an expert at the art of being economical with the truth.

All right, I'll admit it was a blatant lie.

15

A Bard in Beirut

So, like Superman and Clark Kent, and Batman and Bruce Wayne, my alter ego Rafael began work as a troubadour at Chez Pasha, the cosy little restaurant on the Hamra, walking between tables, strumming my acoustic guitar and warbling 'Cuando Calienta El Sol Acqui En La Playa…' to elderly men with their far younger 'wives'. I'd roam towards a table where I felt some reciprocity from the couple, look into the woman's eyes (but also catch her partner's attention on occasion to maintain the equilibrium), and sing those Spanish ballads with a pronounced accent that was certainly all Greek to me. The gentleman would tip me, either out of embarrassment or to impress his lady.

On my third day, I decided to call my friend Anil in Bombay. We spoke briefly, as phone calls were not as cheap as they are nowadays; in the 1960s, they were downright exorbitant. I told him I was staying at the YMCA in Beirut and the name of the restaurant I was working at. He said he'd be flying over in three weeks' time and get in touch with me.

In those three weeks I was averaging about twenty-five Lebanese pounds a day in tips. I think that worked out roughly to about £10 to £12, which was quite a princely amount for the time and certainly enough to justify the lying. I lived fairly frugally as the money saved would go towards my ticket to the UK. Quite often, I'd go to the beach at Gemayzeh and watch the rich, young Lebanese kids having fun. There was a greater openness and less orthodoxy among the people here than in the region I had just come from. No wonder they sometimes called Beirut the Paris of the east.

A month later Anil arrived and found me at the YMCA. It was great to see his familiar face again and for the first few minutes, a Niagara of words rushed out of us as we swapped stories and fell over each other's utterances in our attempts to talk about the last seven weeks.

'So how's Bombay?' I asked excitedly.

'Same as it ever was. Except the morning jam sessions were stopped last week.'

'How come?'

'I think the group they hired wasn't pulling in the crowds. Maybe everyone went back to college. Who knows, yaar?' he said dismissively, with a shrug. 'Anyway, I better go downstairs and see if they have a room for me.'

'You can share my room,' I told him. 'It will save us some money.'

'Don't worry,' he said in that laid-back style of his. 'I'm loaded.'

'What do you mean you're loaded?' I asked, more out of curiosity than meaning to probe.

'I've come out with a coupla grand.' 'Rupees?'

'No. Pounds.'

'How did you get that?' I asked, this time more probing and less curious.

A smile of guilt passed over his lips. 'Dad's safe,' he replied cryptically.

'Oh, shit! Anil!' I exclaimed, more surprised than Caesar must have been when the dagger entered his back. I knew his dad had acted in quite a few English films, so he must have been paid in sterling, which he probably kept in the safe.

'Do you think he's found out by now?' I asked, truly concerned and worried, while Anil looked as nonchalant as ever. His father had let Anil go west only because I was going. I felt the unsubtle hand of guilt on my shoulder.

'Relax, yaar,' was all he said as he unpacked his suitcase and as far as he was concerned, the matter was closed for further discussion. Ten minutes later even I had forgotten it. We were too caught up in the web of our lives and too engrossed in ourselves to dwell on matters that could defile our scruples and principles.

SO ANIL AND I SHARED THE ROOM, WHICH, FORTUNATELY, HAD twin beds anyway. In the daytime we would quite often go to the seafront to have a cola or look at the shops, or go watch a movie and kill time till the evening came, when Chez Pasha called.

'If you ever pop round to the restaurant, remember, I'm Rafael,' I reminded him.

'Okay Raf, I understand,' he said, laughing. He had sussed out the reason for the change of name.

'We should get our tickets to Paris, not London,' Anil reckoned. 'From there we'll go by train to Calais and then by boat to Dover.'

He felt immigration was less stringent there than at Heathrow.

'Okay,' I replied, bemused by it all. 'I can't wait to get on that plane.'

'I hate flying,' he said with a twitch of his lips. 'Packed like sardines in a tin. It's hell.'

A week later, we had our Air France tickets to Paris. The ticket took care of all my savings, but as I worked another week, I had managed to save almost 100 Lebanese pounds by the time we boarded that plane to France. It was, incidentally, my first time on an aeroplane.

As our plane took off and we climbed through the clouds, I looked out of my window at the land below. Little did I know that never again would I experience the Middle East as a place so full of welcoming people, their innate hospitality and their innocence. Soon the world would be a more intolerant place and religion would rear its ugly head and man would fight against fellow man like beast against beast.

I left Beirut at the end of April 1967 and five weeks later, on 5 June, the Six Day War began between the Arab countries and Israel. It would forever change the geopolitics of the region.

But on that plane to Paris, the thought of war did not cross my mind. I was at peace. I gently pressed the button on my hand rest and my seat gradually reclined. Soon an airhostess would be traipsing down the aisle, bringing drinks and peanuts before lunch. If this was hell, I wanted no part of heaven.

16

Channel or Chanel: The Importance of a Consonant

If Beirut was the gateway to the West, surely Paris was the region's boudoir, with its air of decadence, its monuments and its triumphal arches. The city had been largely untouched by the bombings during the German invasion in the Second World War. Though occupied by Hitler's army on 14 June 1940, it had managed to retain its majestic buildings and opulent facades because of the armistice that was signed at Compiègne six days after the occupation. The story – or myth – goes that when the Allied army was about to retake France in December 1944, Hitler ordered dynamite to be placed under bridges, government buildings and at other strategic parts of the city. He vowed that if Paris was going to be retaken it should only be a skeleton of its former magnificence. But apparently, the commandant who was put in charge of Paris had fallen in love with the city and when the Germans had to leave it, he disobeyed orders and refused to allow the place to be blown up, and so Paris's timeless beauty has remained untouched.

We stayed in Paris for just three days, in a small two-star hotel, a room in the attic and a breakfast of a croissant and coffee. But because my focus was on London, I failed to appreciate the finer points of the city. The cafe society, the wide open boulevards that spread out fan-like from a fountain square and, of course, the places the tourists flocked to Paris for – iconic structures like the Eiffel Tower, the Louvre and Champs Élysées. In my naïvety I did not grasp the romance or history of the place. The other big problem was the language. The natives did not speak English. How dare they not? And my idea of Gallic speech was to imitate the shrug of the shoulders when trying to employ a conversation. I found pronunciation of French words horrendously difficult; when I asked passers-by where the 'Champ Elsie' was, I got blank stares in return!

Hermès, Dior and Yves St Laurent were names we in India had never heard of. Back home we had our clothes stitched by the local tailor, our shoes mended by the cobbler round the corner. These brand names meant absolutely nothing to me and I would not have known how to even enunciate haute couture or décolletage, let alone know what they meant. The English Channel yes; Chanel no. So Paris was just a station on the way, although I remember Anil and I walking along the embankment of the Seine one lazy afternoon and marvelling how wonderful and clean the city was with its uniform granite buildings lining either side of the river and boats ferrying tourists along the serene waterway. But like savages unused to the touch of silk or the bouquet of a fine Merlot, we were ready to bid adieu to Paris and head for the Port of Calais.

WE WENT BY COACH FROM PARIS, PASSING COUNTRYSIDE RICH IN farmland and agriculture. We sped by medieval-looking market towns, soft rolling hills and rugged chateaux, which occasionally lifted the scenery. Finally, we reached the town of Calais and weaved through its streets till we arrived at the port and saw a cast of boats and ships bound for different parts of Europe. One of them would take us to Dover, the beachhead of our landing. I won't deny a sense of apprehension and nerves as we clambered up the stairs of our boat. Customs and immigration checks would take place during the journey and I could feel the papillon flying around in my stomach.

There was a queue in one section of the vessel where immigration officials were sifting through the passports and allowing some of the passengers entry into the United Kingdom. There is something frightening or alarming about a man in uniform behind a desk, especially if that man holds in his hand the stamp to your destiny. Anil had been to see him and was given clearance to enter the country. When it was my turn, the officer – who had the look of a walrus – thumbed through the pages of my passport and noticed the numerous entries of the countries I had visited.

'Why are you here?' he asked, unsmiling and with a sense of built-in authority.

'I'm here on vacation,' I answered, with a choke at my Adam's apple, yet trying to give off an air of composure.

'Mmm…' He looked at my passport once again as if the answer lay in those pages.

'Are you sure you have not come here to work?' A smile had yet to introduce itself to me.

'No, sir. I'm here for three weeks to take in the sights and then I'll be going back to India. I have a family back home.' I tried to say this with as much joviality as a man facing the firing squad can muster.

'I don't believe you,' he said, in such a forthright manner that a part of my life ebbed away into the ether. I had not expected such brutal bluntness.

'Honestly, sir,' I begged. 'I'm here simply on a holiday, nothing more.'

He shifted his position, resting his weight on his other leg. He sighed audibly. No doubt he had been through this scenario a million times before. A guy from a Third World country comes to the land of opportunity to better himself and gives the same old excuse. He's only here for a dekko, and then he is heading back to his village.

'How much money have you got?' he asked after a lifetime's pause.

For a brief millisecond I thought the man was looking for a bribe. (You can take the boy out of India, but you can't take India out of the boy.)

'Twenty-two pounds, sir,' I said, flushing out the money and placing it in front of him.

'This won't last you more than a week,' he said. And for the first time a smile of sorts escaped his features; it was a supercilious smirk.

'I believe you are here to find employment.' That stern look was back on his face. 'I'm afraid I can't let you into the country.'

That remark hit me with the force of a Mohammed Ali uppercut. A thousand and one nights of hopes and dreams dashed by the reality of a country's immigration laws. Everything I had worked for, every iota of desire to come to England and finally all that hitchhiking through the Middle East and selling of my blood in Kuwait were being thwarted by the whim of one man. I was close to breaking down. My future was no longer hanging in the balance of his capriciousness. He had given his answer. I could not enter Britain, the land of my former masters.

I had to think; and fast. All that blood, sweat and tears for nothing?

'I do have some more money with me,' I lied in desperation. 'Show me,' he said, as succinct as one can get.

'I have it in my travel bag. I'll go and get it.' I smiled back at his grave demeanour.

I rushed along the corridors of the boat, through the throng of fellow travellers, and found Anil, who was having a cup of tea at the bar, talking to a stranger.

'They won't let me in,' I said palpitating. 'The officer thinks I've come to stay for good. He says I've come looking for a job, not for a holiday. He won't let me in,' I reiterated frantically. 'I can't go back to India. I need some money, Anil.'

Anil opened his case and took out some money.

'How much do you need?' he asked, not really flustered by the turn of events.

'Lend me two hundred pounds.'

I took the money and ran back to the immigration officer who was busy with another passenger.

Finally, he saw me and I showed him the money. He eyed it with some suspicion.

'Why did you not show this to me in the first place?'

'I didn't think it was important,' I said with a shrug of new- found confidence. 'I had the money rolled up in a spare pair of socks. I really am here for a holiday, sir.'

I think the fact that I spoke pucca English and carried a perfectly affable smile may have persuaded him to let me in.

'I'll give you six months,' he said grimly, stamping my passport and handing it back to me.

Never has a sentence been received with so much joy and elation. I wanted to hug the man, such was my appreciation. I can be frivolous about it on reflection, but at the time my world was a heartbeat away from collapsing.

It was 4 p.m. when we got down from that boat and set our feet on solid British soil. I took in the air. It felt different. I walked along the docks, my guitar still by my side and my rucksack bursting at the seams, stuffed with one or two warm items of clothing that I had purchased. I had also bought myself a thick woollen jacket in a flea market in Paris to ward away the late spring chill.

I wore a huge smile of relief – I had finally made it. Nearly four months after I got on that pilgrimage boat in Bombay, I had made it to the land of Shakespeare, Sir Isaac Newton and Norman Wisdom. I looked at Anil; he was smiling too, perhaps caught up in the contagion of my enthusiasm.

An hour later we were on a train taking us to Paddington station in London. The smoky carriage was full of travellers chatting and puffing away. It was like a scene from those old, black-and-white RKO movies I had seen in Bangalore, where the hero, in an overcoat and a trilby hat, has a cigarette dangling precariously from his lips as he looks through the haze of a smoke-filled carriage, summing up the situation.

Outside, the sun had gone down rather hastily and nightfall beckoned. The train hissed into Paddington station and we got out into a world of ant-like discipline. People walked fast and with purpose, looking neither left nor right, talking to no one and heading for the train that would take them to their destination. It lacked the noise, confusion and chaos of an Indian railway station, with coolies running towards carriages carrying suitcases on their turbaned heads followed by passengers – people shouting, babies screaming, hawkers hollering out their wares, and beggars pleading for alms.

Paddington station had a sense of structured serenity about it. I loved it. We got out on to the main road and Anil suggested we walk to a bed-and-breakfast round the corner. I looked up at a darkened sky and offered my thanks to the universe. I noticed that big, friendly star twinkling back. My eastern star had followed me all the way to a western sky.

17

BRITAIN ... AN OUTPOST OF INDIA

WE FOUND A LITTLE HOTEL IN SUSSEX GARDENS. IT was in a row of terraced buildings and every one of them was a hotel catering to tourists, salesmen and weekend trippers. The elderly lady who owned the bed and breakfast was charming and welcoming and made us feel totally at home. It was a lovely room with floral wallpaper, something I had never seen before. There was a radiator at one end of the room and warm, fluffy towels and duvets for us. A clean, modern bathroom was just down the hall. What more could two weary travellers want?

'Have a good night's sleep,' the lady said, after showing us to our room. 'Breakfast begins at 7 a.m. Bacon and eggs all right?' She left us with a wonderful crinkle of a smile.

I wanted to hug the little lady. London was better than I had imagined. I took to it like a vampire to blood. I was totally seduced by the city. I marvelled at the roads, the clean pavements, the wonderfully ornate Victorian street lamps that hung like inverted tulips, the aura of cleanliness and the order of traffic, where drivers followed a single code. And there were no cows or stray dogs in the middle of the road to avoid. We walked the streets and found a plethora of shops and stores with all kinds of tempting goodies within. I saw a dozen varieties of biscuits and chocolates and meats both tinned and fresh at the local butchers'. I gawped at some vegetables I had never set eyes upon before, like broccoli, asparagus and artichokes. In time I noticed the amount of foreigners who had made London their home and realized what an incredibly cosmopolitan city it was, with the most wonderful parks and garden squares. A world far removed from the one I had just come from.

The only disappointment was Buckingham Palace. I had expected a building of some grandeur and magnitude to reflect the power and glory of the British Empire; instead I found one devoid of any stature, splendour or architectural grace. How sad for the Queen. Many corrupt Indian politicians had better homes than this. Even the Mall leading to the Palace lacked the width and pageantry of Rajpath in New Delhi, where the annual Republic Day Parade took place.

Two days later Anil and I found accommodation at the cheaper end of Fulham Road. It was a bedsit, which is basically a large room that serves as a lounge and bedroom. A tiny kitchenette allowed us to do a modicum of cooking and, of course, there was a bathroom at the end of the hall. It cost us three pounds a week and I paid half that, which was all I could afford on my paltry savings. Oh, and there was a little meter in the room where you had to put in a shilling for the electricity. It would last about two hours and then suddenly, like Bangalore, there would be a power cut. So one had to keep a supply of shillings handy just to feed the damn meter. This little steel box, I tell you, took in more money than a Vegas slot machine.

We stayed in the Fulham area for about a month. It was quite a distance from the West End, Piccadilly Circus and Oxford Street, and at that time, Fulham was mainly inhabited by an elderly crowd; it lacked the pizzazz we were looking for. Today, though, Fulham is as trendy as the Left Bank, with bars, clubs and a cafe society, because young families moved in as the elderly passed away or moved on to pastures new.

Although Anil had a tidy sum of money, I was close to being stony

broke. I had a glimpse of a weekly music paper called the Melody
Maker and soon realized there were hundreds, if not thousands, of
singers and groups trying to get up the totem pole of success. This
was not going to be a two-week assault before success garlanded me.
It would be a struggle. I saw some of the singers on television and
even the average ones were better than I was. As for the good ones
… Hare Ram!

Doubts began to creep into me about my ability as a singer. Could
I cut it here in the West? India was a rivulet of flair, while Britain
was an ocean of deep talent, and I realized there is a vast difference
between ambition and ability. Also, the music would have to wait
as my immediate concern was to get some work and cash in hand
to pay the bills. I looked in the classified section of a local evening
paper for jobs and careers. There were numerous jobs available for
young people willing to work hard with a desire to earn a minimum
of £200 a week on commission. Two hundred quid was a fortune in
those days. Forget milk and honey, for a moment I thought I was in a
country where money actually did grow on trees.

SO I APPLIED FOR JOB NUMBER ONE AND WENT TO work in an office
selling carbon paper to businesses. (Carbon paper was used for
making copies of original documents, although this has long been
superseded by electronic photocopying and scanning.) It involved
sitting in a room with four other people, selecting a list of companies
from the telephone directory, then picking up the phone and cold-
calling the stationery buyer of a particular company and talking him
into buying reams and reams of carbon paper.

I lasted in the job for three days. I just could not face ringing
a company and asking the receptionist for the buyer and then, in a
voice as sweet as caramel, enticing him or her to buy carbon paper.
The phone would more often than not be banged down. Sometimes
a curt 'no thanks' would escape the buyer's lips and I would have to
go through the telephone directory to find another company which
might fall for my selling skills.

JOB NUMBER TWO WAS WORKING FOR A COMPANY THAT SOLD paintings by unknown, struggling artists. The paintings were usually done in acrylic and chalk on black velvet material. A motley lot of us would be taken in a van and dropped off at a central point, somewhere in a peaceful, manicured suburb like Surbiton in Surrey. There we would fan out in different directions, knocking on people's doors trying to sell them a painting. The van would pick us up at the drop-off point at 5 p.m. and we would get 25 per cent of any painting sold. I would walk around the streets not knowing where I was or where to go, lost in the new surroundings of a suburb. I had just about made myself familiar with Fulham.

I lasted a week and sold three paintings. Quite often, people refused to open the door to a foreigner standing outside offering a painting for sale. Little old ladies living alone would quiver through their closed and fortified doors, 'Go away or I shall call the police.'

If a man opened the door he was more likely to say, 'Bugger off.' But I persevered and managed to sell a painting to a restaurant owner who planned to hang it in his office and another two were sold to families who were kind enough to open the door to a stranger, who, for all they knew, could have been Jack the Ripper or an illegal immigrant seeking refuge. I made £12 from those sales, not quite the hundreds as advertised. All very disheartening and I knew then not to believe everything one read.

Every week I invested in a copy of the Melody Maker, to see what was going on in the world of music. Groups like Herman's Hermit, the Animals, and the Pretty Things and, of course, the Beatles and the Stones plus heavier rock acts like Led Zeppelin and the Americans like Janis Joplin and the Grateful Dead filled its pages. And all the time another dozen acts mushroomed out of nowhere, each one better than the other. I could not believe this tiny island could have so much talent. The music scene was infinitely more crowded than a slum dweller's hut in Bombay's Dharavi, and here I was preparing to enter this crowded dungeon of musical genius. During this period, the Home Office in their infinite wisdom and munificence extended my visa for a whole year. Freedom means not having to look behind your back every fifteen minutes.

TOWARDS THE END OF 1967, A MOVEMENT WAS TAKING PLACE amongst the youth. It came from America and like a gentle tsunami, this peaceful uprising spread across England and the rest of Europe. It was the hippy movement – the Flower Power era. It was a time of love, peace, sexual revolution, Eastern philosophy and drugs. A joint was no longer a junction or a place to hang out in and dope was no longer an idiot.

London floated in a haze of incense and hashish, and a confection of colour. Anil and I hung out a lot on King's Road and Carnaby Street. On a sunny day, a smiling parade of people would throng the streets in a bedspread of riotously colourful kaftans, scarves and beads. It was a hedonistic summer of love as the 'V' sign of peace was exchanged between strangers.

In fact, 'hi' was not so much a form of greeting as a state of mind.

How I wished I had brought my kurtas and beads from India. Instead, I had to buy them at Kensington Market in High Street, a place which became a Mecca for this hippy subculture. Boutiques like Take 6 and Irvine Sellers played to the peacocks in our society, and Biba's, the mother of all stores, opened with great style and panache in Kensington High Street. It had the look of a courtesan's boudoir and was a meeting place for the young and hip. It was easily the best time to be alive and in London. Suddenly, most things Indian became fashionable. I had to make good this opportunity.

I walked up and down Oxford Street looking for a man called Denny Cordell, a record producer of some repute, who worked for a company called Essex Music. I read about him in the Melody Maker or MM, which had become my new bible. I finally tracked Cordell down and managed a meeting with him. He was an Englishman, soft-spoken with a rather eclectic taste in music. He was at the time involved with an unknown singer called Joe Cocker. I doubt if Cordell had met an Indian before, but Indian music was just beginning to be interesting to aficionados of world music, what with the Beatles' recent trip to see the Maharishi in Rishikesh. So there was a sliver of interest. The man took a liking to me and promised we'd do something in the near future.

'Do you write your own songs?' he asked during our chat. 'Sure,' I said. Since arriving in London I had time on my hands so I had begun composing songs, something I had never tried to do in India, spoilt, no doubt, by Trini Lopez and his rich cache of songs.

'Play me a coupla songs,' Cordell requested.

I unzipped my leatherette guitar case and sang the only two songs I had written. One ditty was called 'Look Out Here I Come' and the other, 'Daughter of Love'. A virgin in the field of song writing, I thought the melodies more mellifluous than anything Puccini had created and the words more significant than the Magna Carta. Ignorance is truly bliss.

'Not bad,' Cordell said, shaking his head in approval. 'Keep writing. You'll only get better.'

That's what I did for the next few weeks. I kept writing. I was the archetypal starving songwriter in his garret, churning out songs, and in my mind, each song was supremely better than the previous one and, once again, I was dreaming of world domination.

One day Anil and I were standing outside one of those ubiquitous red pill-box phone booths, newspaper in hand, wanting to make a call to a landlord apropos a vacant apartment. We were in an area called Earl's Court, which is in the royal borough of Kensington and Chelsea. What a glorious name for a district; the Brits hit the nail on the head with names evocative of history, pomp and regal splendour.

Anyway, while Anil and I were waiting for the young man inside the booth to finish his call, two guys formed a queue behind us, and then another guy – who also looked Indian – stood behind the first two. Soon we all got talking. The two guys were Italians and their names were Aldo and Pietro, and the boy we thought was Indian turned out to be Pakistani. He was affluently dressed in a deep-green jacket, a pale-yellow tie and beige trousers with a perma crease, plus shoes with no scuff marks or worn-out heels. His name was Poncho, obviously a pet name he preferred to go by. He was, we later found out, the son of a Pakistani army general and was related to Zulfikar Bhutto, the country's president. That explained his expensive threads. It so happened we were all waiting to call different landlords about rental accommodation. By the time the guy who was in the phone booth came out, we were all best buddies and decided it would be cheaper to rent a house together. The new guy had overheard us and decided to join the consortium. He was an English lad called Mark.

So this disparate group of strangers standing on the pavement near Earl's Court Underground Station made a collective decision to rent a four-bedroom house in Redcliffe Gardens, not more than 400 metres from where we were chatting, for the princely sum of £28 a week. Only Anil and Poncho looked capable of paying their share of the rent. Although our new home was on a busy thoroughfare, the place was larger and more central than our previous bedsit in Fulham, and the cherry on the cake was that it was barely 50 yards away from a discotheque called the Café des Artistes, which would turn out to be our second home.

We got on rather well in this United Nations of communal living. The two Italians shared a room, as did Poncho and I. Only Anil and Mark had a room each to themselves.

Mark could be sullen at times and had a dark, brooding side to him. The two Italians were likeable and charming like so many Europeans, but could not be entirely trusted. Poncho was an open book – irreligious and naïve; a real Walter Mitty character (as I found out later) without a mean bone in his body.

Money was tight all round, except for Anil. Even Poncho, who got a decent allowance every month from his father back home, was having to borrow after the first two weeks of his profligate spending. Breakfast was usually a mini mountain of cornflakes with milk, no lunch and an early evening meal that consisted of rice with onion and tomato curry. The curry was, as the name suggests, a thin gruel-like gravy made up of onions and tomatoes. On festive occasions like Easter, Christmas and Diwali we added potatoes to the mix. This was probably the cheapest meal designed to fill a hungry stomach. Each day of the week one of us had to cook this meal with Sunday being a day of rest ... from this infernal curry. (That's when we had spaghetti with tomato and onion sauce made by Aldo and Pietro.)

Most evenings, after eating this life-sapping dish, we would head across the road to the discotheque. We usually went in quite early and well before the hour when an entrance fee had to be paid. How we six guys managed to chat up any of the birds in the club with the smell of turmeric lacing our breaths is one of life's little anomalies and remains a mystery to this day.

With the sudden steep increase in rent, I had to go looking for another job. One where the owner would not ask too many questions, as I did not as yet have a work permit. I found a job in Earl's Court itself where I managed to get work three mornings a week in a cafe preparing coffee and sandwiches, then doing the washing-up, preparing bills for the customers, clearing the tables and if time prevailed, singing a song or two in the hope that the additional tips would tip me into the financial league of Anil and Poncho.

It was at this juncture that I wrote a song called 'She', a paean to the unknown woman who dwells in the fantasy of every young guy. I thought it was a beaut of a song, easily the best I'd yet written. In my mind's eye there was only one singer who could do justice to this poem of love, this chanson d'amour. Only one young man whose voice could lift this ballad and soar with it heavenwards, imbuing passion, expression, timbre and a warm baritone to this achingly beautiful piece of music. That singer was Scott Walker of the Walker

Brothers.

I managed to track down the man who looked after Scott Walker. His name was Maurice Katz. I think I got his office number either from the Musician Union's Handbook or from the Melody Maker. Either way, armed with his telephone number, I went to that red pill-box in Earl's Court and dialled his number.

The phone rang a few times before it was picked up by a female voice.

'Yes?' said the girlishly fruity voice at the other end of the line. 'I would like to speak to Maurice,' I replied shakily.

'Who's spayken?' she replied in an accent that flummoxed me. I had been led to believe that all English people spoke with the cultured tones of the presenters of BBC World Service, which I had sometimes listened to in India. In truth, when I came to London I found there were more accents in this little island than there were flies in India.

'My name is Biddu,' I said in a voice rich with expectation. 'Pardin?' Her voice reached for the ceiling.

'Biddu,' I repeated with clarity, sounding slightly foolish for having a foreign-sounding name and not one that a receptionist could get her teeth and ears around, like Cliff, Tab or Rock.

'Howjya spell it?' she wanted to know.

I wanted to know if she was chewing gum. Her pronunciation was atrocious.

'That's B for Britain, I for India, D for Delhi, D for Delhi and U for...' I struggled to find a word for 'U' and at last I got one. 'U for euthanasia.'

'Pardin?' Once again, there was that lilt in her voice which was now starting to irritate me.

'Jaist a minute,' she said. There was silence on the line.

The Earl's Court traffic sped past me while I held on; luckily I had the booth door closed but a smidge of sound filtered through the vacuum of the booth.

'Yes, Boo-Boo?' It was the voice of impatience – the voice of a man in a hurry, deep in tone and sandpaper-coarse.

'It's Biddu, sir,' I replied. It was obvious that dumb-ass receptionist did not get my name right. 'I've come from India with a song that's perfect for Scott Walker.'

There was the briefest of pauses.

'Let me get this right,' his gravel-like voice rumbled. 'You've come from India with a song for Scott Walker?' He asked incredulously, stressing and enunciating each word like he was talking to a bunch of savages or heathens or both.

'Yes sir,' I replied, nervous and yet excited at the same time. 'I have come from India with a great song for Scott Walker. You will love it.'

'Don't be daft,' his voiced boomed. 'Nobody comes from bloody India with a song for Scott.'

With that the phone line went dead. Morte. Muerto. Morto.

I mean dead.

I was left holding the phone with the busy tone echoing in my head. Suddenly the noise from the street ceased. I could not hear the rush of traffic, just that bloody tone which seemed to get louder and louder.

The song 'She' never saw the light of day. It lay on the shelf and died peacefully in its isolation. Missed by nobody but its author. So near and yet so far.

Whistling the sitar line to *'Aap Jaisa Koi'*.

Relaxing at home in casual wear.

The hammock tilts to the right. That's the side I keep my wallet.

Father and son (notice the blue rinse in my hair).

A proud dad.

In Pakistan for the Nazia Hassan tribute concert.

With Tina Charles
after winning the
World Song Festival
in Japan.

With Ashok,
Suresh and Hash,
at Candolim Beach,
Goa: four lotharios
flashing it, without
a woman in sight.
We couldn't pull
a muscle, let alone
a babe.

With Suresh, Deveika and Sue: we could have got two more on the sofa.

With Sue at Vijay Mallya's New Year bash.

With Sue.

Alisha Chinai, with whom I had one of my biggest-selling albums, at my birthday party, Sun and Sand Hotel, Juhu, Mumbai.

Kumar Gaurav, the star of my sole film production, *Star*.

Singer Sophie and I, cutting the cake. Both born on the same day, but different years. Guess who is older?

Sonu Nigam and Adnan Sami at my birthday party.

Two south Indians who obviously share the same dentist.

A fascinated Adnan Sami listens intently, while I tell him the finer points of fly-fishing.

Feroz Khan wearing shades 'cos he can't stand the bright lights, with Sophie and me.

Shaan, a wonderful guy and singer, telling me where
I went wrong in my career, while Sue eavesdrops.

18

Living in the Lap of Penury

I PICKED UP THE PIECES OF MY SHATTERED EGO, my crushed pride and a heart that Mr Katz had unwittingly broken. No one had told me that this snake pit of a business would be easy. In the music business there are no friends, only opportunities. Mine had just slipped through the net. They say youth is wasted on the young. That isn't so. It may only be appreciated by the old, but youth has that ability to bounce off the floor, dust oneself, and carry on like never before.

It was mid-1968, I had been in England for a year; and my music career was heading down a cul-de-sac of despair. Everyone needs a lucky break. That chance which comes along and takes your life by the scruff on an upward trajectory. But more often than not, you have to make your own luck.

So, I tried calling Denny Cordell a few times and eventually got in touch with him. He was a busy man, having just produced a massive hit with a group called Procul Harum. You may not remember the group, but their song 'A Whiter Shade of Pale' is a modern classic. I finally got through to him and went up to Essex Music, where he introduced me to a good-looking young man from the States called Tony Visconti, who was a talented musician and record producer.

'I'd like you to work with Tony,' Denny said in that whisper of his. 'Get to know one another. Play him songs and see what happens.'

During the next few weeks I pretty much set up base at Essex Music, hanging around like an unwanted dishcloth mainly in the reception area, talking to the secretaries when they weren't busy clicking away on their typewriters and striving to be part of the scenario. It was my only link with the music establishment. I was there when a demo of a song came in. We all heard it. The song was called 'Those Were the Days'. The demonstration record sounded a hit to me. Sure enough, the song was given to a young girl who had just won a TV show called Opportunity Knocks. Her name was Mary Hopkins. She recorded the song with Paul McCartney as producer and, two months later, it flew up the charts and stayed at number one for ages.

I also met a young dude called David. He had winter-white skin and rather fine, almost porcelain-like, features. He was a struggling songwriter/singer, and if I remember right, he had just come out of art school. He had already brought out an album the previous year that had sunk without a trace. Sometimes we'd go round the corner from Oxford Street to a nearby cafe and jaw about music over a cuppa tea. Nothing in his persona suggested or trumpeted a future rock star. Eventually, I lost touch with him. Eighteen months later he had his first hit with a song called 'Space Oddity'. The guy's name was David Bowie.

AROUND THIS PERIOD, I MANAGED TO GET A PUBLISHING CONTRACT with Essex Music. It meant anything I wrote during the term of the contract would now be published by them. They were entitled to my songs for life and in return I got the princely sum of fifty pounds a year. It was less than a pittance, but I was in no position to argue. I would have signed the contract for no money, just so I could say I had a song-writing deal with a publisher. It helped that the producer, Tony Visconti, decided to record two songs with me. It would be the first time I'd be going into a recording studio. Was this going to be a lucky break for the boy with gold in his hair?

Alas, it wasn't to be so. I heard the finished recording and my shoulders slumped in disappointment. The tracks were dull and monotonous, the production pedestrian, the vocals passé and the songs itself seemed lachrymose and saccharine-sweet even for the times. 'Look Out Here I Come' and 'Daughter of Love' were not the Holy Grails I had envisaged. Visconti and I parted ways after our brief association. Within a year he went on to better things while I trawled the depths of anonymity. Another missed chance. I, who thought it would take just two weeks to conquer London, was no closer to the triumph I had envisaged.

In a fleeting moment of lunacy combined with a tincture of idiocy, I wanted to kill myself because of this monumental disappointment, but knew straightaway that this was a fruitless and self-defeating exercise. At the end of the day a drowning man thinks only of survival.

To survive I needed money. The advance from Essex Music had long been spent on a couple of weeks' rent which was in arrears, a pair of deep-maroon bell-bottom trousers and an Afghan coat, which cost sixteen pounds and was the envy of Kensington Market. I may have been a struggling musician, but I was on the button in the world of fashion. I needed a regular day job, which would allow me to compose songs in the evenings, unfettered by the mental worry of finding enough money for rent and food.

ONE DAY, WHILE I WAS RIDING ON THE TOP OF a double-decker bus, an idea of sheer brilliance, inspiration and genius revealed itself to me. Why don't I become a bus conductor, I thought? I noticed a lot of drivers and bus conductors were, to put it loosely, from the colonies. The pay was goodish and came with some security. I could pursue my music career in tandem till the next big break came along. They often displayed posters on the sides of buses saying they were looking for drivers and conductors and the salary was always shown in seductively large print. What could I lose? At that moment I was on the periphery of the music biz, my head peeking over the parapet and I was just about managing to hold on through the tenuous grip of my fingernails.

So, on a grey and rain-driven morning, I sloshed my way to the bus depot on Edgware Road with the idea of applying for a job as a bus conductor. Edgware Road runs from Marble Arch for miles and miles, past Maida Vale, Kilburn, Cricklewood and Barnet and probably doesn't stop till it reaches the Mull of Kintyre. It must be one of the longest roads in London.

But, I digress. I walked into the manager's office. It was a small cabin of a room, rather cheaply furnished with a desk that supported an overflowing ashtray, a Bakelite telephone and a tabloid newspaper open to the sports page. A wooden hatstand in one corner supported a black overcoat and a dripping umbrella.

'Hello,' said the manager, looking up as I entered, nervously. He was puffing on his umpteenth cigarette and blew a violent burst of smoke from the side of his mouth.

'Not the best of days to come in for an interview, is it?' I said, trying to create an air of bonhomie by talking about the weather.

'Doesn't really bother me, holed up here.' Another puff of smoke came out of his dragon-like nostrils. We chatted for a minute or two, mainly about the weather, as he emptied the ashtray into a basket by his feet and removed the newspaper from the table as if to make room for something else.

'So you want a job with London Transport, eh?'

'Yes sir,' I replied in a relaxed manner. 'I think it would be nice to work moving around London, out in the open rather than stuck in an office.'

'Know what you mean,' he replied matter-of-factly. 'I take it you have no experience?'

'I'm afraid not. I've never done conducting before. Not even with an orchestra.'

How funny was I, adding a spray of wit to an interview on an overcast morning?

'I see,' he said pensively, oblivious of my remark, or just plain ignoring it. 'Shouldn't be a prob. We run a brief training course. Let me have your P45.'

'Pardon?' I replied, not knowing what he meant by P45. 'Your P45. Let me see it,' he said, just a tad annoyed.

'I don't know what you mean, sir. What's a P45?' I pleaded, a puzzled look on my face.

'I say, your P45 from your previous job.' His irritation was no longer a mask.

'I did not have a previous job. I've just come from India and I'd like to …'

Before I could finish my explanation, he said, 'If you don't have your P45, stop wasting my bloody time. You haven't just come from India. Don't lie to me. You speak perfect bloody English, not like that Peter Sellers.'

'Everyone speaks perfect English in India,' I replied, with breathtaking exaggeration.

'Out of my office,' he shouted, but without any great rancour or venom. And then almost under his breath, and as if I wasn't in the room, added, 'Bloody time waster.'

I walked out of the bus depot, not totally dejected or devastated. In fact I had to laugh when I saw the irony of it. Fancy me being a bus conductor and running into a few of my friends or fans from the Venice days. The rumour would get back to Bombay faster than a carrier pigeon could coo. Poor Bidz was on the bread line, having to make ends meet by working as a bus conductor issuing tickets to tourists and daily travellers. What a fall from grace! I had started my journey from India eighteen months ago with nothing … and I still had most of it left.

I kept in touch with my mother through letters. Once every six weeks, regular as clockwork, her aerogramme would arrive with news of back home which I would scan very quickly. I would write back, usually a litany of lies of how well things were going and how that elusive success I had come for was almost in my sights if not in my grasp.

It was the beginning of 1969 when I finally got a decent job working in a hamburger restaurant. Not just any burger place, but one that was a replica of an American diner. It was called Yankee Doodle and I was employed as the chef. It was based in a side street off Oxford Street. This was before the advent of malls, and Oxford

Street was the premier place for shopping at the time. It stretched from Marble Arch at one end right up till Tottenham Court Road about 4 km ahead, an avenue of pavements, people, cars and buses merging into a melange of traffic and noise.

I, WHO HAD NEVER BEEN IN A KITCHEN BACK HOME and had just about managed to scale the culinary equivalent of a hillock with the infamous tomato and onion curry, was now responsible for the eating habits of thousands of Londoners. With one foul swoop, I could reduce the population of the city by a quarter. I was given a white chef's uniform and hat to hide my long hair and told to get on with the business of making burgers. The restaurant had a central U-shaped bar with a lot of neon, very much like the ones you see in a modern-day American deli. Customers could sit at tables or choose the informality of the bar and have their coffee and doughnuts while perched on high revolving stools, watching the chef turn the meat patties on the grill with a flick of the wrist and spread mayo and ketchup and slices of lettuce and tomato with the dexterity of a performing artist. It was a theatre of sorts, if your imagination was limitless. The place also had a doughnut-making machine which I mastered in minutes; the little spherical-shaped dough waded through a river of boiling oil and was then dusted with a monsoon of sugar. When hot they were yummy and I loved making and scoffing them.

The owners of the burger joint were two Jewish gentlemen who took a liking to me and treated me with great kindness. I had my own washer-up and two young, attractive waitresses to attend to the tables. One day the owners asked me if I would make doughnuts for the American Embassy, which was in Grosvenor Square, not far from the restaurant. They would drop me some extra money for my troubles and since money is the root of all wealth, I said fine. So I would come in at 6 a.m., make fifty to sixty doughnuts and then, at 7.30 a.m., whisk them around to the Embassy and give them to the marine who stood sentry at the door, stiff as an erection. Morning coffee and doughnuts were de rigueur for America's finest. Then I would head back to Yankee Doodle and make some more doughnuts for our customers before the doors opened at 9 a.m.

Around the same time, the collective at Redcliffe Gardens was beginning to disintegrate. The Italian boys went their own way, teaming up with some other Italians and rented somewhere near Shepherd's Bush, while moody Mark, the Englishman, also decided to leave. That left Anil, Poncho and me. We moved away from Earl's Court and the Café des Artistes to an apartment in Cornwall Gardens near Gloucester Road, a big step up from our previous location. Luckily, a discotheque called Blaizes in South Kensington was close at hand. We had a large ground-floor flat which suited us fine. With my new job at Yankee Doodle I could afford the slight increase in rent and frequent visits to Blaizes. Occasionally, a decent act would perform at the club. I saw Tina Turner who was trying to make a comeback after the split with her husband Ike Turner, and I remember seeing an animal of a man who played the guitar like the way the Devil himself would have wanted to play it. He could make the instrument scream in pain and squeal in ecstasy as it echoed his tortured soul. He was a slim man with an Afro hairstyle like Sai Baba and wore purple velvet trousers, floral patterned shirts and Cuban boots. The guy was called Jimi Hendrix.

Anil, in the meantime, had acquired a very attractive girlfriend called Jane who moved in with him. It would be a summer of love as far as he was concerned. Poncho and I were still single and hugely available. We made a new friend called Peso, a guy who had come from Bombay and, eventually, he and Poncho moved into an apartment down the road from us.

Money was tight for Anil. The cash he had brought from his father's safe had long been spent. He had been to India six months ago and came back with some more money. I didn't ask and he did not tell me where he got it from. But now that he had a girlfriend, the money flowed like water down an unclogged sink and he was close to broke. His girlfriend, incidentally, came from a wealthy background.

(Her folks lived in Jersey, a tax haven in the Channel Islands.) While I was making burgers and doughnuts, Anil and Peso were cooking up a plan to make some quick money and not necessarily the legal way.

19

Hash for Cash

One morning, a bespectacled young man walked into the restaurant, sat at the bar and asked for a coffee. He had a friendly enough face, was plump of features but in all other ways, quite nondescript. This man popped in quite often and in time an unhurried acquaintance developed between us. Often, I would not charge him for the coffee and sometimes when no one was watching, I would give him one of those sizzling-hot doughnuts. I found out that Gerry Shury, for that was his name, was a copyist. At first I did not know what that meant, till he told me.

A copyist was the one who wrote down the detailed musical score for an orchestra, after the arranger had written out the different parts for violins, cellos, trumpets, bass and drums, etc., and passed it on to him. The bigger the orchestra and more varied the instruments, the greater the amount of parts to be written out. It was a laborious, detailed and time-consuming job, appreciated by no one. Because no one knew a copyist even existed. He was one of the many unknown and unsung men who worked behind the scenes in the making of a recording. His name would never appear on the album sleeve and apart from a flat fee of £11 for his services, no other kudos was forthcoming.

I was rather fascinated by this job. Not that I wanted to be a copyist. Far from it. But my ability to score music was, at best, amateurish and as I planned to produce my own records some day soon, the idea doing the rounds in my head was that I could work with Gerry.

I gave him another free doughnut.

BACK AT THE APARTMENT, THE IDEA OF 'HASH FOR CASH' was hatched by the boys. As I mentioned earlier, swinging London was in a fug of fog created by hashish, pot, grass, dope, shit, Lebanese gold, or whatever else one called it. If it smelled funny, the chances were that someone was smoking the damn stuff.

Anil and Peso wanted to go to India and come back with a suitcase or two of hashish. The idea was that the two guys and Jane would go, source the drugs and come back with a couple of suitcases filled with blocks of the stuff, suitably disguised. It would be a one-off trip and they would invest the money from the sale in a proper, legit business and life would forever be rosy with a rainbow's arc sweeping the horizon. The boys thought it was for an honourable end but through dishonourable means. To get through customs and immigration, they would fly back from Bombay to Paris, change flights at Orly airport and head for London.

The logic was that, for obvious reasons, a Paris–London flight would demand less scrutiny than a flight arriving at Heathrow from Bombay. Factor in an attractive English girl with them and the chances were that customs and immigration would be looking at her shapely ankles, rather than at the suitcase the men were bringing in. There was one very important caveat or requirement to this plan of theirs, which I shall reveal a little later.

Back at Yankee Doodle, things were really smoking. The doughnuts and burgers were selling rather well. I had already saved £150 in my three months at the restaurant, and I needed another couple of hundreds before I could hire an orchestra and make a record.

By sheer coincidence, I found out that Polydor Records, a major music label, was on the other side of the road, across from Oxford Street, literally no more than 100 metres away. What luck! Within the complex, they had a very spacious eight-track studio, which I went to check out. The control room looked like the inside of a cockpit, with its array of dials and knobs, limiters, graphic equalizers and various other electronic gizmos needed for creating the layers of sound that go towards making a record. All this science was new to me, having been in a studio just once to put my voice down on the song 'Look Out Here I Come' and the record's flip side. Alas, it wasn't just my voice that needed putting down!

One lazy summer afternoon, Anil was getting back to the apartment on Cornwall Gardens and when he approached the house, he realized he did not have the key to the front door. Remember that we had a ground floor flat. The window that opened into the lounge was slightly ajar because of the hot weather, so Anil managed to scale along the side of the window ledge and, with some difficulty, pry open the window fully. As he was about to scramble in, a passing policeman saw him and thinking he was an intruder, stopped Anil midway through getting in.

Now, how often would you see a policeman walking along a leafy side street of central London at that precise moment? An alien invasion would be more likely, I would think.

Anyway, the policeman questioned Anil, who in turn told him he had forgotten his keys and could prove that the place was his and that he was no thief. To cut to the chase, the policeman allowed him to go in through the window and open the front door and show some identity and proof of ownership.

When the policeman entered the building and walked into our lounge, he noticed a red-and-white, plastic traffic cone placed decorously by the side of the fireplace.

'Hello, hello, hello. What have we here then?' I imagine the copper must have said.

It was illegal to take a traffic cone from the street and one could be fined if caught doing so. Hundreds of Londoners, however, had them in their homes as a show of bravado or cavalier stupidity. In this case, it was certainly a foolish exhibit. The policeman promptly issued a warrant, which demanded that Anil would have to appear at Hammersmith Magistrate's Court in seven days' time. It was a negligible misdemeanour, but not in the eyes of the law.

A WEEK LATER I WAS DRAGGED ALONG TO STAND SURETY for bail. The bail was set at £50, a rather paltry sum, which in some ways reflected the trivial nature of the offence and Anil was ordered to appear in two weeks' time before the judge for sentencing. We assumed a fine of £100 would be handed down, at best. Thus, no more thought was given to this intrusion.

A few days later, Anil and Peso told me briefly about their plan. There was no visible halo around my head, but I didn't do drugs in spite of looking the archetype dopehead with shoulder-length hair and an Afghan coat.

'You guys are crazy,' I said, on hearing their plot. 'You're taking one helluva chance.'

'Piece of cake, yaar,' Peso replied with a laconic grin, not bothering to elaborate.

'We have a foolproof plan,' Anil echoed. Then he explained their modus operandi. If it was meant to soothe my fears, it had the opposite effect.

'I think you both are nuts, forget it,' I remonstrated. 'It's far too dangerous and what if you guys get caught? They have sniffer dogs and stuff, you know that?'

For me, my two biggest fears were (and still are) potholing and prison. And if I had to pick one of them, spiralling down narrow caves in search of subterranean excitement would just edge out a prison sentence.

'We won't get caught,' was their unsubtle answer. It seems they were determined to carry out their plan of bringing two suitcases full of hash, and no amount of gentle persuasion would deter them from it.

'I don't know…,' I said, leaving the question hanging in the air. Perhaps I should have taken a stronger stance and argued them into changing their minds, or even gone to the police. But I did not.

Four days later, the pair of them and Jane were winging their way to Bombay. I met up with Poncho and told him about Peso and Anil's reckless scheme. He was aware of it and, in fact, had given the boys £300 towards the trip.

'What for, Poncho?' I said angrily. 'That's the stupidest thing you can possibly do, you know that?'

'I've been promised a grand when the stuff is sold, so I'll have enough to buy a yellow E-Type,' he replied, smiling broadly and unaware of what his actions might get him into. He wanted an E-Type Jaguar to go cruising down King's Road, because it was a babe magnet. Poncho, like me, did not smoke, but I could only think all that passive inhaling was definitely doing his head in.

Three weeks later, I got a letter from India. It was from Anil. A simple letter asking me to come to Paris on a certain date. It was apparently imperative for the execution of their plan. The reason behind this request was juvenile in the extreme. If I went to Paris to tie in with their arrival from Bombay and flew with them to London's Heathrow, then walked alongside them through customs, the focus would be on me, because of my looks and dress sense (the Afghan coat was requested). I would be the perfect decoy, enabling Jane to walk with the suitcases of contraband, with nary a look from the customs officer while I was being questioned and probably searched with nothing to declare but my concealed musical genius. There was only one chink in this plan: I hated it and did not want to get involved any which way.

My musical career may have been spluttering and in need of a kick-start but I could not jeopardize it with this foolish foray of getting involved with drugs and the law, even if it was to help a close friend. It was too dangerous, as far as I was concerned. Anil had been a good buddy and had helped me out at Dover by lending me that money to get into the UK, and I guess, in a way, I was indebted to him and owed him one, but this idea of going to Paris just did not sit well with me. His letter interrupted the equilibrium of my days.

I was torn between loyalty and friendship and my own need for self-preservation. My coming to London was a career move because I wanted to make it on the big stage. It was a dream I had nurtured through a thousand shows I had performed in India. Mine was a vision that kept me going on that crowded pilgrimage boat to Basra, an ambition that drove me through the endless sands of the Middle East, till I was finally able to give my dream a home. True, success had eluded me so far and I was surrounded by the trappings of failure, but mine was not a flight of fancy or a whimsical trip to do some sightseeing, bed a few birds and go back to India if things did not work out. I was in London for better or worse, my resolve to work towards my vision entwined deeper than a marriage vow, and I could not put at risk my future or my destiny.

I spoke to Poncho, who was planning to go to Paris to meet the returning heroes.

'Let's go together, Bid,' he said cheerfully. 'It'll be fun, Paris and all.'

To add further fuel to the fire, I got another letter from Anil. '… arriving on such and such date. See you in Paris…' was the gist of it.

I could see the peer pressure starting to build on me. On one hand I did not want to let my friends down but on the other neither did I want to help them. That old cliché, caught between a rock and a hard place, never rang truer.

20

THE DRUG BUST

IT WAS A SUNDAY MORNING WHEN PONCHO AND I boarded the plane for Paris. I was a bag of nerves, my throat drier than a prehistoric fossil. Poncho, oblivious to the seriousness of the situation, was as dapper as ever in an amber-yellow jacket, pale- blue shirt and gold tie. I was strictly out of Haight Ashbury, with love beads, gold headband, Afghan coat and the rest. As we sat next to each other on the plane, a more ridiculous and unlikely couple you had yet to see.

We landed in Paris a short while later and walked along the airport tunnel towards Immigration, as the Tannoy played muffled messages of information in French and people walked past us, consumed with Orwellian seriousness. Poncho's passport was first looked at and he was allowed to pass through. When I handed the officer my passport, he thumbed through it a couple of times, then looked at me rather sternly. I wondered if it could have been my attire.

'I do not see your visa?' he said, with a faint trace of irritation.

'Visa!' I exclaimed, genuinely surprised. Nobody had told me about a visa.

The man told me, in fractured but decent English, that Indian nationals need a visa to enter France.

'What about my friend?' I said, pointing to Poncho, who was

standing on the other side of the yellow line.

'There is no requirement of a visa for Pakistani nationals,' he said with a shrug of the shoulders and without a hint of a smile to calm my nerves. 'I am afraid I cannot allow you in. Please stand to one side.'

I found it unbelievable that a citizen from Pakistan, a country created from India's rib was allowed the freedom of France, while its neighbour, an infinitely larger country with 5000 years of history and a democratic government to boot, was being treated like the bastard son!

'Oh dear,' I sighed dramatically, but inwardly I breathed a sigh of relief. Not being allowed to enter was a godsend. I had tried, but the immigration laws of the country had prevented me. My friends would understand.

'Sorry Poncho,' I said, looking crestfallen. 'Explain it to the guys, huh.'

'Sorry yaar,' he said, then turned and walked away till he was lost in the throng of people allowed into the country.

I was sent back to London on the next flight. Someone was looking out for me.

The next day the world came to an end. Or at least it did for some of us. Briefly, this is what transpired.

The three returnees plus Poncho caught a flight to London. They were disappointed I wasn't there to meet them in Paris, but Poncho explained my visa problem. Bravely or foolishly, they landed at Heathrow and as they stepped off the plane, the police were there to meet Anil. He had skipped bail on the traffic cone offence and there was a warrant out for him. The police took him away to a room for questioning, which threw the other three into total confusion. Without their leader, they were like headless chickens in panic mode. The suitcases circled on the carousal and as fear gripped the three of them, those suitcases continued circling. Poncho, Peso and Jane left the airport terminal without the cases, too frightened to collect them in case they were searched.

AFTER BEING QUESTIONED, ANIL WAS RELEASED BY THE POLICE. HE rejoined the rest of the team and they took a black cab back to London. But their suitcases containing the black stuff were still tirelessly circling in the luggage hall at Heathrow. Either common sense had deserted them or asininity had befriended them, but once they got home they rang up Heathrow's Lost Luggage counter and mentioned that their bags were still on the carousal.

'No problem,' said the crisp voice at the other end of the phone line, 'once we've located them, we can have them delivered to you. There is a small fee of course.'

Grateful for the accommodating and helpful attitude of the airport official, Anil requested the bags be sent to a certain room at the Royal Garden Hotel, a five-star hotel in Kensington. The idea behind this was he did not want to reveal his home address to the courier. How this would have helped or hindered the outcome I don't know.

Anyway, Poncho had gone back to his apartment and the other three headed for the hotel. If you're interested to know where I was, remember it was a Monday afternoon, so I was busy at Yankee Doodle, mixing the minced beef with seasoning and then flattening the burgers before putting them on the griddle, quite oblivious of the drama unfolding on the other side of Hyde Park.

THE THREE SAT AND WAITED IN THEIR ROOM AT THE Royal Garden Hotel. Soon there was a knock on the door. It was the bellboy announcing the arrival of the suitcases. I can only assume there was a collective sigh of relief from the weary travellers.

The suitcases were brought in and placed on the bed. A generous tip was handed to the bellboy. In the surreal silence of the room, and with just a hint of trepidation, they opened the first suitcase. As they pushed back the top, a spray of burgundy powder jettisoned onto their clothes and face, marking them with the colour. Inside the suitcase some of the packets with blocks of hashish could be seen. In the ensuing confusion and panic, the door was burst open with a master key and as the hotel manager stood to one side, four plainclothes policemen dashed into the room to catch Anil, Peso and Jane, red-handed, smeared with the telltale powder.

A week later I moved out of the Cornwall Garden flat as I could not afford the rent on my own. The three of them had been taken away by the police from the Royal Garden Hotel and held in detention, being searched, questioned and god knows what else. If I remember right, the boys were sent to Wormwood Scrubs Prison. What had happened hit me like a thunderbolt; I hated to think what they were going through. How they must have cursed and regretted their monumental act of madness. I felt terrible for Anil and Jane. Whatever they had done, they were still my friends, especially Anil. Had he been deluded into thinking he could get away with it? They say money is often a curse. The lustful desire for it can be an even greater hex. Had Jane been drawn to the idea like a fly trapped in the web of Anil's love? I really didn't know.

A part of me felt the guilt of being responsible for the plight of my friends, till a certain rationale prevailed. Karmic-ly, I wasn't meant to be with them in Paris. I wondered what the outcome might have been, had I been allowed in. Would my presence have helped them in going through customs with the suitcases? Would the pangs of guilt in aiding and abetting my friends in something totally illegal have stayed and drowned me in remorse and shame?

But this was a great wake-up call for me. No more dawdling about. I had to get my career off the ground and start chasing pavements again.

Suddenly things began to happen in double quick time. I moved into a flat in Astwood Mews, just around the corner from Gloucester Road Tube station. I was now sharing with two brothers and their sister. It was a convenient arrangement and the four of us got on rather well. My work at Yankee Doodle was bringing in a small but steady stream of revenue.

I also managed to get out of my writing contract with Essex Music, pleading that slavery had been abolished in 1833. I then promptly signed a song-writing deal with Warner Brothers Music also based on Oxford Street. This time the signing amount was £100 per year, a marginal improvement on the £50 that Essex Music had paid me, though still ridiculously low for a writer. On reflection, the words 'frying pan' and 'fire' come to mind. My business acumen was shining through like a miner's lamp gasping for air.

I MADE PLANS TO RECORD TWO SONGS AT POLYDOR STUDIOS, which, as I said earlier, was a stone's throw from the restaurant. I worked with Gerry on the arrangements and went in to record the songs. I had nearly £400 with me, which would cover the studio costs of £8 an hour, plus musician's fees at, I think, £12 pounds per three-hour session. I had a rhythm section of drums, bass guitar, electric guitar and keyboards plus a string section of six violins and two violas and a small horn section of two trumpets and two trombones. The session was going well, when the studio door opened and a gentleman popped his head in.

'Nice music,' he said, with a cheery grin. 'I could hear it in the corridor. Whose is it?'

'Mine, sir,' I replied, with a modicum of hubris. In those days I tended to address anyone in a tie or a suit as 'sir'. Perhaps it was a throwback to the British Raj, but that's what we were taught at Bishop Cotton School.

'I know you're busy, can I talk to you after the session?' he whispered like a collaborator in a conspiracy.

After the session, the gentleman came back and introduced himself to me.

'I'm Roland,' he said in that casual manner that affects show business and then asked, 'Would you be willing to produce a group for us?'

Like Dracula at a blood bank, I could not refuse.

I found out that the group in question were the Tigers, a four-piece band from Japan. Roland Rennie was either sufficiently impressed by the ribbon of music he had heard seeping through the studio door, or he had tried every other producer in the phonebook and they were either too busy doing needlepoint or visiting their mother-in-law to be bothered to produce this act. Although the group was unknown in the UK, it was huge in Japan; massive, in fact. They wanted to cut a song in English for the Japanese market and because the boys did not speak a word of English they would have to learn every word by rote. They were due in two days' time for a three-day stay before flying back to Japan. That was all the time their busy schedule allowed them.

It was their dream; and I, a novice in the world of record producing, was chosen by the head of Polydor Records to make this dream come true. It was akin to asking a passenger to fly the plane.

THE NEXT DAY I WAS GIVEN A BUNCH OF SONGS by Roland and asked to select two songs for the recording. I went through them and picked two written by an upcoming group called the Bee Gees. The songs were 'Rain Falls on the Lonely' and 'Smile for Me'. The melodies were fine, but not as clever or contagious as the songs that Barry, Robin and Maurice would write in the near future.

The following day, I met the Tigers who had just got off their flight from Tokyo. They were four lads, cute as buttons with their pudding-bowl hairstyles. They bowed and smiled a lot, as did I. This was our one way of communication, although they did have a man from the Japanese record company who spoke a smattering of English and acted as a translator. I then sat with the boys in their hotel room and taught them the lyrics syllable by syllable, word by word and line by line. They had trouble with their R's but that Japanese work ethic persevered and although 'Rain Falls on the Lonely' kept ending up as 'Lain Falls on the Lonely', after a hundred attempts and a million laughs we got a respectful rendition of the lyrics, good enough for the Japanese market. A smarter and more experienced producer would have picked a lyric with no R's in it!

21

IF MUSIC BE THE FOOD OF LOVE ...

I LOOKED UP AND THERE SHE WAS, AT THE top of the stairs, framed against the luminous glow of a street lamp, this girl and her friend. Both modishly dressed, with a vast halo each of blonde hair on their delicate heads; they were debating between themselves whether to come in or not.

I was at the bottom of the stairs at the basement entrance to Blaizes, a discotheque, chatting to the receptionist.

Slowly and at a measured pace they came down the steps, their long legs descending like willowy praying mantises.

They stood in front of the window rummaging through their purses for coins to pay the entrance fee. I noticed they had eyelashes like talons; these girls were beyond what one would call merely attractive. They were tall, quite stunning and, in my opinion, cut from the finest of silk.

'Can I sign you girls in?' I asked. It was an impressive opening gambit from me. It relayed a frisson of power and wealth. Both of which I was bereft of.

'No, thank you,' they replied with hollow smiles. 'We can do it ourselves.'

PERHAPS THEY DID NOT BUY INTO THE POWER AND WEALTH bit, seeing how I was dressed in soft brown suede trousers trimmed with short tassels and a suede jacket with extra-long tassels hanging from the arms. I had a crucifix on my bare chest, and with a gold headband circling my forehead, looked more Apache than Onassis!

It should have been a closed chapter after that, but somehow during the evening the girls and I got talking. They told me their names and around 2 a.m. we decided to leave the club and go to the Empire Grill opposite Gloucester Road Tube station for a cuppa tea. In those days it was the only cafe open after midnight.

However, I only had enough money for one cuppa. Those outfits I wore cost every shilling of my Yankee Doodle wages. So the girls had to pay for their own tea, which must have impressed them no end.

We chatted for over an hour, nursing our teas. The girls could talk for Britain, that's for sure and whenever they stopped for breath, I managed to squeeze in a sentence or two. They were to jabbering what Marcel Marceau was to mime.

Tea over, I walked the girls home to their friends' house where they were both staying.

'Would you like to come in for a coffee?' one of them asked out of politeness rather than desire when we'd reached the front door.

'Sure,' I replied, although I was up to my gills in tea. It was close to 4 a.m. by now and already a filter of dawn brushed against a cerulean sky, so another hour with two lovely girls wouldn't kill me and if it did, what a way to go. In the lounge, there was a guitar leaning against the wall yearning for someone to play it. I wasn't trying to impress, honestly, but I picked up the lonely, discarded instrument, tuned it and languidly caressed a few chords and sang a number from my Beirut repertoire of love songs while we sipped cheap foul-tasting coffee.

IT WAS 7 A.M. WHEN I LEFT THAT HOUSE. THE streets of London were just beginning to awaken to the trickle of traffic and the sound of hastened footsteps of a city going about its work. People huddled in their overcoats and scarves like figures in a Lowry painting. A cold

November wind beat against my open chest, but I was radiating my own body heat. You see, when singing 'Cuando Calienta El Sol', I had noticed more than a scintilla of appreciation from one of the girls.

Two weeks after producing the two songs with the Japanese group, I decided to give up my job at Yankee Doodle. I allowed the resonance of that occasion to go to my head. I was now a proper record producer, no longer a short order cook. Four months behind a griddle with the ensuing heat and smoke, and soon the joys of cooking began to wane with alarming speed. I thanked the two owners of the restaurant for the opportunity of working with them and, without a tear to mist the moment of departure, I wished the staff goodbye.

From now on, music would occupy my mind and my working hours 24×7. It was the only way, I reckoned, to crack it into the upper echelon of the biz. Those poor starving marines at the US Embassy would have to find someone else to make their doughnuts because I was glued to my guitar, coaxing melodies and lyrics in the search for chart domination.

It was Christmas 1969, and I was on my own, with just my Afghan coat for warmth and company. You see, Anil was in prison, as were Poncho and Peso; the prosecution was building up a case against them and the boys had aligned themselves to being deported, so a veritable balloon of gloom hung over their heads.

One of the blonde girls I had met at Blaizes, the one who made infinitely bad coffee, had gone to her parents in deepest Essex as was the custom with most Brits around Christmas week. She and I had met a few times since that eventful night, taken in a film together, had a meal at the Chelsea Kitchen on King's Road and, quite frankly, I was being drawn to her like the Mafia are drawn to crime, like the needle of a compass is drawn to the north, like decadence is drawn to rich, dark chocolate, like a moth is drawn to a flame, like … well you get the drift.

ON CHRISTMAS EVE I GOT A PHONE CALL FROM HER.

'I was telling mum all about you,' she said excitedly. 'And mum said, "Poor thing, if he's all on his own why don't you invite him over?" So will you come and spend Christmas with us?'

I felt a welcoming lightness in her voice.

I had never met an English family before, up close and personal, let alone stayed with one. I was familiar with Christmas and all its trappings, but still a minute serving of nerves betrayed my outer calm. I went out and bought a bottle of Chivas Regal whiskey for her father and chocolates for her mother. I knew she had three brothers who played rugby and called themselves 'The Dangerous Brothers', but I would have to work on them when I met them.

IT WAS A CHILLY AFTERNOON WHEN I GOT OFF THE train at the town of South Benfleet, where the family lived. It was a one-horse town, but on that particular day, the horse was missing. The Golden Angel was there to meet me at the station. She stood out against the bleak and desolate scenery of the railway platform, her blonde hair falling to one side, smooth as a waveless sea. We met with a gentle embrace, uncertain of how much affection to parade in a public place.

She drove past the town centre, which was devoid of any of the sparkle of Christmas and turned right into Kent's Hill Road. A row of neat houses with trimmed hedges lined the pavements on either side. In my nervous state, I counted twenty-two houses before we arrived at her parent's place. It was a pebble-dash, semi-detached house with a front porch to park the car in and a decent-sized yard at the back with a facsimile of a lawn, bordered by the gentle fragrance of clematis, honeysuckle and rose bushes.

Her parents were lured into appeasement with the gifts I presented them. They seemed totally delighted, even though the father did not drink alcohol. He loved the shape of the bottle.

The mother said, 'Oh! You shouldn't have,' as I gave her the chocolates, and seemed immensely pleased by the gesture.

The three brothers, Aryan-looking with blond hair and light-blue eyes, stood looking at me like the guards at Nuremberg Gate not knowing what to make of me. Apart from my Afghan coat, I was wearing soft lilac bell-bottoms in velvet, a deep-purple shirt with ruffles down the front, a gold headband round my forehead and an assortment of beads and that crucifix on my chest.

'We hear you're in the arts?' Alec the oldest one, said to me. 'Yes,' I replied, with an engaging look.

'Which one?'

'Martial,' I said, without missing a beat.

'Good. We thought it might be flower arranging,' he replied tersely, before cracking up.

That broke the ice. We laughed, shook hands and then sat round the table to play a game of cards, while the mother made tea and ham sandwiches for everyone.

During the game, the boys cheated and afterwards while watching television I told them so.

'So how come you won then?' Phillip, the youngest, asked as a quizzical look materialized on his face.

'I was cheating, too,' I replied, wearing an enigmatic smile, reminiscent of a famous painting hanging in the Louvre.

'You're our kinda fella,' Alec said it as if it was a compliment.

'Yes, we hope you're going to marry our sis?' the middle brother, Richard, butted in, then added, 'We've been trying to get her married off for years.'

'Yeah! Please take her,' they chanted. 'We've got a dowry ready: two cows and a blanket.'

'Yeah! The blanket's to cover her face,' said Richard.

This was followed by boisterous laughter at our expense. 'Boys!' the blonde screamed in mock distress. 'Honestly!'

She looked a tad embarrassed. Our eyes met and held for a moment.

'Ooh! Look at them,' the boys cooed effeminately, ganging up on us and bringing colour to our cheeks.

Christmas Day was unique for me. We all gathered in the

front room, while a gas fire roared in the background, and began the ritual of unwrapping our presents. The family had taken the time and consideration to buy me little gifts to open. Presents like an ice-scraper for the car windows and a pair of red socks embossed with reindeer pulling Santa on them. Regardless, I had a grand time and we all got on like a house on fire. Christmas lunch was historic; no wonder the boys were all of a large size.

On Boxing Day, the brothers, their sister and I went out in the morning towards the sea coast. Lunch was going to be chicken with gravy and roast potatoes, plus a variety of greens like sprouts and beans. It all sounded wonderful as the mother was a divine cook of the old school and I was really looking forward to it. But in her over-generous hospitality, wanting to make the boy from India feel at home, she was going to make me a curry. I had tried to protest that this was quite unnecessary, but she would have none of it. So a curry it was going to be. It would be her first attempt and she was looking forward to it.

I must add that this was a time when the British were not too familiar with curries or any kind of food from beyond the English Channel. Any cheese apart from Cheddar was considered foreign and salads were unknown. As for asparagus, forget it. Anyway, I thought this a rather nice gesture on her part and in a way I was looking forward to a home-cooked chicken tikka masala with pulau, mango chutney and a stack of poppadoms.

WE GOT BACK FROM THE COAST, OUR APPETITES MADE MORE ravenous by the long walk and bracing sea breeze. While the family tucked into their roast, I was served Uncle Ben's rice from a packet, with turkey, carrots, peas and raisins mingling in a paprika-induced curry sauce. To say it was tame and tasteless would be giving it a build-up. The food was prison-awful. But I persevered, while watching the others slice into a golden-brown, herb-scented chicken with well-done roast potatoes and al dente vegetables drizzled with piping hot gravy.

I could have cried.

22

SCOTLAND YARD IN MY BACKYARD

THE RECORD, 'RAIN FALLS ON THE LONELY'/ 'SMILE FOR Me' by the Tigers came out in Japan in the New Year and went straight to number one. My first production and my first hit. I bought a copy of Billboard, the American trade paper that listed the top ten chart positions of major countries around the world and there it was at number one in the Japanese charts. I was elated. I had made the right move by throwing in my job at Yankee Doodle; now the work would come flowing in and with it the money and the good life. Quite frankly, producing a record was easy peasy.

I NOW HAD IT ALL: A HEAD FULL OF HAIR, a lovely blonde girlfriend and a number one record. The only thing missing from this equation was money. Since leaving my job at the restaurant the previous month, I was living on my meagre savings. It's uncanny how money slips away when you most need it and soon, I was down to my last five pounds. The rent was due every week and since I ate on a daily basis, there were food bills to pay plus other expenses that cropped up like unwelcome relatives. Luckily, this hit record would save me the embarrassment of penury. I had been through this cycle before and finally I could feel myself breaking free from the tentacles of indigence.

I was down to my last two pounds with my back against the wall, if not going through it, when I decided to go and see the record company about an advance on the record. I caught a bus to Oxford Street and wormed my way through the crowds of shoppers till I got to the office. I managed to see Roland Rennie, the gentleman who originally asked me to produce the record. He told me I would have to go see the managing director, Jeffrey Black, who was the head honcho at Polydor Records at that time, regarding monies and royalties. So I went across to Mr Black's office and requested his secretary for a quick meeting. Ten minutes later, I was in Jeffrey Black's expansive office.

He sat behind his desk and did not get up to greet me.

'Yes?' he said, looking up. Apart from a George Michael-like growth on his face, he looked a regular sort of guy. 'How can I help?'

I told him I had produced the Tiger's record, which had gone to number one in Japan, and showed him my copy of Billboard.

'I've seen it,' he said, not bothering to look at the magazine.

I also had with me a copy of the record, which credited my name as 'producer' on both the sleeve and disc.

'I would like an advance of £100 against future royalties,' I said in my best cut-glass accent.

'All right,' Jeffrey Black said, leaning back in his chair. 'Can I see a copy of your contract?'

'Contract,' I exclaimed. A feeling of déjà vu set in, reminding me about the time when I was asked for a P45.

'Yes, your producer's agreement with us,' he replied. 'Have you got it?'

'I'm afraid no one offered me a contract,' I stuttered, meekly. 'I don't have one.'

'If you don't have a contract, I'm afraid I cannot give you an advance.'

There was a prolonged silence while my heart sank and then journeyed up to my throat.

'Can I have fifty pounds?' I gulped. It was all I could think of.

'Listen, if you don't have a contract, I cannot advance you any money.

It's as simple as that. I need proof. I'm sorry.'

It may have been simple, but this simpleton had not the brains, or even a replica of it, to ask for a contract when he made the record. Since none was offered at the time, the idea of a written agreement had not occurred to me.

I thrust the disc in front of him.

'Here's my name on it,' I argued. 'That's proof isn't it?'

He shook his head. 'Listen, without a contract I cannot authorize a payment.'

'Can I have ten pounds, please?' I said, not wishing to sound desperate.

'I cannot,' he replied stubbornly.

'Can I have five?' A clear sign I was desperate but frankly I didn't care if he knew. Of the two pounds I had when I'd left home, I'd already spent 50p on a Mars bar and the bus ticket. If there's a word that's more befitting than desperate, I was it.

He finally picked up the phone on his desk and spoke to his secretary outside. A spray of relief spread across my face. Maybe there is a God after all, I thought to myself.

'Daphne,' he said 'change that booking for dinner from 8.30 to 9 p.m.' He put the phone down and told me one last time he could not give me any money.

I stood up, gutted and broken. He too got up – a tall man he was – and led me to the door, making sure I was no longer in his orbit. Sitting in his ivory tower, he had forgotten how others lived; he was unaware of their needs, their desperation or their desolation. For all his height, he was a pygmy of a man with no heart. There was absolutely no reaction to my pleas. What would it have taken for him to give me a fiver out of his own pocket? What kind of a man was he? Obviously, one whose emotions had died at birth.

I walked out of his office with one salutary thought that has stayed with me the rest of my life: to always have time for others and if I did not, to make it my priority to find time. After all, kindness costs very little. A part of me felt that fate had brought this about because human beings need a moral compass to teach us that while we are immersed in the self, we should not be unaware of the less fortunate.

I went back to the apartment totally deflated and broke. My hangdog expression spoke volumes about the way I felt. My flaxen-haired beauty tried to cheer me up by telling me there were people worse off than I was in Africa. She could have mentioned Merthyr Tydfil, Glasgow, Hackney or Bootle which were nearer home and as amply deprived. Things could not get any worse for me, could they?

There was a knock on the door of our Mews flat. I went down the stairs and opened the door to see two men dressed in suits, sombre of expression, standing outside on the cobbled path.

'Are you Mr Biddu?' one of them asked.

I sensed that something was wrong. Their demeanour was like those of agents from the Federal Bureau of Investigation, but this was London.

'Yes,' I replied hesitantly.

'We would like to talk to you,' one of them said, presenting his credentials. 'We are from Scotland Yard.'

'Jeez,' I whispered under my breath. What would Scotland Yard want with me? My passport was in order. I wasn't an illegal. I hadn't strangled Jeffrey Black, much as I had wanted to.

'May we come in?' suit number two said. 'We want to ask you a few questions. This shouldn't take up too much of your time.'

'Yes, yes,' I replied, taking them up the stairs and into my room. I did not want to take them into the small lounge in case our conversation was overheard by the others in the flat. To quote Shakespeare, that ultimate wordsmith, 'The better part of valour is discretion.'

ONCE IN THE BEDROOM, I PULLED UP TWO CHAIRS FOR the men to sit on, while I sat on the bed, nervously chewing my nails down to the cuticles.

'You are aware why we have come to see you?' they asked. 'No,' I replied, shaking my head, with a look of innocence that would melt most mothers' hearts.

'Are you a friend of Mr Anil, Mr Peso and…'

It suddenly hit me why the men were here. I had forgotten all about the drug bust, immersed as I was in my own well of despair.

'Erm, yes,' I said, a shiver of apprehension running through me.

The men spoke softly and slowly to put me at ease. On reflection these guys were pros, they could see the anxiety in my eyes.

'You have nothing to worry about,' one of them said.

'Just so long as you tell us the truth,' the other one finished the sentence. I could see they were a double act like Cain and Abel or Jekyll and Hyde.

'Do you take drugs?'

'No, sir. You can ask my friends – I don't drink alcohol or do drugs.'

'Have you ever been involved in the sale of drugs?' 'No, sir.'

'I see,' they replied, and there was an uneasy silence as they looked at each other.

What were they thinking? I wondered. A cocktail of emotions raced through my body; two parts fear and one part panic with a slice of dread.

'Were you aware your friends were transporting drugs into the country?' suit number one finally broke the silence.

'Erm…' I stuttered.

'It's better you tell us, rather than us finding out later,' the other man said, noticing my hesitation. 'If you come clean, it will be in our report and the judge will take this into consideration.'

Judge? Hold on, this was way above my head.

Do you have a cigarette?' I asked them.

One was proffered to me. I was not a smoker, but this was as good a time as any to start. I lit up and took a deep drag and coughed and spluttered and wheezed like a dragon.

'I've never done this before,' I gasped, searching for air, my eyes watering from the effort. 'Thanks.'

I noticed a whisk of a smile shared between them.

But who wouldn't be a bundle of nerves, having two men

from Scotland Yard sitting in your bedroom and questioning your involvement in a drug heist?

Ten minutes later, they got up.

'We'll come back tomorrow,' one of them said, checking his watch.

'Yes. Take it easy. No strain. Think about what we've said,' the other added.

'Sure,' I replied.

No strain, the man said. Easy for him to say so; here I was, bound and gagged on the tracks with the train speeding towards me. And I'd have to wait till tomorrow to see how it all ended.

23

AN END AND A BEGINNING

I SPOKE TO THE SUNSHINE OF MY LIFE THAT EVENING and told her all about the two guys from Scotland Yard, and the background to it. She offered me sympathy and kisses and told me I had nothing to worry about as she was 100 per cent sure I was innocent. I was thinking of ditching her as my girlfriend and taking her on as my lawyer.

The next day, Batman and Robin were back. We took our places in the bedroom, and the interrogation began.

'So have you had a think about it?' one of them asked. 'About what, sir?' I replied.

'About your involvement with your friends in the import of drugs.' The tone of voice was just that bit harder.

'I told you I wasn't involved.'

'But you were aware of what they were doing, were you not? You were an accessory to their crime. Yes?'

'They told me about it, and I asked them not to do it,' I replied feebly. 'I didn't think they would go through with it.'

'You could have gone to the police,' one of them said, snookering me.

I sat there looking at my feet, not knowing what to say. The silence rolled on forever.

'Listen,' he sounded exasperated. 'We would like to search your room. We don't have a search warrant, but we can come back later with one if you insist.'

'Please look around.' I said, as if I had a choice in the matter.

The room had a double bed, a chest of drawers on one side and cupboards on the opposite side, in which I hung my clothes; there was also a writing table with a mirror above it. My guitar stood as silent witness against one corner of the wall.

Within minutes of searching, they had found the letter from India which Anil had sent me, asking me to come to Paris. Once again, with my brain cells more scrambled than an egg, I had forgotten to tear up the letter and flush it down the pan or bin it. Instead, it had been lying in the top drawer, waiting to be discovered. They read the letter to themselves and then looked at me.

'So you were involved,' they said, shaking their heads as if to indicate it was all over bar the sentencing.

'When did you go to Paris?' suit number one asked.

'I keep telling you I wasn't involved. I did not go to Paris,' I said, as defiantly as possible under the circumstances.

'We have it here,' he said, waving the aerogramme. 'Here is the proof. They asked you to meet them in Paris.'

'Let's see your passport please,' suit number two demanded.

Even as I opened the drawer to get out my passport, I felt relief cruise through me.

I handed them my passport, as an imperceptible smile sprouted inside me. They went through the pages once, twice and then a third time. They could not find an entry stamp for France during the preceding two months.

'So you didn't go to Paris, then?' one of them said with a baffled look on his face.

'I told you, sir, I didn't go and I wasn't involved.'

I didn't know if the two men were disappointed, but I lit up my third cigarette of the session. This time I inhaled slowly, not too deeply and let the smoke spiral its way out into oblivion. From that day on, I was hooked on cigarettes. Not having a visa had disallowed me from entering Paris and thus saved me from going to prison.

As for my three friends, they were each given a one-and-a-half-year prison sentence, with time off for good behaviour. At the end of their term in jail, they were to be deported from the UK. Jane was given a suspended sentence, as the judge believed she acted under the influence of her Svengali. It was a miserable end to a sad chapter, but an inevitable one.

Anil, Poncho and I met for one last time when they were released from prison. It was quite surreal, and there was no sense of recrimination or acrimony between us. We talked for about an hour, but the conversation lacked the fluidity of the past. In fact, it was punctuated by long silences; a sense of gloom pervading the atmosphere. One was going back to India, the other to Pakistan. How they would have loved to stay on in England. But in seventy-two hours they would be winging their way back to their respective countries, courtesy of Her Majesty the Queen.

'I'm sorry guys,' I finally mumbled.

'Yeah, sure.' Anil tried to raise a smile. 'It wasn't your fault.' And we hugged one another.

'Look after yourself, okay?' Poncho said, also giving me a bear hug. 'Stay away from trouble.' It must have been an effort for him to put on a weak smile.

'I'll miss you guys,' I replied softly. I never saw my friends again.

A week or so later, I received a letter from the States. I hurriedly opened it, wondering who it could be. Surprisingly, it was from my friend Suresh who had just finished his studies at Boston University. He wrote that his ex-room-mate, a guy called Marc Etra, wanted to cut a record and since I was the only one he knew that was vaguely connected to the music business, the request was for me to come to New York and produce a couple of tracks for the guys. Marc Etra's parents would pick up the tab for my airfare to the States and I could stay with the family in Laurence, Long Island, which was about an hour and a half's drive from Manhattan.

It was a most unexpected and opportune intrusion, but one that was more welcome than desert rain.

The letter lifted my spirits no end, especially after the recent court case. The pendulum of my existence was as ever swinging from side to side, the highs and lows and the ups and downs, all part of life's twisted and unfathomable tapestry. Two weeks later, the ticket arrived and I kissed my lady-love goodbye with the promise I would see her in a month's time. I had sixteen pounds on me, the remnants of my fortune from a part-time job. With that and a suitcase of clothes, I was ready for the Big Apple.

AT HEATHROW AIRPORT, I SAT WAITING FOR THE BOARDING ANNOUNCEMENT. My flight was due to leave in an hour, when suddenly over the Tannoy and above the general cacophony of an international terminal, I heard the announcer's voice.

'Will Mr Biddu please come to the BOAC information desk? Will Mr Biddu please come to the BOAC information desk?' the announcer repeated.

'What now?' I thought to myself as I found my way to the desk, wondering what it was they wanted from me. I had a visa for the States, so no problem on that score.

'I'm Biddu,' I said to the lady behind the desk.

'A call for you, sir,' she said, handing me the phone. 'Yes?' I said, mystified.

'It's me, darling.' I heard the lilt of her dancing voice. 'What's wrong?' I asked, expecting a problem. 'Nothing,' she replied. 'I'm missing you.'

'I haven't gone yet. I'm still at the airport.' 'I know, silly. I'm making the call.'

'Flattery will get you nowhere,' I said, happy to hear her trill. 'I've given in my notice at work. I'm going to join you in America in two weeks,' she said.

'Can't live without me huh?' I teased, happy that we wouldn't be apart for too long.

'No, I just want to see New York before I die.' She giggled flirtatiously.

We spoke for another two minutes.

'Gotta go,' I said hurriedly. 'They're calling my flight.'

We blew kisses over the phone.

'Put the phone down,' I said.

'You do it first,' she replied.

'No, you first,' I answered.

'No, you,' she cajoled.

'Ladies first,' I said dutifully.

'No, you.' She was adamant.

I finally put the phone down. She would always have the last word.

New York did not let me down. It was everything my imagination told me it would be. Big, bold and brassy, with buildings of glass, chrome and concrete reaching for the clouds. Actually beyond the clouds, they were reaching for the sky. Their cars were the length of playing fields and as wide as British roads. The city looked like a hundred movie sets come alive and made London look placid. It made London look genteel and it made London look quaint.

I drank it all in – Times Square, Broadway, The Rockefeller Center, SoHo and Central Park. I ate it all in – hamburgers, chilli dogs and pizzas the size of hub caps. It had the buzz of a thousand hornet's nests. Even the steam rising from vents on the street was mystifying and magical.

In two words, New York was 'bloody awesome'.

Marc was a good guy. Friendly, warm and self-effacing, but yet made no bones about the fact that he was seeing a psychiatrist, because his girlfriend had recently left him. That broken heart was costing him $60 an hour, twice a week to unravel his emotions while lying on a couch talking to a shrink. Hello, I thought, what planet are we on? He could have opened his heart out to me for far less money. I soon found out that for most well-off Americans, a shrink was de rigueur.

Suresh, Marc and I would drive from Long Island into Manhattan most mornings in Marc's Pontiac, a car big enough to house a swimming pool. Well, maybe that's an exaggeration, but definitely big enough to host an ex-Kamikaze pilots' reunion. We'd take a look at studios and try to get to visit record companies with the idea of selling our potential disc. In the evenings, we'd head back to Long Island. Marc's parents, Ma and Pa Etra, were wonderful hosts, extremely friendly and generous and when my English Rose arrived from London three weeks later, she was welcomed with open arms by the family. They say house guests should never stay more than three or four days because, like fish, they tend to go off. But we stayed with the Etras for six weeks and were made to feel such a part of the family that I briefly flirted with the idea of converting to Judaism. I resisted, however, when I realized bacon sandwiches would no longer be on the menu.

While New York was fun and we oohed and aahed at Macy's and Bloomingdale's, from the point of view of work it just didn't pan out. The studios were expensive and we did not know of any musicians we could call upon to play on the sessions. We met the owner of Colossus Records, a gentleman called Jerry Ross, who thought it wouldn't be a bad idea to record the songs in a setting I was more familiar with. He was also prepared to buy the track and release it, if it sounded good. So, we decided to fly back to London and record the songs there.

We were sad to leave America and in particular, Laurence, Long Island. It was an oasis of absurd wealth in a sea of riches. Almost all the houses were low and bungalow-style, with manicured lawns leading to the front door and rooms the size of London's apartments. The people in the area were really taken up with my cherub's British accent and found me, shall I say, rather interesting. Sometimes neighbours would knock on the Etras' door and ask politely, 'Can we take the Indian out?' I kid you not. Most of the rich white people in the village had never seen an Indian before. What with their annual median income per household of $90,000 in 1970, Planet America cosseted and isolated them from the realities of existence elsewhere on earth.

Back in London, the three of us went into a studio and recorded the song 'Love a Little Longer', written by Suresh with help from me. It sounded polished and professional and we were happy enough with it. Jerry Ross of Colossus bought the tracks and released the single in the States on his label. It unfortunately did not get any airplay on American radio (the oxygen for a record's success), and so the record passed into oblivion with a speedy and painless death, lost amid a thousand songs that suffered a similar fate every year. At least Marc wasn't out of money, having recouped his costs from the advance I negotiated with the record company. It was the one other thing I had learnt from making the Tiger's record.

THEN BEGAN A PERIOD OF INTENSE ACTIVITY ON MY PART in making music. I started by recording an album with the actor Jack Wilde who had played the lead in the movie Oliver. I met him at the offices of Hemdale Films, a film production company I was smooching around, hoping to score some work. Jack was immensely popular following the release of Oliver and he wanted to make an album. Doesn't everyone? In any case, I was roped in to write and produce the songs.

Jack was a lovely kid, who unfortunately did not have much of a singing voice, but it was a job that paid my rent and some. So I took it. The album came out and did reasonably well both in the UK and the States, selling mainly to his fans. This gig, however, led to me doing the title song for a movie called Embassy, starring Richard Roundtree the actor from Shaft, a film that was famous for being the first to have an all-black star cast. Its iconic theme song, with its sexy spoken line, 'Shaft, can you dig it?', had been composed by Isaac Hayes.

I composed the title track for Embassy with a frenetic, pulsating and dramatic melody written in a minor key, and conscious-awakening lyrics. The song was called 'Somebody Stop This Madness' and I needed a strong, intense lead vocal to do justice to the melody.

I had heard a group called Gonzales, a loose collective of

musicians who played when the fancy took them or when gigs became available. I saw them at one of the London clubs and noticed their singer had a voice as fluid as mercury, a soulful tone and near-perfect pitching. His name was Carl Douglas. I met with him after the gig and asked him if he would sing my theme for Embassy.

He sang the number impressively and we stayed in touch with one another. I thought his was a voice with that special indefinable ingredient that separates the wheat from the chaff, and I wanted to use him again one day, when the time was right.

EMBASSY RELEASED TO A LUKEWARM RESPONSE BUT I GOT A thrill out of doing a song for a movie. It was my first and a learning curve in my career. I had made a few shillings from these two productions and for the first time, my pockets were jingling. I had enough money to consider taking a trip back home. My mom and I had kept in touch those last four years through letters and the odd crackle-infested phone call, but it would be nice to see her in the flesh.

So, in February 1971, I finally took that trip back to Bangalore, after an overnight stay in Bombay, where I met up with my old friend Ashok, the one who gave Brian Epstein a run for his money when it came to managing acts. He had just met and fallen in love with a French girl who was flying with Air India. Not as a passenger I hasten to add, but as an airhostess. So, jet- lagged and exhausted as I was, I had to listen to him go on and on like the never-ending cascade of a waterfall, about Annelise, his 'cherie amour'.

The next day I flew to Bangalore. Nothing much had changed except it had got more crowded with the influx of people from major cities like Bombay, Delhi and Calcutta.

But seeing the look of joy and happiness on my mother's face was worth a hundred journeys. Nothing beats a mother's unconditional love. A love that is trampled on, ignored and often unappreciated but still remains undiluted in its essence, to cocoon you in its maternal blanket of devotion.

It was also good to see my sister, who had married her tennis partner and was in the process of producing children when not on the tennis court. My brother had given up the estates and was now an apprentice horse trainer under one of India's best trainers, a Mr Byramjee. The racing season in India is almost around the year. My sister-in-law had opened a burger joint called Ice and Spice and Mom supervised the staff in the kitchen at home and made sure the burgers were made to certain specifications. She could have run McDonalds.

DURING MY THREE WEEKS IN INDIA, A WANDERING MYSTIC, PSYCHIC or fortune-teller or whatever they call themselves, knocked on our front door. My mother, more curious than a cat, let him in and suggested he read my fortune. The man sat on the floor and laid out his talisman, some cards and seashells. He asked me a dozen questions to which I gave him short, succinct answers. He looked at my palm and then said this was my last birth and I would not be reincarnated any more. To a practising Hindu (which I am not) achieving moksha is the ultimate beyond nirvana. He also said I should marry on 2 June, which also happens to be Queen Elizabeth's birthday; not that the mystic was aware of this.

I was missing my duchess a lot, and I spoke to her once on the telephone from Bangalore. Trying to make a long-distance call from India was an achievement of sorts in those days. You had to book a call with the local operator a day in advance to make sure that a call could be made. So I decided to send her a telegram asking her if she was free on 2 June and if she was, would she marry me. She replied, saying there was a possible window of opportunity open on that day.

On 2 June, my lady love and I got married at St Luke's Church in Redcliffe Gardens, Earl's Court. Being non-religious, it really did not matter where I got married, so long as it was to the right girl. Invitations were then sent out to close friends to attend our 'Farewell to Freedom' party. Our close friends like Ashok and his wife Anne; Hash, who had made it to the UK with his wife Loretta; Pauline and Abbas, her Iranian boyfriend, who soon became her husband; Jane and David Coulson; Barry and Ruth Berman; Esther and Victor Fieldgrass; Jonathan Rowland; Vivy and David Butler; Dee

Page; Cathy; and my cousin Ashok from Bangalore and his lovely wife Mangla were all in attendance. (Sorry, but I was coerced into mentioning them.)

It was a gloriously sunny day and the bride looked radiant in an outfit of cream silk with tiny pearl drops delicately stitched on, while I wore a deep-green velvet suit, shirt and a borrowed tie. We had hired a vintage Rolls Royce to drive the bride and her father to the church on time and, ironically, the Rolls had an insignia of Lord Ganesha on the bonnet instead of the Spirit of Ecstasy. Spooky, that!

We walked down the aisle to a sensual, instrumental piece I had composed called 'Song for Sue' which would later be featured on my first album. It was a simple, joyful but daunting ceremony.

After the vows we all adjourned to our one-bed apartment, which was also in Redcliffe Gardens, where we had finger food and drinks. By late evening it was all over. The wedding celebrations that is, not the marriage. That has lasted as I write this autobiography and hopefully will continue to do so when the book is published and long after you've read this.

From that day on, my bride became Mrs Sue Biddu and for ever she would walk two paces ahead of me.

24

KUNG FU ON THE MENU

I BEGAN LOOKING FOR NEW ARTISTS TO PRODUCE AND trawled the music and trade papers to find them. I met a singer called Faith Brown who played the cabaret circuit. She was an attractive girl with a powerful voice, but her main assets were that mother nature had gifted her a pair of enormous breasts. In fact, she made Dolly Parton look downright flat-chested.

She would stand in front of me and joke, 'Can you tell me what colour shoes I'm wearing today?'

We recorded a couple of singles that were released on Pye Records but they didn't trouble the charts. Pity really, as both her records were meaty, beaty and good. Faith Brown went on to bigger things (no pun intended). She became a comedienne and a star in the Midlands and the north, with frequent appearances on television.

I met the singer Jimmy James, from the group Jimmy James and the Vagabonds, a popular club act, and recorded a song with him called 'A Man Like Me'. This song had a Tamla Motown vibe, a style of music I was enamoured with since those early Beirut days.

Although it did not get national airplay, 'A Man Like Me' continued to sell well over a period of five years, always hanging around the lower end of the charts and eventually became a cult hit.

It was big in the clubs, especially up north where there was a booming club culture playing a style of music called northern soul. Many years later, copies of 'A Man Like Me' were changing hands at £50 per vinyl at specialist record stores.

I also recorded an American singer called Johnny Johnson. A guy with a great soul voice whose vocals pulverized and cut through a track like laser through steel. He had, many years previously, had a hit with a song called 'Breakin' Down the Walls of Heartache'. Johnny's new single only tickled the bottom rung of the charts.

AROUND THE SAME TIME AS I WAS WORKING WITH THE above artists, I composed a song called 'Stop What You're Doin' to Me (I Like It)', a tease of a lyric line with a strong Motown feel to the music. I got a couple of girl session singers, paid them a fee and recorded the song under the group name of the Playthings. Once again, it did not receive a single play on any radio station, but somehow it managed to sell a certain amount. Somewhere, somehow, someone was getting to listen to my records and buying them, albeit in small numbers. I could only think it was because of the clubs, which incidentally were now being called discotheques- one French word I had no trouble getting my tongue round.

I REALIZED THAT WITHOUT AIRPLAY, THE CHANCES OF HAVING A big hit were, in the words of the boxing promoter Don King, slim to nil. And slim was out of town. Every week, around fifty new records were released in the UK and there was only one major national station. That was Radio One. If Radio One did not play your song you could kiss its chances of success goodbye. The station had a play list which they adhered to and about five or six songs were added to that list every week. When you took into account the new releases of well-known artists from the States and the UK, whose records would certainly go on to that play list, you had a better chance of finding a nugget while panning for gold.

I realized that the only way to circumvent this problem was to make dance tracks that could get played in the discos and hopefully those punters would go out and buy the record. I had noticed this happening with many of the songs I produced and figured radio would only disintegrate my hopes and never break my records.

WHEN I LOOK BACK ON IT, THOSE FRUSTRATING YEARS WERE my learning period. They taught me more than just the rudimentary skills of songwriting and production. They educated me in how to construct a record. I deduced that a record should begin with a musical introduction that catches the listener's attention and draws him to the song, making him want to listen to the rest of the piece. The introductory motif should be distinct, melodic; perhaps a unique sound, or an unusual instrument playing it. The verse of the song should be interesting and set a mood for the rest of the song, with a slight build-up of the melody and arrangement on the bridge before it opens up and motors on with a chorus or hook that is as catchy as measles and won't leave your memory. It didn't hurt to often start the song with a chorus for instant appeal, which could then lead into a verse. A good production should have plateaus and peaks but never valleys and troughs.

A good vocalist is the icing on the cake. An average singer blessed with Pavarotti's looks and not his voice can make a good song sound ordinary and dull, while the same song, if sung by a dynamic vocalist can raise the fine hairs on your arm by making it sound like music from the heavens. I had a weakness for violins, or 'dancing strings' as I called them, and this became the leitmotif on most of my productions. I also tried to remember what Steve Cropper, the famous guitarist, once said: 'It's not what you play, but what you leave out that's important.' In other words, don't layer the track with everything, including the kitchen sink. Instead, allow a track to breathe without clutter and musical confusion.

All this is easier said than done. Quite often with all the best intentions, a record could come out sounding quite unlike how it had sounded in your head. But making records was and is a gamble. All you're trying to do is shorten the odds in your favour.

Towards the end of 1973, we bought our first apartment in Pimlico, an affordable area on the fringes of Chelsea. It was a small, two-bedroom maisonette down a treeless cul-de-sac called Westmoreland Terrace; it cost us £13,000. I had to put down a deposit of £1300, 10 per cent of the asking price, and get a mortgage for the balance amount. I managed to scrimp together a little over £1000 and the balance was given to me by my father-in-law. The duplex came with a tiny garage that housed our beat-up but still mobile Morris 1100.

Owning a property made infinitely more sense to me than paying rent to someone else. But finding the money for the monthly mortgage repayment and sundry utility bills was a big headache. The trouble with being involved in the arts without a regular job or income meant no regular pay cheque at the end of the month, so I was continuously chasing my tail. But this is the road I had chosen, so I wasn't looking for sympathy; just a massive hit record.

THE WORLD WASN'T IN A GREAT STATE EITHER. THE OIL crisis which began towards the latter part of 1973 caused a huge problem of recession for the industrialized nations. The Organization of Petroleum Exporting Countries, or OPEC, proclaimed an oil embargo because of America's support for Israel in the Yom Kippur War. OPEC used its leverage to hike the price of crude and, this in turn, began hitting the developed countries as OPEC was the predominant supplier. Britain went through a period of stagnation during 1974, which wasn't helped by the stock market crash. But when the going gets tough, you either go shopping and faff around doing nothing, or put your thinking cap on, and hope that one among the many moneymaking ideas swirling around in your head will bear fruit.

One day, the idea came to me to form my own music and production company. The plan was to sign an artist or writer to my own mom-and-pop outfit, self-finance the production of a record with the artist and sell the finished product to a major record company, like, for instance EMI. The record company, if they liked the product, would pay an advance, which would more than cover my costs plus a royalty of, say, 12 per cent on future sales of the record. The record label would do all the work in marketing and promoting the record; if it clicked and the record was a hit, the royalties would hopefully pour in. Are you with me so far?

The percentage of royalties paid out on an externally financed project was at least twice as much as an in-house production that the record company would have initiated and paid for. Although I would have to pay my singer his or her royalties from the 12 per cent my company received, it would still leave a very substantial amount for me and my little company.

The next step was to negotiate a publishing deal for the copyright of the songs in my company with Chappell Music, a huge global company that would look after my repertoire and collect any and all revenues due to me or my writers. Because every time a song is played on the radio, television or club, they have to make a payment to the collecting agency of that country for the use of that song. The collecting agency (Performing Rights Society in the UK) collects that money and sends it to the publishers who then make half-yearly payments to the writers of the song. There are a few other revenue streams of money that come in on a record, but I'm beginning to sense you're stifling a yawn so I won't bore you with technicalities and detail.

Anyway, I received an advance of £1000 from Chappell Music against forthcoming royalties and decided to use this money to finance my first home production for my fledgling company, Subiddu Music, an obvious amalgamation of my wife's and my name. I liked the name Subiddu – it had a musical ring and rhythm to it. A few years later, Sinatra would paraphrase that name in the reprise of his song 'Strangers in the Night'. The bit at the end where he goes 'doo be doo biddu'. Thanks Frank, I owe you one.

I found an American song called 'I Want to Give You My Everything', which I thought sounded like a hit. It had been released in the States with a modicum of success but for some reason, had not been released in the UK. I wanted to do that song as my first home production. All I now needed was a singer who could deliver what I needed vocally. I remembered Carl Douglas from the time he did the title track for the film Embassy, so I got in touch with him. He was at a loose end and looking for a record deal. I offered him the opportunity of signing up with me and making a record. It was a straw, but he clutched it.

We met at my maisonette a few times to rehearse. His super-smooth vocals were just right for the song. On the third day of our rehearsal, we had honed the vocal to perfection and with time to kill, I casually asked Carl if he ever wrote songs.

'I have some lyrics here,' he replied, producing a crumpled sheet with some lyrics scrawled on it.

I looked at the sheet. 'Everybody was Kung Fu fighting, those cats were fast as lightning,' it read.

I went through the rest of the lyrics.

'Interesting,' I said. 'It might make a good B side.'

I picked up my guitar and started working some chords and Carl began to hum a melody. Pretty soon we had the song shipshape, and Carl added a few Chinese-type instrumental riffs, which I thought would sound good on violins and flute.

ON THE DAY OF THE SESSION, I SPENT MOST OF the time on the perceived A side, concentrating on 'I Want to Give You My Everything'. With fifteen minutes of studio time left, I got the musicians to record 'Kung Fu Fighting'. By now I had a regular pool of guys I worked with. Of course there was the old Yankee Doodle mate Gerry Shury on keyboards, Chris Rae on guitar and Frank McDonald on bass. I often used Pip Williams on guitar and arrangement, and Clem Cattini, Barry D'Souza or a young guy called Jon Richards from a well-known pop group called the Rubettes on drums.

In the afternoon session I added the violins and flutes and Carl came and sang his vocals. Since this was going to be a 'B' side, which meant not many people would hear it, I thought it would be fun to add some grunting sounds on the track. I had a writer with the exotic nom de plume of Lee Vanderbilt signed to me; so he, Carl and I added the chopping 'huh' and 'hah' vocals on the track which, on reflection, gave 'Kung Fu Fighting' its aggressive, streetwise edge. We also added the 'oh ho ho ho' on the intro to the song, which gave it that distinctive opening motif. Later that evening I mixed and mastered the track with my extremely capable and consummate recording engineer, Richard Dodd.

The following day, I took the tapes of the two songs to Pye Records, which was spitting distance away from the studio. I met with Robin Blanchflower, a soft-spoken gentleman with glasses and a doctor's calming influence. He was head of A&R (Artiste and Repertoire) at the company. We had a good working relationship, as I had made the Faith Brown and the Playthings records for him. Anyway, I was all excited with my new master and I handed him the tape, which he promptly spooled on to the tape recorder.

The first track, 'I Want to Give You My Everything', came on and Robin listened, his head bobbing to the groove and when it was over he said one word: 'Good.' He said it in that soft, mellifluous voice of his.

'Anything else on the tape?' he asked, before making any further pronouncements on the song.

'Nothing special,' I said. 'Just a quickie B side. It only took fifteen minutes.'

'Let's hear it anyway,' he replied nonchalantly.

'Kung Fu Fighting' came through the speakers and halfway through it, Robin got up and stopped the tape.

'This should be the A side,' he said, with tremendous prescience.

'You sure?' I asked, more than a little surprised.

'Yes,' Robin seemed quite sure about this. 'I think it has a chance.' There was a moment's hesitation on my part. But wisely, I gave in to his thinking. In hindsight it was probably the best decision I ever made in my entire career.

The week before the record came out, Carl's father, who was very ill in Jamaica, took a turn for the worse. Carl needed to go and see his dying father, and I gave him £500, which I could ill afford, for an airline ticket to Jamaica. The record came out in July 1974, while he was away. As usual, radio ignored the song and I thought, here we go once again – the death of a record due to no airplay. It was an unfair system, but then nothing's fair in love, war and the music business. Fair is just a state of complexion.

During the first three weeks of release nothing happened. Sure, I moaned to the record company that their promotion department was asleep at the wheel and they in turn complained that radio did not see fit to put the record on the play list and without it being on that shortlist there was very little they could do. It was a classic Catch 22 situation. In sheer frustration and in an attempt to breathe life into the record, I thought I would go to a large record store in Bond Street and buy a couple of copies of it. This might stimulate sales, I hoped.

I went into the store and asked for the record.

'I'm sorry sir,' the store assistant replied. 'We don't stock it.' 'Why not?' I asked with restrained annoyance.

The man just shrugged his shoulders with a 'dunno boss' attitude. He looked at me blankly and said, 'We can't stock every record that's released. Only if there's a demand.'

At that very moment another shopper came by and asked him if he had a copy of 'Kung Fu Fighting'. The request was met with a rejection, but before he could walk away, a young girl came and asked for the same song. For three unrelated people to ask for the same record was either a cosmic coincidence or a miracle.

Again the sales person made an excuse for not stocking the record.

'I produced that song,' I said proudly to the two customers. They smiled wanly, made their excuses and left.

'You've got to order some copies,' I urged the salesman. 'See, everybody in the world wants the record.'

We talked for a few minutes. I told him he held the key to my future happiness, the state of my marriage and my very existence on this earth. I restrained myself from being too dramatic.

'Okay, I'll order some copies,' the salesman said with a little laugh as he toddled off in the direction of his office, which had a 'Staff Only' board hanging on his door.

A shiver of excitement coursed through me. If this scenario

was replicated in a hundred record stores, who knows what could happen? My palm began to itch. This punk was feeling lucky.

CARL RETURNED FROM JAMAICA WITH THE SAD NEWS THAT HIS father had passed away. At least he was there during his dad's final moments. If this was the yin, I was waiting for the yang. The following week as if by magic, the record entered the lower rung of the charts. There was a buzz at the record company. Their field staff relayed the news that people were clamouring for the record and stores were running out of copies. The week after its low chart entry, the record zoomed to number nine. This was a big leap forward and achieved without a single play on radio. Every sale was from a punter hearing it in a club somewhere in the country.

Carl appeared on Top of the Pops with Lee Vanderbilt and me providing the backing vocals. Sue fitted us out in black kimonos with a snarling tiger motif on the back. I had a few old scarves, which we wore around our foreheads and midriffs and we managed to look like fearsome Ninja warriors or Japanese paddy farmers. It was hard to tell the difference.

Suddenly the radio stations were forced to play the song and with airplay now on, the record leapt to number one in the hit parade and stayed there for three solid weeks.

25

WHERE THERE'S A HIT THERE'S A WRIT

THE DAY THE RECORD WENT TO NUMBER ONE SHOULD have been a momentous and memorable occasion. It was. But for all the wrong reasons. That night, around ten, there was a knock on my front door. On opening it, I saw a tall, bespectacled man standing under the porch light.

'Yes?' I said, surprised by this late call.

'My name is Eric Woolfson and I am Carl's manager,' he said, in a voice laced with arsenic.

'Oh!' I replied, taken aback. 'I didn't know Carl had a manager.'

'I've just signed him to a management agreement. I'd like to talk to you. May I come in?' he asked brusquely.

It all happened so fast, that it threw me. The record went to number one in the morning and by that evening, Carl had signed up with a guy he had never met before.

'Yes, yes, come in,' I said, accommodatingly.

We went upstairs to the lounge and while I sat on the sofa, this tall man stood in front of me and, wearing the look of Dr Death, started berating me, 'You've taken Carl for a ride. Look, you have a nice place of your own here, while Carl lives in a rented flat. You're taking all the money.'

'Excuse me, I have had this place for over a year,' I pleaded. 'I just signed Carl a coupla months ago. I've already given him a number one, and he gets a percentage of the royalties. I even sent him to Jamaica for his father's funeral.'

I was being forced to prove my innocence in front of this insidious character.

He went on for another ten minutes, telling me I was a crook taking advantage of Carl and how he would earn Carl a fortune in future deals and he was going to nullify the existing contract with me, etc., – in the music business there is a saying, 'Where there's a hit there's a writ' – while I sat there, stunned into disbelief at what this man was saying. There is an ancient Vedic proverb that goes: 'We are given two ears and one mouth to listen twice as much as we speak.' But I think I was taking this mantra too literally.

Suddenly, my wife, who may have been listening to his tirade, came from the bedroom into the lounge.

'Who are you to shout at my husband?' she said, sounding like Wonder Woman. She raised her voice, 'Out! Get out of our home immediately.'

The man, surprised by this sudden feminine onslaught, walked downstairs, unable to breathe a word of protest and saw himself out of our home. He had harangued me for nearly thirty minutes; it was half-an-hour of my life I wouldn't get back.

THE NEXT MORNING I SPOKE TO CARL, WHO SHEEPISHLY ADMITTED he had signed to Woolfson the previous evening.

'How could you, Carl?' I complained. 'After all I've done for you. The record's at number one. You don't even know the guy.'

He seemed unrepentant. 'Eric says he'll make me millions.'

As he spoke, I felt the sting of his betrayal, but I hid my disappointment under a bushel of hope. 'Don't be silly, Carl. You're killing a good thing. Come on, man!'

I had been working on Carl's album and we still needed two more songs to finish the project. Carl, however, under instructions from his manager, would not attend the studio sessions to finish the tracks. I had eight songs ready and it was imperative to record the other two to complete the album. I racked my brains, wondering what to do. In the meantime, the unscrupulous manager had gone and worked a deal behind my back with Louis Benjamin, the chairman of Pye Records. When I found out about this, I approached the chairman and told him he was acting illegally and had also broken the tenets of our deal. He looked at me guiltily and said, 'I didn't think you would mind.'

I could have gone to court on these issues. But frankly, I was not that way inclined. I'm a writer, not a fighter. I had never employed a lawyer till then and I wasn't about to start.

I thought, fine, if Carl doesn't want to be with me, I can't stop him. The old adage 'you can take a horse to water but you can't make it drink' came to mind. I could have sued Carl, but then it would have cost me a year of worry and a small fortune, and the only people who would win would be the lawyers. There'd be other singers, I told myself, and the chairman of Pye made an overture of reconciliation. After all, his A&R man, Robin, and I got on rather well and so to maintain the peace, I acquiesced. I had one solution for the unfinished album. I wrote an instrumental piece over five minutes long, which, in those days, was considered an interminable length of time for a pop melody. It, however, allowed the album to have a decent running time. The instrumental was called 'Blue-Eyed Soul' and I placed the track on Carl's album called Kung Fu Fighting and Other Great Love Songs.

By now Carl's relationship with me had disintegrated into a fractious one. There was still a fair bit of television and promotion work to do on the single, 'Kung Fu Fighting'. A month or so later, and quite inexplicably, Woolfson decided Carl should go and live in Germany. Carl told me it had something to do with future tax planning and VAT. I could never understand this game plan, but he was sent off to live in Munich. Through this tenuous relationship we somehow managed to make a follow-up album, ironically called Love, Peace and Happiness, but the ties that bind two people in a working relationship had been severely damaged. There was no love, no peace and certainly no happiness between the two of us.

'Kung Fu Fighting' was released in America, Europe and the rest of the world. It went to number one in every territory and had cumulative sales of over nine million copies, which included three million in America alone. This was phenomenal and went some way to ameliorate the pain and disappointment resulting from Carl's behaviour. As for his manager, the only phrase I can bestow on the man without appearing unduly rude is to say, he had a head and a body.

I decided to move on with my career. The worldwide number one brought with it an avalanche of financial gain in royalties. My cherub and I decided to move from our maisonette in Pimlico to a big house in Notting Hill Gate, an area that would soon become ultra-fashionable. I was in a position to send money home to my mother, which allowed her to buy a small place of her own and we were also able to help Sue's parents financially towards a new home they were moving into.

We went to India that Christmas to spend time with family and friends. India had not changed much, still stuck in the mire of its outmoded and moribund ways. In Bombay, my buddy Suresh had fallen for the charms of a dazzling damsel called Devika and marriage was on the cards, if not in his horoscope. In Bangalore, my mother was on tenterhooks at the prospect of meeting her son's bride. Would this girl be worthy enough for her special one? I need not have worried. The two women in my life got on fabulously. Sue had a growing and underlying quest for mysticism and Eastern philosophy, and India just happens to be the ideal country for a person seeking a spiritual awakening, rebirth or renaissance. Amidst the heat and dust, the grinding poverty and teeming crowds, there is an essence of devotion among the Indian people for the pantheon of gods and avatars. Sue dived into the waters of India's spiritual ocean, seeking answers to her questions on god, the meaning of existence and the duality of life.

While I was in India, the instrumental piece 'Blue-Eyed Soul', which I had written to complete Carl's album, became a big club hit. The song had a lush melody with sweeping strings, a catchy baseline and a driving hi-hat-led rhythm. CBS Records (later to become Sony Music) wanted to sign me up as an artist. I called my friend Stuart Reid from India and asked him to negotiate the deal on my behalf. Stuart and his partner in crime, Frank Coachworth, had a small company called Mautoglade Music, and they looked after my accounts and did my bookkeeping. A deal was quickly struck with CBS and that's how the Biddu Orchestra was born. It was February 1975.

ON OUR RETURN, I BEGAN WORK ON THE BIDDU ORCHESTRA album. I picked some well-known songs with beautiful, dramatic and pathos-filled melodies like 'Summer of '42', 'Exodus' and Rodrigo's 'Concerto De Aranjuez'. I worked on the core elements of the melodies, taking just the main themes and with my friends, Gerry Shury and Pip Williams, scored musical arrangements to give the songs a glossy, orchestrated sound with a very danceable disco rhythm. I also wrote a slew of new instrumentals like 'Northern Dancer' and included a new version of 'Blue-Eyed Soul', which gave the album its eponymous title. We released a single with the instrumental 'Summer of '42', a provocative idea against the plethora of vocal-fronted songs. But it was a beautifully hot summer in 1975 and the song caught the mood of a nation basking in sunshine. It went up the charts and helped launch the album and me as an artist.

I also spent time looking for another artist to sign, now that Carl was no longer with me. I found two.

I met up with the singer Jimmy James, with whom I had worked in the past, and signed him to my company. We made a record called 'I Am Somebody', a five-minute opus in which Jimmy talks the lyrics rather than singing them. Today it would be called rap, but that word had yet to find its way into street jargon. The lyrics carried a message of love and peace and the chant 'I am somebody' in the chorus had the vibe and feel of a Baptist Church chant coupled with Martin

Luther King's 'I had a dream'. The song was released in America and sold well via the clubs and Black Radio.

My friend Lee Vanderbilt told me about this young girl singer with an amazing and powerful voice. I soon found out she was singing with the resident band at the Cat's Whisker, a nightclub in Streatham, London, and I went to meet the petite singer. Her name was Tina Charles.

26

MILAN, MONZA AND MOUNTAINS

IN AUGUST '75, MY WIFE HAD HER OWN NUMBER ONE production: Zak, a lovely little boy with a mop of brown hair and, thankfully, his mother's good looks. When he was three months old, we left him with his toys and his English grandma while Sue and I went to Los Angeles for a holiday. I had been touched by the base metal of wealth and success had gone to my bank account.

It was my first trip to the West Coast and I was really looking forward to it. If New York was exciting, LA was totally enticing. We lived it large by staying at the Beverley Hills Hotel on Sunset Boulevard. I was walking the set and living the movie. I had a rictus of a grin as I sat behind the wheel of a huge limousine driving down the open highways and boulevards of Los Angeles and around the streets of Hollywood. It was tacky, for sure, but we hadn't come looking for elegance. Our hotel was the meeting point of film stars, their agents, producers and directors. Often we would come down to breakfast and find Donald Sutherland at the next table in deep conversation with someone, perhaps his agent, discussing a script. Life begins early in LA.

I ONCE SAW WARREN BEATTY TALKING WITH A MAN. IT was unusual

to see him without a woman by his side; a bit like seeing Dean Martin with an empty glass in his hand. Beatty was a good- looking man with, allegedly, over 2000 bedroom conquests. No wonder Woody Allen wanted to come back as Warren Beatty's fingertips in his next life! Some days, my ammorata and I would drive majestically along Sunset Boulevard and around Bel Air, looking at the magnificent homes of the rich, the lawns tended to by Mexican gardeners and with Honduran maids tidying the bedrooms. Los Angeles was man's idea of paradise and we were buying into it briefly. The two weeks just flew by and soon it was time to say goodbye to La La land and hello to London.

Refreshed from the break, I got back into the blur of work. By now, 'Summer of '42' was doing well in Europe and there was a request from someone at the record company in Italy to go there and perform the song on an Italian daytime TV show. My English record company thought it was a great idea as it would boost sales in Italy and domino onto other neighbouring territories.

So I flew out one windy October morning to Milan. I was met at the airport by some personnel from the TV company, and unfortunately none of them could speak any English. My Italian was limited to cappuccino, spaghetti, ravioli and Gucci, which is fine in a restaurant or shopping arcade, but absolutely useless anywhere else. Anyway, I was taken in a van like a smuggled immigrant and driven along the auto route to a town called Monza. During the journey, the Italians chatted amongst themselves, intermittently breaking away to look at me with limp smiles and flashing teeth. At Monza, I met a few more people from the television company. Fortunately, one of the men could speak a little English with a lotta accent.

'We shooter you in the mountains,' he said to me by way of introduction.

'Mountains?' I asked puzzled.

'Yes,' he said cheerfully. 'We taker the you to the mountains in the helicopter and er shooter the you.'

Thank God! That explained everything. Frankly, I was none the wiser, but I remained silent. Who knew how these TV directors worked? But it did seem strange that a song called 'Summer of '42' was going to be shot in the mountains. Plus, the idea of going in an Italian helicopter filled me with dread. Fear was another sensation I was beginning to feel.

'Doah you need the anything,' he asked kindly.

'Cappuccino,' I said in fluent Italian. I needed something strong to take all this in.

So there I was, in a helicopter, its rotor blades whirring noisily, two hours after arriving in Milan, climbing ever upwards towards the Italian Alps with the pilot and a cameraman. Fortunately, I had worn my fur coat from London, so at least I would be warm up in the mountains. As we climbed the series of snow-covered mountains, the scenery was breathtaking. We whizzed between mountain passes and far, far below, one could see a picturesque little village. It all looked so magnificent. I wanted to be down there in the village, not up here in a copter.

Then suddenly, we neared the top of a mountain and all around me I could see the jagged, dagger-like panorama of silver mountains stretching endlessly, foreboding and unnerving, their craggy architecture blowing away my calm. The helicopter slowed down enough for us to remain a few feet above the snow, its rotor blades furiously churning the snow into a mini blizzard. There was a bit of unsteady movement as the helicopter struggled to maintain an even balance. Then the pilot opened the door.

'Down, down,' he pointed to the snow below. 'Pardon?' I said, above the noise of the blades.

'Down. You er down,' the pilot repeated in his expansive and erudite English.

'No comprendo,' I said, sounding like a damn tourist.

The cameraman decided to join in by doing a mime. I was to jump down and they would film me. I finally gathered what the storyline was all about – I was to play a lost hiker and as the helicopter kept swooping down on me, I was to yell and wave my hands as if looking for help and the helicopter would finally rescue me. What a fabulous storyboard! My language deficiency precluded me from arguing why on earth I should do this and what did it have to do with my song. At that moment, I was prepared for the record to flop.

Too late. I was gently pushed out of the helicopter. Luckily, I landed on my feet, but I did not realize – coming as I did from a land of snakes, tigers and monsoons – that virgin snow on the tops of mountains is soft and pliant. As I landed, I went right through the snow and up to my armpits. I was now in nearly five feet of snow. To make matters worse, the whirring blades were sucking in the air around me and creating a vacuum, thus depriving me of oxygen to breathe. Plus, the rotating motion was causing the snow on my hands and face to freeze into ice. Fear took over. I looked at the two guys as the helicopter kept coming towards me and then drifting away, and then returning once again in repetitive moves. The cameraman was busy shooting, while the pilot's attention was rightly focused on keeping the machine on an even keel. My fur coat was wet at the edges, my hair was dripping, my shoes were soaked and my fingers were freezing but those were the least of my problems. I waved in sheer panic to the two men and tried to catch some air at the same time, wondering if I would ever get out alive; I got the thumbs-up from the cameraman. It was exactly the kind of shot he wanted. What a trooper this Indian fellow is, he must have thought. This scene shooting went on for a dangerous ten minutes, at which point I think the pilot recognized my predicament and told the cameraman that it wasn't method acting on my part but something more serious. So the helicopter landed inches above the snow and I was hauled in shivering like a frightened puppy.

I was taken back to base in Monza; my hands were icy-cold and a tingling sensation of pain shot through them. I was greeted and taken into the studio where they were going to do an indoor shoot of the song, to complement the outdoor shooting we had just completed. My hands looked normal. There was no redness or anything untoward, but boy, was it painful. I did not want to sound like mama's little boy, so I bore the pain in silence like a good martyr.

The indoor shoot required me to sit by a piano, pensive, looking at the score of the song. Another scene had me by a fireside, pensive, looking at the score of the song. The final scene had me standing by a window with my reflection on the window pane, pensive, and looking at the score of the song. The only thing I was pensive and apprehensive about was the stinging sensation in my hands. It felt like I had been resting my hands on a residue of burning ashes. I finally told them I wanted to get back to Milan and to my hotel, so I could catch the next morning's flight back to London.

ONE OF THE CREW DROVE ME BACK TO MILAN, ONLY about 20 km away, but it felt exceedingly longer, due to the throbbing of my digits. Finally, ensconced in the womb of my hotel room, the first thing I decided to do was lie in a hot bath to try and take away the pain. It was close to 7 p.m., so a bath, some food and a good night's sleep before catching the flight the next morning sounded perfect, if not ideal.

The only minor problem was I could not undo my trousers. My hands were in such excruciating pain and in such a state of numbness that I could not undo the buttons on my fly. How I wished for a zip. I tried for half-an-hour to undo my trousers, but I just could not. I was starting to perspire with the effort and bearing in mind that this was October, you can understand the struggle I had trying to undo them. Finally, by going through the barrier of pain, I undid my trousers and shirt and slunk into the hot bath.

But this was not the balm I was looking for. The hot water only seemed to increase the pain. I got out of the bath and decided, to hell with dinner, only sleep could help me. I hoped to fall asleep and wake up in the morning to find that the previous day's happenings had been just a bad dream. I tossed and turned for a few hours in pain, wondering if my hands would have to be amputated, would I be able to play an instrument again? If not, would I get a disability pension? Would I be able to hail a taxi without any digits? Would my wife still want me? Would I be able to hug my children? Finally, I could take it no longer. I got out of bed slowly; very slowly I got dressed and went down to the hotel reception.

This being Italy in the 1970s, there was a nationwide strike on. Don't ask me why. There was only one man holding fort at reception, and most of the lights were not on.

'Strike,' the receptionist said in halting English to me, when I queried what was going on. 'No power, only small generator. Strike.'

This explained the dimly lit hotel rooms. And I thought it was for atmosphere.

'I need a doctor or hospital,' I said, not caring if the world was on strike, so long as my hands could be healed.

'Strike,' he answered again. 'No any doctor.'

'But surely there's a hospital in the city,' I begged. This was a First World country after all, a country that had given us Sophia Loren, Marcello Mastroianni and that painter fellow, da Vinci. He shrugged his shoulders. I looked at my watch; it was 1:30 a.m., so I went out of the hotel and walked along a deserted road, looking for a taxi. I walked a few hundred yards and there was not one taxi plying the streets. How I wished for London, where taxis roamed the streets like vigilantes. Finally, I saw a man walking in the opposite direction and I went up to him,

'Hospital, hospital, senor.'

He did not understand me. Now you'd think hospital, like police, sounds pretty much the same in any language. Finally, he understood what I was getting at and pointed me in the direction of a hospital, which was about 400 metres away. Once inside the building, I got to see the night nurse and the doctor on duty. Another language problem ensued. I showed him my hands, I pretended to shiver, I screwed my face in pain and I said, 'Mount Everest.' Now I'm sure you get the picture but they didn't. Fifteen minutes later, the penny dropped. In fact I nearly did.

They put some cream on my hand and gently massaged it in. They gave me the rest of the tube of cream and sent me back to my hotel, with the written advice that I should use it every day for a week. When I went to see my local GP in London, he said it was a mild case of frostbite, nothing to worry about. I hate to think what a more serious case would be like, where the skin turns black and the ends of toes and fingers almost fall off.

Gradually over a seven-day period, the pain disappeared completely, my fingers moved like a concert pianist (which they had never done before) and the experience was soon put to the back of my mind. The moral of the episode: the only heights I would scale would be musical ones. Someone else could scale the Everest for all I cared.

27

SCALING MUSICAL HEIGHTS

FOR THE NEXT FOUR YEARS, MY LUCKY STREAK IN music seemed to hold. During this phase of fecundity, I played at the Albert Hall, as the opening act for the American artist Gladys Knight and the Pips. I conducted the orchestra, played a few of my hits and even sang the Neil Diamond song, 'Girl You'll Be a Woman Soon' which would soon be featured on one of my albums. It was my first live gig since those Venice days in Bombay. I had, by now, signed Tina Charles and took her into the studios. She had a massive number one with a song that has a little anecdote behind it. I shall endeavour to relate this to you, as briefly as possible.

One evening a German gentleman, whom I did not know, rang me out of the blue.

'Hello, my name is Peter Peters,' he said in sparkling English with just a trace of an accent. 'I am in London and I was wondering if we could meet.'

I was about to make an excuse for not wanting to meet him, preferring to relax at home. But then my conscience went into overdrive. I thought about the poor guy being alone in his hotel room, and that Polydor incident played on my mind.

'Do the decent thing and spend an hour with him,' the angel on my right shoulder whispered.

'Sure, come round,' I said, and gave him directions to my place which he could relay to the taxi driver.

Peter Peters turned up and told me he was involved with a lot of acts in Europe. He had a tape of songs he wanted me to listen to. So we spent an hour listening to tunes while he sipped a beer and I closed my eyes in the contemplative pose of a producer at work. As I listened, nothing he played caught my fancy.

'Thanks, Peter,' I said, trying to bring the evening to a close. 'But I don't see a hit in what you've played me. Anything else?' 'Yes, I have just one more song, but I don't think you will like it.'

'Well play it anyway,' I said, not expecting too much.

He played the tape and after the first thirty seconds I knew this was a number one song. It had a few faults; it was far too long and the lyrics had a reference to Ginger Rogers and Fred Astaire, which was totally uncommercial, but nothing that a producer could not wield an axe to.

I love this song,' I said, sounding excited. 'I have a new artist I'd like to use this song with, but I need to make certain changes to the song.'

'No problem,' the German replied, sounding like an Indian.

THE SONG WAS CALLED 'I LOVE TO LOVE'. THE MUSIC had been composed by a Frenchman and the lyrics were by an American in Paris called Jack Robinson. A week later, I recorded the backtrack to the song. But it didn't feel right.

'Can you boys come back tomorrow?' I asked the musicians in the studio.

'You're paying,' they said, or something to that effect.

The next day, I made the boys play along to a rhythm box with a samba rhythm. This click track gave the song a bouncy Latin feel and sounded closer to what I was hearing in my head. Tina came in and did a great vocal. I then asked her to sing the lyrics towards the end of the song an octave up.

'You're joking?' she replied. 'I don't think I can do it, and if I could I'll shatter the glass between the studio and the control room.'

'You can do it,' I said encouragingly.

She sang the ending a whole octave up. It took the song to a stratospheric level.

'This is a number one,' I said to anyone who would listen.

I ran to CBS Records, the company I had signed Tina to and told them I had a number one. They heard the track and its relevant B side, a song called 'Disco Fever' written by Lee Vanderbilt. The marketing people loved B side.

'Disco is big,' the promotion head told me. 'And with a title like "Disco Fever", the clubs are going to lap it up. It's gonna be a smash. This should be the A side, not "I Love to Love".'

'Okay,' I said, after a few minutes of debate, giving into the collective opinion of the promotion and marketing guys. I also remembered that meeting at Pye Records, when I first played 'Kung Fu Fighting'.

LATER THAT EVENING I SAT AT HOME, BROODING ABOUT THE decision. The more I thought about it, the more obvious it seemed that 'I Love to Love' should be the single. So the next morning, I picked up the phone and rang Morris Oberstein, the head of CBS.

'Morris,' I said pensively, 'I'm going to bring back the recording agreement between us on Tina and return the advance.'

'What for?' Oberstein asked, in that high-pitched croaky voice of his.

'I think "I Love to Love" is a number one and I cannot see "Disco Fever" as a hit,' I replied, with just a hint of agitation in my voice.

The line went quiet for a moment.

'Listen, Biddu,' he said calmly. 'I have great trust in my promotion and marketing people, but if you are so concerned, we'll bring out "I Love to Love" as the A side, but if in three weeks nothing's happening on the record, we'll flip it. Okay?'

'Fine,' I said, relieved that the company was going with my choice of song.

The record came out; within three weeks it was number one and once again stayed at the top for a few more weeks. Like 'Kung Fu

Fighting' it went on to become number one all over Europe, Canada and South America.

At the same time, I was recording Jimmy James and the Vagabonds. Two of the songs I did with him climbed the charts: 'I'll Go Where the Music Takes Me' and 'Now Is the Time', the latter just missing the number one slot.

Tina had another major hit with 'Dance Little Lady Dance' and her version of 'I'll Go Where the Music Takes Me' also charted. In fact, this song was also recorded in French by Claude François, the composer of the original version of 'My Way'.

In 1977, I released a Biddu Orchestra album, which contained the instrumental 'Rain Forest'. The song won the Ivor Novello award for Best Instrumental. I was also awarded an Ivor Novello for songwriter of the year, a huge accolade by any measure of merit. The Novellos are the equivalent of the Grammies in the States. The previous year I was fortunate to win two Ivor Novellos for 'Kung Fu Fighting' as best song.

The next year, I brought out a mainly instrumental album called Futuristic Journey. It contained one song that had a distinct Indian vibe to it; it was called 'Eastern Journey' and the main melody line was played on sitar and violins, augmented with tables and a percussive groove. It was my first foray into a quasi- Indian sound. I released a single from the album called 'Journey to the Moon' with its female chant of 'We're all going to moon', which tickled the charts, once again helping the album to sell in large quantities.

It was also the year when Tina won the World Song Festival in Japan, with a song of mine called 'Love Rocks'. It was a thrilling moment when, in front of 20,000 people at the Budokan Hall in Tokyo, I was called up along with Tina to collect the cash prize, which was, mercifully, in dollars and not yen!

Disco music was all the rage and it was only a matter of time before a movie was made utilizing a disco soundtrack. One day I met an American lawyer called Marty Machet who asked me if I would do a couple songs for a forthcoming English film.

'Sure,' I said, and asked him for the name of the film. 'The Stud,' he replied, without batting an eyelid.

I took a little gulp. 'It sounds like a porn film.'

'It's soft,' he answered casually. 'From the Jackie Collins book. Her sister is going to be in it.'

'Who's that?' I asked purposefully. 'Joan Collins. Have you heard of her?'

'Yeah,' I replied, remembering Joan Collins from magazine and newspaper articles, although I had never seen a film of hers. She was a stunning-looking brunette, although her career had been languishing in the dark room of yesteryear, pretty much like the British film industry at that time.

'Well, she's playing the lead and we want to use a disco soundtrack of well-known tunes, but we also need some original material. I'd like to rope you in on this. What do you think?' Marty said in that unhurried manner of his.

'I'm going to Los Angeles for a coupla weeks,' I told him. 'Maybe we can meet and sort out the music on my return?'

'Great! Joan will be in LA with her husband Ron Kass. You guys should meet up,' he drawled. 'Where will you be staying?'

Joan Collins and her husband came to pick us up from the Beverley Hills Hotel. She was extremely glam, friendly and talked as much as my wife, if not more. The four of us had lunch at a restaurant, the name of which escapes my memory. Although I remember Ron paid the bill. Or did I? At lunch, the conversation went something like this.

Joan: 'So you're going to be in the film?' Biddu: 'Yes, Joan.'
Joan: 'As the male lead?'
Biddu: 'No, as the music director.'
Joan: 'Ah! Pity really.' Then she let out a throaty laugh. Oh! This Collins woman can tease, I thought to myself.

OUR THREE-YEAR-OLD SON ZAK HAD ALSO COME WITH US TO LA. We'd left him with the babysitter arranged by the hotel while we'd had lunch with Joan. The next day the three of us were invited to Joan's house for tea. It was a sumptuous place, like most of the homes around the Bel Air/Beverley Hills area. Low-built with manicured lawns and the ubiquitous swimming pool. Zak was too young to appreciate having tea with a star, but Sue and I lapped it up.

A few days later, we met Tony Curtis at the hotel, a real Hollywood star if ever there was one. I remembered him in Spartacus, The Defiant Ones and Some Like It Hot. He still had his looks, much of his hair and that strong Bronx accent of his. He was a real charmer, chatty and effusive, making us feel like long-lost friends and with that open and welcoming friendliness that many Americans seem to have in bucketloads. We were invited to his house for tea and to peruse his paintings. Curtis was a pretty good artist and the walls of his house hung with numerous portraits and sketches he had completed. He took us around his place, showing us every single painting and giving us the background to how that painting came about. We also met his lady; a rather tall woman, taller than the Boston Strangler, although with her stilettos I could have been mistaken. She was quite buxom with a very peroxide blonde bouffant, which gave her even more height. Any taller and she would have suffered a nosebleed!

28

BIMBOS AND RAMBO

THE MUSIC FOR THE STUD CAME OUT JUST PRIOR TO the release of the film. The publicity machine whirred into action. 'Joan Collins in soft porn, raunchy movie', the tabloids screamed. The male lead opposite her was a hunk of an actor called Oliver Tobias, who was almost as beautiful as Joan. A sex scene between Joan and Tobias, in a caged elevator that she stops between floors (every male's fantasy), helped put more bums on seats. Both the film and the music were a huge success. We were number two in the album charts for weeks, kept away from the number one position by another soundtrack album from a film that was infinitely superior and cleaner than ours. That film was Saturday Night Fever, and the music by the Bee Gees was one of the best soundtrack scores ever. Since the time I had used their songs with that Japanese group all those years ago, the boys had gone on to bigger and better things. I'm glad I gave them a leg-up. As for Joan Collins, the success of The Stud re-established her as a modern-day legend.

And as for me, I was riding the crest of the disco wave, seeking and finding success in my music, while in a neat juxtaposition, my wife was seeking spiritual enlightenment. She found it in another man. He, too, was Indian. His name was Meher Baba, a spiritual master who had passed away in 1968, leaving behind his message and a band of disciples in the unwelcoming heat and dust of Ahmednagar, a town some 300 kilometres from Bombay.

Ironically, Sue heard about this guru or master in the hedonistic town of Marbella in southern Spain in early 1979. A follower of the master by the name of Robert Bloeme and his wife Brigitte gave my wife a book on Meher Baba to read. The revelations and knowledge contained in those pages were the answers my wife was searching for, and the spark of light and love could shine no brighter. The pupil had arrived and the master was waiting. This path of love was no fickle affair. From that day to this, my lady has been a devoted follower of Meher Baba.

GRADUALLY, OUR PERIODIC TRIPS TO INDIA BECAME A YEARLY AFFAIR. This was fine by me. I would dash to Bangalore to spend time with my mother and siblings, while Sue would spend a few weeks with the disciples at the Meher Baba Ashram in godforsaken Ahmednagar.

Then to shed the cloak of austerity from the extremely spartan living at the pilgrim centre, we would go for a few days to Kerala and spend time at a beach shack, soaking in the rays, and while madam meditated, I would indulge in some gentle yogasanas. I have often been asked how I feel about my wife's spiritual journey and about sharing my life with another man, an avatar at that. My answer is: What is the purpose of life if your life has no purpose? This spiritual path has been my wife's raison d'être. To follow the path of love creates no harm, only harmony. So, in a nutshell, I quite admire her for this. It gives her a purpose apart from family and friends. Sometimes, I think she's a bit doolally, but at all times lovable. Then again who truly understands a woman? Certainly not a man!

The tremendous success of The Stud demanded a sequel. After all, in show business nothing succeeds like excess. Jackie Collins had another book called The Bitch whose title (like the first one)

made me blanch. Once again Joan undressed for this soft porn film and I was roped in to write four songs, including the title track. I composed the title theme and had the lyrics written by Don Black, a very likeable Oscar-winning lyricist. He had written the lyrics for a couple of James Bond films, and for 'Ben', the song made successful by a young Michael Jackson.

Marty Machet, the lawyer, decided that it would be a splendid idea if Sammy Cahn, the eminent American lyricist, penned two of the songs. It would also lend some gravitas to the film. This, I write with tongue stuck firmly in my cheek. Sammy Cahn was an icon who had worked with Sinatra, Henry Mancini and more stars than there are in the firmament. He had written the lyrics for 'Three Coins in the Fountain', 'Love and Marriage', 'Time After Time' and many, many more.

SO OFF MY WIFE AND I WENT TO LOS ANGELES, and on my second day, I went to Sammy's house which was very near the Beverley Hills Hotel. He was a slim man, with a salt-and-pepper moustache, glasses and, at around sixty years of age, still as bouncy as a jack rabbit. He had a wife half his age; that could have been the reason for his bounce.

Anyway, we met, and like most Americans, he had that friendly and extrovert take on life; so within minutes we were like buddies who'd spent time in 'Nam.

'Hello Mr Cahn,' I said, on meeting him.

'Call me Sammy,' he countered enthusiastically. 'All my friends do.'

We sat in his office. He behind an aged typewriter, probably older than him, a sheaf of yellow A4 paper by his side and a cupful of pencils, sharpened to a point like arrows from the quiver of a tribe of headhunters in Borneo. I sat across the little table in reverence, guitar in hand.

'Hum me the melody, Biddu,' he said, his fingers suspended over the typewriter keyboard like a concert pianist about to bang out Beethoven's Fifth.

As I hummed the melody, he hit the keys and began typing almost in sync to the lines I was humming. When I had finished humming the tune, he stopped and ripped the paper away from the typewriter and showed it to me. I read it slowly, scanning the phrasing.

'I'm not sure about this word June,' I said, perusing the lyrics. 'The rhyme with moon is a bit old-fashioned. Don't you think?'

I said this nervously, not totally sure if my candour came across as rude and impolite.

He looked at me, and then grabbed the paper from my hand.

'Okay,' he said. 'Let's start again. I'll get something fresh.'

He wrinkled up the sheet and threw the paper in a little wicker basket by his side and off we went again. I kept humming the song and he kept typing away furiously. A mini mountain of screwed-up A4 papers piled up in the basket, till finally we both felt the lyrics had the meaning, depth and originality befitting a film called The Bitch.

I CAME BACK FROM LA CLUTCHING SAMMY'S LYRICS. IT HAD been quite a trip. We had met Sylvester Stallone on one of the evenings. He was riding high with his Rocky franchise (and later with his Rambo series of hits). He invited us to come up to Holmby Hills and see him in a polo match, which we did. We sat in his box at the tournament, sipping champagne, while he and a bunch of Argentinian friends played hockey on horseback. After the game, we chatted for about an hour; he told us all about himself and his ideas for future productions. One thing I noticed about those American stars was that in real life, they were exactly as we saw them on the screen. Their mannerisms and voice inflections were the same. Only their height changed – they looked like giants on the big screen.

This was our third trip to the States in six years and while I was fascinated by the country, intoxicated by its abundance and had nothing but admiration for the people's positive attitude towards life – a can-do attitude which helped that vast country grow into the most supreme economic power in the world and the Mecca of materialism – it still left me feeling disappointed. Like a meal that surfeits but does not satisfy.

Back in rain-soaked London, my wife found out she was pregnant again. This time we were blessed with a little girl. We called her ZaZa. She was a gorgeous, exotic little beauty, with light-olive skin and chestnut-brown hair. The reason for giving the kids names beginning with 'z' was to teach them patience. In school they would have to learn tolerance as the teacher called out the pupils' names during morning roll call, usually in alphabetical order beginning with the letter A. It was a zen of an idea!

Around the time that ZaZa was born, a new form of music was evolving. The music was raw, crude and anarchic. It was the sound of young white kids, some from dysfunctional families raging against the establishment. It was their form of rap; cluttered, amateurish and vitriolic, thrashing away (often tunelessly) on their guitars, drums and bass. This was punk music, and one of its earliest heroes were the Sex Pistols. Personally, I found this form of music quite abhorrent, with its swearing and cussing. Perhaps I was being old-fashioned or elitist, accustomed as I was to the finesse of well-played rhythm sections with an overlay of strings and brass, all very professionally executed with vocals in tune and augmented by perfect harmonies. But gradually, punk was overtaking the disco sound as the music of the day.

Initially it did not worry me. I thought this music would die of natural causes, like lack of talent, or songs so malnourished and bulimic they wouldn't be able to carry a tune. Also I was preoccupied with finding artists to sing the songs for the soundtrack of The Bitch. One of the songs, 'Almost', a slow romantic number, needed a sexy, sultry male vocal on it and I met a singer called Bill Fredericks from the group the New Drifters. I thought he would do a commendable job on the song. Bill, I must tell you, had a voice deep as a ravine, so rich in resonance that it was lower than basso profundo. The earth trembled when he spoke and women had orgasms when they heard his velvet-toned growl and animals slunk back into the safety of the woods in which they dwelled. His speaking voice was unique. He made Barry White sound like a tenor. Bill knew his allure lay in this voice of his and he played on it, especially when women were around.

ON THE DAY OF THE RECORDING, I HAD BOOKED THE Roundhouse, a recording studio in Chalk Farm, North London. Joan Collins, her sister Jackie and the producer of the film decided to come for the recording, as they had never been to a music session before. So we sat in the control room, the four of us making small talk, when the door opened and in walked Bill Fredericks, nattily dressed, wearing a black polo-necked sweater and a beige blazer, looking the epitome of an Italian gigolo, if that gigolo was black.

'Hi Bill,' I said by way of greeting.

'Hey man, my apologies for being late. How is everybody?' Mr Sex-on-legs said in that bottomless voice which sent a mild tremor across the room. My cup of coffee quivered on the console table. I looked at the two women and saw their eyes widen in amazement. Bill Fredericks was trowelling the charm in heaps. I introduced him to Joan, Jackie and the producer. They eyed his every movement. The room filled with the sound of silence and expectation.

'May I ring my missus at home, to tell her I'm at the studio?' Bill asked in that sensual rumble, reaching for the phone on my console desk.

'Sure,' I said, fascinated.

He dialled the number and a few seconds later spoke into the mouthpiece, using his cavernous voice.

'Hey babe, it's me,' he purred like a finely tuned Ferrari.

There was a moment's silence. Then, 'It's me, babe.' His voice rose in pitch but just a hint. More silence.

'It's me, babe.' This time his voice was pitched even higher. A moment's silence. And finally an agitated and high-pitched voice emitted from him, almost a falsetto: 'It's me, babe – Bill!'

His missus finally cottoned on to who it was on the phone. The four of us laughed our guts out, as Bill finished his call and looked sheepishly at us. Who did his wife think was calling? How many men did she know, who could undress one with their voice alone? We teased him no end.

The movie and the soundtrack of The Bitch came out and although it did very well, it wasn't the massive success its predecessor was. I have noticed over time, in music and films, rarely does repetition reach one's expectations. However, a friendship of sorts had developed between Joan and my wife and I during the making of these two films. We often went to her house in South Audley Street, Mayfair, for dinner, meeting and air kissing celebrities of the film world. Joan, in turn, came to our place in London and once to our house in Haslemere, Surrey, to a Hawaiian-themed party that we were throwing.

The idea was that everyone had to come dressed in some tropical outfit and the winner would receive the first prize of a week in Tehran. The second prize was two weeks in that same city. (Yes, it's a joke.) Our house in the country had a long stately driveway from the road and huge gardens, in which a marquee was set up for dinner. For seven days prior to the party, dark cobalt-grey clouds roamed the countryside and emptied themselves of their burden. It rained the proverbial cats and dogs. The lawns were inches deep in water, and my wife worried that the party would be a damp squib and all our efforts would amount to a soggy evening. But the angels were smiling on us and on the day of the shindig, the sun came out in all its glory, soaked up the rain and saved the day.

A steel band played during the evening, welcoming our guests as they walked up the drive. Joan was at the Chichester Theatre, nearby, acting in a play; it was a Noel Coward play, I think, the name of which escapes my mind. She came over after the show. My friend Clive Limpkin, an unmitigated extrovert, came dressed as a hula girl. He wore a skirt made of straw, two coconut shells attached with string to form a bra, and a blonde wig that sat askew on his head, because blondes have more fun. On his feet he wore Hawaiian sandals and his body was covered in an orange suntan lotion to take away the surf-white of his skin. He walked up the driveway with his long-suffering wife Alex in tow and we all thought he looked hilarious. More so, when he told us he had to stop on the motorway dressed the way he was to change a flat tyre. I don't know if this last bit was true, as Clive had a propensity to exaggerate. We danced the night away to the steel band and Joan was in her element on the floor. The dance floor, I hasten to add.

The financial success of the two movies thrust Miss Collins in the spotlight. She soon became Alexis Carrington in the long- running American TV series, Dynasty, and destiny allowed her another bite of the cherry.

In 1984, I sold my house in the country to a wealthy Pakistani politician (are there any poor ones on the subcontinent?) called Mustapha Khar. An entire book can be written about this man. But briefly, he was one of the founders of the Pakistan People's Party (PPP) and a close of friend of President Zulfikar Bhutto, the father of Benazir Bhutto. In the internecine corridors of Pakistan power politics, his star rose and waned according to the whims of his party leader or the leader of the country. At one time he was languishing in jail during Zia ul-Haq's presidency, and later went on to become a federal minister of water and power, during Benazir's regime, though he eventually fell out with her. He was married many times and one of his wives, Tehmina Gill, wrote a book called My Feudal Lord in which she describes the suffering and alleged abuses she went through with Khar.

He bought my pile in Haslemere, but when I drove past the place five years later, it was in a desolate, decrepit state. A beautiful house, looking lost and lonely. The fourteen acres of garden with its wild flowers and rhododendrons had fallen into a state of neglect. Perhaps he was in prison again. There you go, a little bit of historical tittle-tattle.

29

THE ORIGINAL KING KHAN

I WAS NEVER TRULY INTERESTED IN DOING FILM SOUNDTRACKS, enjoyable as they were, and the two I had completed had literally fallen into my lap. Think of someone waiting for ages at a bus stop with no sign of a bus and then suddenly three arrive at the same time. Similarly, another offer to do a song for a film came my way, but this time from India.

A film actor from Bombay called Feroz Khan came to London to meet me. He had heard my various instrumental albums and was keen for me to do a song for a film he was making called Qurbani. He was a charming gentleman with a well-modulated speaking voice and impeccable etiquette. His accent was a fusion of Indian inflection, a BBC newsreader's plummy-ness and the suggestion of a Yankee drawl. He was a lovable rogue with a cavalier attitude. We met at an apartment he was renting near Claridges Hotel in Mayfair. This is one of the most expensive parts of London and I could tell Mr Khan was used to a certain amount of luxury.

'I'd like you to do a song for my film,' he said when we met. I wasn't sure if I wanted to get involved in anything to do with India. And quite frankly, I didn't know anything about Indian films or Indian music.

'I don't know,' I replied, with an air of uncertainty.

'Listen, you and I come from Bangalore. We are both Bangalore boys.' Feroz was using the old 'boys from the 'hood' routine. 'Come on, do it for a friend. Your mama will be so pleased.'

I deliberated for a moment. My mother would be happy if I did a song for an Indian film, that bit was true. None of my success abroad had really touched her. It had all happened so far away from home that as far as she was concerned it didn't really count. I decided maybe I should do it for Mom.

'Okay,' I replied, still not totally convinced.

'Great, man,' the actor drawled, pumping my hand.

LITTLE DID I REALIZE THAT THIS MAN HAD GONE OUT on a limb by asking me to do a song for his film. The local music directors in India were up in arms that he was going to 'use a foreigner' to do music for one of the songs. Apparently, there was talk of boycotting the production, and worse. But Feroz stuck by his guns. He was a bit of a maverick, a risk-taker. He wanted me and he was going to get me, come hell or high water.

'I don't want to do the recording in India. I know nothing about the studios over there,' I told him.

'No problem,' he answered. 'I'd rather you did it in London anyway. We want your London sound.'

My eyes arched in surprise and I played my advantage. 'I don't want to use any of the playback singers from back home.'

This was a tough one. Almost every song from a Hindi film which needed female vocals was sung by one of two sisters who were to music what water lilies were to Claude Monet. Their names were Lata Mangeshkar and Asha Bhonsle, household names in India and veritable nightingales.

'Okay,' he replied. Once again he was playing with fire. Who knew how the singers in India would react?

'We'll need to find a singer in London who can sing in Hindi,' I said, unsure if we would find one.

'I know a Pakistani family in town whose daughter can sing a bit, I believe,' he replied. 'Shall I fix up for you to meet the parents and the girl?'

♫

Two days later, I went to an apartment in Century Court, opposite Lord's cricket ground, and met the parents. Over tea, biscuits and small talk, they asked their daughter to come out from her bedroom. The girl, no more than fifteen or sixteen years old, appeared in pigtails, standing gawkily against the wall. Her name was Nazia Hassan. Her brother, only marginally younger, looked more assured; his name was Zoheb.

'I'd like to hear your voice. Will you sing for me?' I said, wondering if this was going to work.

She mumbled a yes, which I hardly heard. This is encouraging, I thought. Regardless, I took my guitar and asked her to sing anything and I would accompany her. She sang a verse and chorus of 'Dance Little Lady'. It was one of my songs. This kid was smart. Her voice did not have the piercing sharpness of most Asian singers. The pleasantness in her voice was around C3, from middle C to G4 – warm, expressive and nubile. It wasn't a great voice. But it was different, and it was this that made the difference between using her and someone from the old school in India.

'Sounds fine,' I said, when she had finished singing. It was agreed she would sing for the film.

Feroz then came round to my house with the lyrics for the song. Now my speaking Hindi is laughable and appalling, but fortunately all those one-hour-a-week classes at Bishop Cotton twenty years ago would finally pay off. I could read and write Hindi fairly well. I read through the lyrics that Feroz had given me, not knowing or understanding what any of it meant. The song title was 'Aap Jaisa Koi Meri Zindagi Mein Aaye'.

'Yeah! That's fine,' I said, not wishing to admit my ignorance.

Two days later I had the melody ready and played it to him. 'Great,' he said. 'I like it, Bidz. Give it that touch, okay?'

I liked his familiarity. His bonhomie was infectious.

The following week I went into Red Bus Studios near Paddington Green, with my able engineer Richard Dodd to give it 'that touch'. Somehow, everything I did on that song made it sound better. I had a catchy introductory riff played on the sitar; I used syn drums, which had never been used in a Hindi song before. The syn drum made a sound not unlike my name. It went 'bidoo' every time you hit it and I double-tracked Nazia's voice to give it some oomph. Once again, I used a rhythm box with a Latin beat to give it a hip-swaying groove.

'Aap Jaisa Koi Meri Zindagi Mein Aaye,' she sang, her voice sounding young and sexy as the song came alive.

When I played it to Feroz, he was all smiles.

'Wow! I love it, man,' he enthused. 'Bidz, you've done a damn fine job, my friend. This is a smash.'

I gave him the master tapes of the song, he paid me and went back to Bombay. And I soon forgot all about the song and the session. It was for India after all. Ten thousand kilometres away.

30

DISCO FEVER

I GOT BACK INTO THE ROUTINE OF MY LIFE – one eye on my music and the other on helping my wife bring up our two kids. Perhaps it was tradition and my cultural inheritance speaking to me through the deepest stratum of my subconscious, but I wanted to be a hands-on father. I was beginning to see the break-up and desecration of the family unit in the West and, more pertinently, in the UK. Vast numbers of old people lived in isolation, detached from the umbilical cord of their children's touch and concern. It was a time of Thatcher's Britain and though she took us out of the economic quicksand we had sunk into, and felled the power of the unions like a dragon-slayer, she had also taught us to worship at the temple of materialism and that greed was good and no price was too high to pay for it. We were turning into an 'I, me, my' society. I was a part of that society and yet I wanted to be apart from it. Easier said than done, I'm afraid.

THEN, ONE MORNING, I GOT A CALL FROM FEROZ. HE sounded decidedly upbeat.

'Bidz, the song is killing them, man,' he said with typical filmi hyperbole. 'They are going crazy for it.'

'What are you talking about, Feroz?' I asked, unhinged from the chore of changing little ZaZa's nappies.

'The song, man! "Aap Jaisa Koi". The song you did. People are going crazy about it,' he said.

'I see,' I said phlegmatically.

Neither my indifference nor the crackling telephone line would dampen his enthusiasm. It slowly began to dawn on me that the song I had composed for his film was making tsunami- size waves.

'I'm happy for you, Feroz,' I finally said, cheerfully.

'The film opens tomorrow in Bombay and next week in Bangalore. I want you to come for the premiere in Bangalore.'

'I can't, Feroz.'

'Man, I'm sending you a ticket, you got to come. You're a Bangalore boy,' he said, not willing to settle for a no.

So THE FOLLOWING WEEK, I FLEW TO BOMBAY AND CAUGHT a connecting flight to Bangalore, reaching there at 5 p.m. I stayed with my mother, who was as pleased as punch and attended the premiere that night. The next morning, I did the journey in reverse, returning to London. The whole tamasha took forty- eight hours.

Qurbani was a massive hit. It wouldn't be wrong to say that while the film was pretty good, it was the music and two songs in particular, 'Laila O Laila' and 'Aap Jaisa Koi' which lifted it to super-hit success, if I may indulge in some filmi hyperbole myself. 'Aap Jaisa Koi' went on to become one of the most successful film songs of all time. It was choreographed on a delectable young actress called Zeenat Aman. Feroz was holding three aces. The man's gamble had paid off and he deserved it. He had put his money where his mouth was. I always think of him as the last of the Mughals.

IRONICALLY, DESPITE THE IMMENSE SUCCESS OF MY SONG IN THE film, there was no stampede to my door in London W8. In fact not a single film producer came knocking. It wasn't as if I was hiding in some isolated Hebridean island, my number was in the phone book. But perhaps Indian producers at the time were illiterate and could not read, and certainly judging from some of the scripts and storylines there is some credence to this theory. Anyway, almost a year passed by without so much as a tinkle when my doorbell did ring one afternoon and standing outside was a young man from the London branch of an Indian record company.

His name was Vinod Kumar and he represented the largest Indian music company, called HMV (later to be known as SaReGaMa). He introduced himself to me, and after my initial surprise, I invited him in.

'We would like you, sir, to make an album with Nazia Hassan, the singer,' he said respectfully. The way he put it, I assumed there was also a Nazia Hassan who was not a singer.

I probed him with a hundred questions about the Indian record company.

'Our head-office is in Dum Dum,' he said, enthusiastically. 'Where, where?' I asked, jokingly.

'Dum Dum in Calcutta,' he clarified. 'We have the largest repertoire of film music in India, dating back to the forties.'

'How many non-film albums has your company released?' I asked.

'None,' he replied, looking at me as if I was dumb. 'All music in India is from films.'

I suddenly remembered that this was true. Apart from a few religious albums – of bhajans – which sold about a hundred copies each, it was only film songs that dominated the market. On average, a Hindi film had between seven to eight songs. It will probably be easier to locate Osama Bin Laden than find a Hindi film without songs that allowed the actor to run around a tree wooing his love, or a female lead coming out of the waters of a gentle stream, her wet and dripping sari clinging to her buxom figure.

'So you want me to do a non-film album with Nazia?' I looked at him, incredulously.

He nodded, which I took to mean yes.

'How many copies do you think you can sell?' I said, worriedly.

'We hope with both your names we can achieve sales of forty to fifty thousand,' he replied optimistically.

In his opinion, this would amount to the album being a major success. With no film or television to back this product, the figure of 50,000 that he quoted would indeed be phenomenal.

'What about royalties?' I asked. It was my favourite word after discount.

'We don't pay royalties. Only a token lump sum for producing the album,' he replied.

'I don't work without royalties,' I replied firmly. There was an uneasy silence in the room.

'Can I speak to my boss, Mr Sood, in Calcutta, and get back to you in a day or two?' he said apologetically.

'Don't bother if there are no royalties involved,' I said, sounding marginally annoyed.

No one in the West worked in the music industry without royalties. The Beatles were earning around £5 million a year from various royalty streams from songs and records they made in the 1960s and '70s. Royalties were a musician's insurance against penury in old age.

Young Mr Kumar called back the next day. 'Yes, royalties will be payable to you. This is an unusual case, because we don't normally pay royalties.'

'Your company should get used to it,' I replied. 'That's how it works in the West. It's only fair.'

WE MET ONCE MORE, THIS TIME WITH NAZIA AND HER brother Zoheb. I was not keen on composing all the songs for the album as it would be too much of a workload trying to be creative in a style I was not familiar with, so it was decided that Zoheb would work a few tunes as well. I set about composing the melodies and in a couple of weeks, I had a batch of songs I felt extremely happy with.

I must say I also derived a certain amount of joy and satisfaction in composing those tunes. I was doing something new, almost novel; so a certain amount of passion went into the composing. Zoheb for his part also came up with three songs of merit. Bearing in mind he was only sixteen years old, I was highly impressed.

We went into a small studio on Finchley Road as the budget for the album was half that of producing an English album. But quite often, necessity is the mother of invention. Nazia sang most of the songs, although Zoheb sang on two tracks, plus on a duet with his sister. The recordings went like clockwork and three weeks later I had a finished album.

The master tapes were couriered to Calcutta, and four days later I got a call from HMV India. It was the secretary of Mr Sood, the managing director.

'Mr Biddu,' she said over the ubiquitous crackle of the line. 'Mr Sood would like to know what you want to call the album.'

Frankly I hadn't given it a thought. 'I have absolutely no idea,' I said, candidly.

'We have some suggestions, sir. Please can I tell you what they are?'

'Sure. Go ahead.'

She rattled off some titles and among them were two names that caught my ear. One of them was Disco Party and the other was Music Ke Deewane.

'What does deewane mean?' I asked the lady. I liked the sound of that particular word.

'It means crazy or mad,' she replied. A thought went around my head.

'Can we call the album Disco Deewane?' I asked in total ignorance 'Just a minute. I shall ask.'

She went off the line for a moment; then she came back on. 'Yes, if you want, Mr Sood says you can call the album Disco Deewane.'

I loved the flow and alliteration of that title and I liked the rhythm of the words.

'Listen,' I said, getting all excited. 'Tell Mr Sood to hold on. I'm going to write a song called "Disco Deewane" and I'll send the tapes over in three days. We can't have an album title without a song of the same name.'

'All right, sir. I'll pass on the message,' the secretary replied dutifully.

I put the phone down, and immediately picked up my guitar. The title was screaming for the melody that was forming in my head.

I composed the melody in one straight run-through. Three minutes later I had the song ready, including the introduction. If I may be immodest on this page, it was an inspired moment.

I picked up the phone, called Nazia and told her I had a new song for her and she should come to the studio in the morning to record it. I sang her the melody on the phone and the lyrics I had on the chorus.

'Work some more lyrics for the verse by tomorrow,' I said, the adrenalin rushing through me. I then rang the musicians and booked them for the next day's session.

The song was recorded, vocalized and mixed in one day and I knew instantly we had a mega hit on our hands. To me, it was the best song and production I had ever been involved in. Till today, I never tire of listening to the melody. I gave the tapes to Vinod Kumar, who sent them on to Calcutta.

A few days later, it was Mr Sood himself on the line.

'Great song,' he said, in a soft, singsong voice. 'We are printing up 100,000 copies. It's never been done before, but I think we can sell it all.'

THE ALBUM CAME OUT IN APRIL 1981 AND SOLD 100,000 copies on the first day of release. It went on to sell nearly three million copies and became the soundtrack to a vast number of young people's lives in India. Without the ballyhoo of a motion picture, radio or television, it sold like hot samosas. I went to India and did a short promotional tour, as did Nazia and her brother. The tour consisted of visiting record stores and signing copies of the vinyl and doing interviews for newspapers. The album ticked all the boxes required for a massive hit. The music was melodic and fresh, the sound quality was vastly superior to anything that was produced locally, and the product had an attractive young singer fronting it, with a voice that was sparklingly different.

The album was a massive hit right across Asia, South Africa and a few countries in South America as well. It went on to become the biggest-selling pop album in Asia and Nazia was the first in the seldom-peopled galaxy of Indian pop stars.

31

A 'STAR' IS BORN

BACK IN LONDON, I WAS SURPRISED BY THE TRAJECTORY my career was taking. Suddenly India was playing a part in picking up the slack in my music. What with my wife's annual trip to the ashram in Ahmednagar, it seemed as if some hidden force was pulling me in that direction. Like the lithe and supple fingers of a danseuse whose arms arc and twirl in sensual flight and beckon you with their unbound eroticism, I found the pull of India inexorably powerful. Yet, I resisted or, at least, tried to. But fate or karma had many ways of spinning its scheming web to entice me and soon, my family and I would spend six months in the teeming metropolis of Bombay. But first, let me explain how it started.

MY FRIEND SURESH, WHO WAS NOW WORKING IN HIS FATHER'S plastics company, came over to London to buy some machinery to take back to India. As usual, he stayed with me. I noticed that during his stay he was continuously on the phone to India. There was a slightly harassed look about him.

'What's up?' I asked him, one morning.

'Yaar, nothing but hassles,' he replied. 'The workers are planning to go on strike again.'

He then explained the industrial situation back in India. It seemed downing tools and going on strike was the favourite pastime of factory workers in India.

'I know exactly how you feel,' I said. Which, on reflection, was a stupid thing to say, since the only knowledge I had about strikes was the miners' one in 1974, also known as the 'winter of discontent'. But one often says the most brainless thing when trying to show sympathy or solidarity.

'Sometimes I wish I was in some other business,' he remarked despondently.

'Me too,' I answered. 'It can be boring sometimes, just sitting and writing songs all day. Day after day. Wish I was doing something more exciting.'

'Like what?' Suresh asked, not really sure where this confab was leading to.

'Like opening a restaurant,' I said excitedly.

'Or a bar,' he replied, caught up in the virus of my sudden enthusiasm.

'What about a movie? What say we make a movie?' I continued dangerously.

'Great idea.'

Now the conversation was beginning to flow like an unsilted River Ganga. It was unanimously decided we would make a movie in India to allay the boredom we were going through and inject some buzz into our lives. We were like two guys in the early period of male menopause. I went to sleep that night with a tributary of ideas in my head.

As we sat down to breakfast the next morning, I opened the conversation.

'Suresh, I've got a great story for a film. It came to me last night in bed. I could hardly sleep.'

'Let's hear it,' he said, breaking into a soft-boiled egg.

I gave him a brief synopsis of the storyline. It was about a young boy who wants to be a singer; after the usual pitfalls and hardships and against all odds, he finally makes it in the last reel of the film.

That was all I had. The skeleton of a story and the title for the film.
'What's it called?' he asked. 'Star,' I announced proudly.
'I love it,' he said approvingly, as we tucked into our breakfast.

I'm not sure if this was a case of the blind leading the blind, or the dumb leading the dumber. But we were on a high and with no chemical inducements.

That morning a star was born. Within the hour I started work, feverishly writing the screenplay in English. The idea was to then have it translated into Hindi by someone in India. I had never worked on a screenplay before; neither Suresh nor I had progressed further than a Brownie Box camera, but somehow we were ready to make a movie. This was thrilling stuff.

The first thing we needed was a director and then a male star to carry the film. The director, we found in London. We heard there was a chap called Vinod Pandey, ex-BBC (in what capacity we knew not, nor did we bother to find out), who had just made an art film called Ek Baar Phir, which had met with a modicum of success. The man was in London, so we got to meet him. He wore blue jeans, which impressed me no end. At least we had a dude on the same wavelength.

In the meantime Suresh went back to India to deal with his factory problems. We signed up Vinod Pandey as the director. Next, we had to find a hero. In one of her letters, my mother had mentioned a young actor who looked the spitting image of me, and had just been in a film that was a mega hit. The film was called Love Story and the kid was now a real heartthrob. His name was Kumar Gaurav and, as luck would have it, he was coming to London to promote his film. Arrangements were made for me to meet him in the foyer of the Cumberland Hotel in Marble Arch. Come the day and I was dressed in blue jeans, boots, cowboy hat and a leather jacket. I walked into the foyer and standing in one corner was this innocent-looking youngster dressed in blue jeans, boots, cowboy hat and a leather jacket. And what's more he looked like a younger version of me, only better-looking. My mother, bless her, had forgotten to mention this last bit.

WE STARED AT ONE ANOTHER, INCREDULOUS AT THE SIMILARITY OF our clothes and looks. There was no way he wasn't going to be the lead in our film. We got on like two peas in a pod. The added bonus was that his dad was an icon in the pantheon of Indian film stars. His father's name was Rajendra Kumar; he had been nicknamed Jubilee Kumar, because all his films celebrated at least twenty-five weeks, or a silver jubilee, on release.

Now that I had a hero and a director, the rest fell into place. I flew to India and as I disembarked from the plane, the darkened surroundings illuminated by the sepulchral lights around the airport, the familiar smell of Bombay hit me. A smell that can corrode your senses. Not unlike the odour of an aged and sickly uncle, whose orbit of pong clings to your nostrils till finally you get used to it. And on the journey from the airport to my hotel, I witnessed the teeming mass of humanity sleeping on the pavements or under shopfronts. I reeled at this sudden onslaught on my senses. I felt the guilt as I always did when coming to India, about the dichotomy of our lives. I had come to make a movie in a sea of poverty. But, like most people, my conscience and I would learn to live with this guilt.

I MET UP WITH SURESH AND WE WENT THROUGH A couple of film magazines and whenever we spotted someone attractive we decided he or she should be in the film. In this scientific manner we made our selection of cast for the film. Certainly, the female lead – a pretty young actress called Rati Agnihotri – was found this way. We also signed up Saeed Jaffrey, the London-based actor, for the role of the gangster.

I handed my finished English screenplay to Vinod Pandey who insisted on doing the Hindi screenplay.

'Shouldn't we get a proper screenplay writer?' I asked, in all innocence.

'They'll only screw it up. I'll do it,' he said, verging on the pompous.

I liked the confidence of the man. So I gave him my English script and as a parting shot, added, 'Don't forget to keep the humour in it. Keep it pacey, like Saturday Night Fever. Remember, people have the attention span of goldfish.'

'Don't worry, yaar,' he said in a rather laconic manner. Frankly, I should have.

I WENT BACK TO ENGLAND, WHERE I MADE PREPARATIONS FOR the family to come out and stay in Bombay for the duration of the film. The shoot would last approximately six months. During that time we were going to rent out our home in London to an actor, coincidentally from India. His name was Kabir Bedi and he was going to be in London for six months, working on the James Bond film Octopussy.

I HAD COMPOSED EIGHT SONGS FOR OUR FILM – VIBRANT, catchy melodies with modern dance grooves and sounds. I felt I had a couple of winning tracks, including one surefire hit called 'Boom Boom'. To add to the pot, Nazia Hassan and her brother Zoheb were going to sing all the songs for the soundtrack. The record company was thrilled. They sensed a hit album on their hands, as the brother-sister duo was extremely popular with the masses. I then flew back to Bombay for pre-production work on the film, including discussions with the set and costume designers, meetings with various film distributors who were interested in releasing the film all over India and arguments with the various actors' agents on availability of dates for shooting. Suresh and his team headed by Natubhai were also handling the admin and business side of things.

My family would follow in two weeks' time. I had taken the top floor of the Sun 'n' Sand Hotel on Juhu Beach for us to set up home in. So far, so good.

I WAS AWARE THAT INDIA PRODUCED NEARLY 700 MOVIES A year and was the largest film producer in the world, followed by Hong Kong, Hollywood and Nigeria. Bombay itself produced nearly 200 films a year, while the balance was made up by films in regional languages like Tamil, Telugu, Kannada, Punjabi, Bhojpuri and Bengali, to name just a few. The Bombay film industry was shambolic in its running. Films could take years to complete, depending on funding and, more often than not, the rumour mill had it that the local mafia financed some of the films in an attempt to launder their money. But all this was mere gossip compared to the problem I was faced with in getting my screenplay ready.

A week before the shoot was to commence, the Hindi screenplay was not ready.

'What the friggin' hell's going on?' I said to my director. 'You've had six weeks to get this ready, man.'

'Don't worry. It will happen, ya,' he repeated in that indolent manner of his.

I WAS INCENSED WITH HIM AND HIS CASUAL ATTITUDE TO film-making. I was now having doubts about my choice of director, but frankly one couldn't change horses midstream. So I counted to ten and simmered inside. Here was a major film being funded by my buddy and I, the trade papers were writing up the film as the next big thing, and yet this director was messing us around. It wouldn't have been half as bad if he was busy with other projects, but he had only our film on hand.

I did find out much later that his time had been taken up in working a storyline for his next project, another arty-farty low-budget opus. It was obvious that art was closer to his heart than a commercial venture. This was his chance to break into the big time, yet he was faffing around. In life you get one, maybe two, chances to hit the jackpot. Perhaps he wished to skip chance number one and was happy to wait for break number two.

'Don't worry. I'll have it ready,' he repeated like he was reciting a shloka.

Two days later I went round to his place but no further work had taken place on the script. I took the unfinished script to a screenplay doctor who promised to have it ready a day before the shoot.

Mrs B and the kids arrived from London and my wife was happy to be back in her spiritual home. Within two days we had organized the children into a school at the Theosophical Society on Juhu

Beach, not far from our hotel. Sometimes, when the heat was quite unbearable, especially in April and May, classes would be held in the open air under the shade of a large jackfruit tree, and lessons would take place to the subtle sound of lapping waves kissing the shore against a Krishna-blue sky. It was an idyllic setting for six-year-old Zak to be in and ZaZa would often attend the nursery section, taken there in the arms of her mother, with nanny in tow. This being India, we had a host of staff to look after and pamper us.

THE FIRST DAY OF SHOOTING FOR A FILM IS AN incalculably exciting event. We were like kids in a candy store sitting in our producers' chairs, waiting for the opening shot. A casual conversation between two friends at breakfast had, three months later, morphed into reality. But before the cameras could roll, we had to have the mahurat for the film. This is a ceremony which, I think, has some spiritual or superstitious connotation to it. A diya or lamp is lit, a coconut is broken and some prayers are chanted and the first shot for the film is taken while Indian delicacies are passed round for the cast and unit. The mahurat is supposed to take place on the best date and at the right time for beginning any work. It's an auspicious occasion. Suresh and I stood solemnly with our wives Devika and Sue as the puja was performed and the cameras rolled briefly. The next morning would be the first day of filming.

THE FILMING PROGRESSED FAIRLY SMOOTHLY, THOUGH NOT WITHOUT DAILY HICCUPS. The biggest problem was dates from the stars. Since most Indian films are star-based, the main actors were often working on three films at a time. So we were constantly shifting our shooting schedule. Our hero Kumar Gaurav, or Bunty, as he was affectionately called, became a close buddy of ours. He and his family became surrogate parents during our stay in Bombay and we were deeply grateful to them.

When filming was completed, we sat in a preview theatre and saw the first cut that the director had assembled. Parts of it were rather good, but there were sections of the film that had an overtly artistic mood to them. The theme of the film was youth and the songs carried through that theme, but somewhere between the storyline (which was mine) and the execution of the film (the director's), we had reached vertigo-inducing heights of mediocrity. It was only when the film had been completed that I noticed the flaws in my storyline.

In India, the hero never loses the girl; in mine he does. And to his older brother at that. In India, the hero beats the hell out of the baddies single-handedly. If fifty goondas or baddies come to attack him, he says, 'Bring it on.' With a smirk, he fights them and wins, without a blemish on his face.

'Remember, a film is made on two tables. The writing table and the editing table,' Rajendra Kumar had said to me, prophetically, at the beginning of our shoot. 'You cannot have success without a proper script and a good editor.' I now understood what he meant.

We tried to salvage the film with some additional editing to hasten the pace and it took on a better shape, but there was a nagging feeling in my head that it wasn't the blockbuster I had hoped for.

The soundtrack to Star came out and started doing well. This buoyed us into thinking it might help to carry the film. We had a premiere and a lavish party at the Oberoi Hotel (now, the Trident) on Marine Drive. If we were going down with the ship, we would do so eating at the captain's table, the men in tuxedos and the women wearing tiaras.

As I had feared, the film did not do well. It was not the success we had envisaged it to be. The youth in the cities loved it and could identify with it, but it wasn't a commercial success. Perhaps the film was ahead of its time. For sure, the storyline would be more acceptable in today's climate.

But we had a fabulous time making the film. Some moments made us smile, while others had me wanting to tear my hair out. However, the memories – some good, some bad – have always remained with us.

ONE OF THE MORE HUMOROUS MOMENTS I REMEMBER WAS WHEN Sue's brother Richard came to India to see us on his way to China on business. He visited the sets at Mehboob Studios in Bandra, where we were shooting a disco scene in which a fight breaks out between the hero and a villain. It was quite a lavish set that replicated a modern discotheque. Our hero, who plays this singing sensation, finishes a song and is attacked by one of Saeed Jaffrey's thugs. There were at least a hundred people milling around the set: spot boys, tea-wallahs, lighting men, gantry shifters, carpenters, the make-up man, extras, hangers-on and VIPs. In this melee sat my brother-in-law in pride of place, behind the cameraman, about to watch the sequence of events. He was the only white man on the set and was, thus, the focus of most people's attention. Everyone was fascinated by his white skin, blue eyes and blond hair. Plus he was a relative of one of the producers of the film. This gave him VVIP status. He had a tea boy standing by his side with an urn ready to fill his glass at the merest nod from the White Raja.

The set was lit and the okay given by the cameraman.

'All quiet in the studio,' the assistant director barked and a gradual hush enveloped the set.

But first, let me describe the scene they were going to shoot. This thug jumps up onto the stage where the hero has finished his song and grapples with him. A fight ensues. It was going to be a short scene but a very important and integral one to the film. We also needed to shoot as fast as possible with no real mistakes or too many rehearsals, because Kumar Gaurav had to leave in fifteen minutes for the airport to catch a flight to another city, where he was due on the set of another film. Speed was of the essence and so there was a certain amount of tension in the air. 'Quiet please,' the assistant director shouted again, as a smidgeon of chatter could still be heard. Finally, total silence.

There was a thumbs-up from the sound recordist, a shake of the head from the cameraman and our director called, 'Action.'

Richard and I looked at each other as a smile played on his lips; his first time on a film set.

The camera whirred silently as the baddie leapt from the crowd onto the stage, and as he made this giant leap, his black trousers ripped alarmingly all along the seam of his backside, till his briefs could be seen in their surf white glory.

'Stop camera,' shouted the director and, suddenly, raucous

laughter filled the studio.

The extra who was playing the baddie climbed down from the stage, looking embarrassed as his trousers had an opening the size of the Panama Canal.

Then panic set in, when we realized the hero had to leave in ten minutes. Somehow the shot had to be completed. The seamstress was in another building of the huge studio complex. There wasn't enough time to take the trousers to her, get them mended and returned in the few minutes we had available. So we started looking around the crowd of people to see if anyone was wearing a pair of black trousers. Lo and behold! Someone was. That someone was Richard the Lionhearted. All eyes were riveted to him or, at least, at his trousers.

'No way,' he said, firmly. And then pleaded, 'I can't. Please, I'm a guest from a foreign land.' He was almost begging.

Four pairs of hands plundered his trousers even as he cried for mercy. His buttons were undone in a jiffy and his trousers were at his ankles before he could gain his composure. There he stood, in front of a hundred brown-skinned people, his lily-white legs poking out of his boxer shorts, his white shirt creased at the parts that were previously tucked into his trousers, and a pair of calf-length blue socks rising from his black leather shoes. I must say, Richard took it like a good sport and he saved the day for us. After the shot was taken, the trousers were returned to him and as he put them on, the crowd burst into spontaneous applause.

32

THE FOURTEEN-YEAR FILM

I HAD SPENT NEARLY A YEAR IN BOMBAY MAKING star and with its release, it was time to head back to London. The children were taken out of their school and we made our farewells to the people who looked after us – the driver, the nanny and the dhobi who washed and ironed our clothes with enough starch to stiffen a spineless back. The Sun 'n' Sand had been like a second home to us and the staff members became our friends. During our stay, Sue and I would come down from our terraced rooms, while the kids were being readied for school and we would walk past the swimming pool and the glass-domed conservatory, where hotel guests were served their breakfast. The watchman would give us a subtle greeting and open the little gate so we could go onto the beach. We would stroll along the sand as daylight began its arc and the Arabian Sea shimmered in the first rays of the morning sun. It had been our daily ritual and allowed us to face the chaos of the day that Bombay threw at us.

We said goodbye to the numerous friends we had made during our stay in India. I had the opportunity to see my mom during sorties to Bangalore. For Suresh and me, it had been an adventure, a roller-coaster ride of highs and lows, but with no regrets. We even managed to recoup 80 per cent of our investment.

We boarded the Air India flight and waved goodbye to Mother India, our sadness tinged by the fact that the film I had made was, unfortunately, not the success I had wanted it to be.

For the next few years I walked the wilderness of my career like a rogue elephant abandoned by the rest of the herd, unsure of which direction to go. The winters in London felt colder as I drifted into the tundra of no man's land. In the absence of further success, my indecently large royalty statements were proportionately reduced, but still ample. Computers were beginning to take over the world of music and musicians were rarely involved in recording sessions.

I either had to play catch-up or be left behind. I had the time; now all I needed was the inclination. So I decided to learn about computers interfaced with synthesizers, sound cards, modems, modules and such like. Every sound imaginable could be produced on a keyboard that was linked to a module that contained a thousand sounds, from a sitar to a didgeridoo to a string quartet. One would have five or six modules attached to your main synth which meant you could access up to 6000 sounds while programming your song. It was a hard learning curve but I could not allow myself to succumb to the changing world of technology unless I wanted to be a window cleaner or on the factory floor. Gradually, the pieces fell into place like a giant jigsaw that takes shape bit by bit till the final big picture emerges.

One day, I got a call from a man with a gentle singsong inflection in his voice that told me it had to be someone from India. Allow me to relate this jewel of a snippet, which will also lift the cloud of gloom from the previous paragraph.

'My name is Chandru,' the caller said confidently. 'Chandru Asrani. You don't know me but I want you to do two songs for my film.'

I wasn't sure if the caller was a hoaxer. Everyone in India wanted to either be in films or make one. 'What film are you talking about?' I asked. I thought it a pretty rational question.

'The film is called Ramu To Deewana Hai and I am the producer.'

'I see,' I replied. 'Who's acting in it and who is the director?' Having made a film in India I had garnered sufficient knowledge about some of the stars and the names of a couple of directors.

'I am playing the lead role and I'm also the director,' his voice had a ring of total assurance.

Wow, I thought to myself, this guy is so talented, so rich or so deewana.

'We'll have to meet, before I can say yes or no,' I answered.

'You will definitely say yes once I relate the story to you. I am most certain of that. That's why I've come to London to see you,' he blabbed.

'Fine,' I replied, more to get him off the line.

THE NEXT MORNING CHANDRU CAME TO MY HOUSE. HE WAS a pleasant- looking fellow with graying hair, a few wrinkles and a ready smile. I made him welcome and noticed that while he wasn't unattractive, he certainly wasn't hero material. A slight paunch did not go unnoticed by me.

My better half brought in a tray of assorted biscuits and tea, said a pleasant hello to our guest and left us alone. Wise girl.

'I have come all the way to London, because I want you to do two songs for my film,' my guest said, stirring his tea.

'I know, you told me this on the phone yesterday,' I replied, politely.

'Do you want to hear the story?' he said, eagerly.

'Briefly I said, aware that when people were selling themselves, they could go on and on, till the veranda lights needed switching on.

CHANDRU BEGAN HIS STORY. I DON'T REMEMBER TOO MUCH OF it, because within the first twenty seconds, it sounded no different from a thousand other Hindi films that followed a formulaic storyline of good son versus bad son or good cop versus bad cop, rich girl falls for poor boy and parents object or rich boy falls for poor girl and the boy's mother threatens self-immolation. My attention drifted to whether I should have a rich-tea biscuit, the Scottish shortbread or the chocolate-coated ones. In the end I had one of each.

'So what do you think, yaar?' he was beaming proudly and widely.

'Er, I think I'd like to see the film,' I said hesitantly, not having heard his pitch.

'I've finished 90 per cent of the film. I have only 10 per cent more to do.'

'Are you saying you haven't completed the film yet?' I asked, surprised.

'No. I have come for some funds promised by my friend. Then I'll go back to Bombay and finish the thing,' he said with alarming honesty. 'But I have a VCR of bits of the film shot so far. Shall we see it?'

Why not, thought I, it may not be half as bad as I imagined or expected. So I put the video in the machine and we sat back on the sofa to watch it. The film started in black and white.

'When was this shot?' I asked, puzzled by what I saw on the screen.

'I started it in the late '60s, early '70s,' he said, without any discomfiture or embarrassment.

The Chandru on the screen looked a lot younger, infinitely slimmer, minus wrinkles and hair as dark as newsprint. Ten minutes into the recording and there was a new section of film; our friend looked decidedly older in this than during the earlier recording, as did the heroine.

'This was shot a few years later,' he added, lest I hadn't noticed.

Then the film moved forward and suddenly it was in colour, obviously filmed recently when funds became available.

'Chandru!' I exclaimed. 'The film is in colour.'

'Yes,' he said excitedly. 'It's in Kodak.'

'But half the film is in black and white,' I tried to reason. 'What to do? I could only shoot when I had money. You see, there are no distributors for the film, so I can't get any advance.'

'But…' I stuttered.

'Do you think anyone will notice? Black and white to colour … what does it matter?' he asked matter-of-factly.

What worried me more than the unsubtle change from monochrome to colour was the ageing of the actors, the girth and looks. I could have sworn the heroine in colour was not the same one who started in the film, although I cannot be sure. But if she was, she needed to go to Weight Watchers! And our man was playing the college lover in his late forties. He could have passed off for a college professor!

'Chandru, I cannot do the two songs. I'm sorry,' I said apologetically.

'Please, Biddu,' he begged. 'You have to do the music. I need your name on it. Two bloody good songs and I will be able to sell the film.'

I doubted it. But having made a film that hadn't done well I felt some sympathy for the guy. I thought about it for a minute. The last year or two had not been good for me career-wise. I was in a building called writer's block and whatever I composed didn't have that elusive vibe to make a hit. I had heard of writer's block in an article on John Lennon, when he went through a fallow period of music. All creative people go through this and I had known many years ago that this would happen to me one day, but like death, I had wanted it to be some time in the far distant future.

Doing two songs for this man would not hurt. But then again if the film was awful – and from what I saw, awful was a euphemism – it could hurt my career. While I ruminated over it, Chandru butt in.

'I will pay you well,' he said, pleading his desperation.

'Maybe I can help you out,' I said, like a harlot in Harlem. 'After all, you've come a long way.'

'Yes,' he replied. 'All the way from Bombay.'

'No. I meant from black and white to colour,' I replied as we shook hands on a deal.

'By the way, how long have you been working on this film?' My curiosity was aroused.

'It's taken me fourteen years to try and complete this film,' he replied with frightening honesty.

'I see,' I replied, shaking my head in disbelief.

'I want two Abba-type songs,' was his brief to me.

Six weeks later I gave Chandru the two songs for his film. They were catchy little numbers with elaborate arrangements sung by a female group. It was cut-price Abba.

Chandru went away, happy. I never saw him again and I don't know if his film ever came out. In fact I'm sure it didn't. He probably didn't get that last bit of funding to complete the film. Sadly, I heard he passed away a few years ago, unable to realize his dream. Ramu To Deewana Hai with my two songs is languishing somewhere.

33

Taking Sun City by Storm

I MADE TWO MORE ALBUMS – YOUNG TARANG AND Hotline – with Nazia and Zoheb Hassan; both met with a degree of success in India, Pakistan and among the Asian diaspora elsewhere. Both albums were recorded at the house of a young Sri Lankan musician friend, Winston Sela. While working on these albums, Winston and I had written a song called 'Don't Tell Me This Is Love', a pop and R&B dance tune with an ingrained hook. We had all but forgotten about it until one day my friend Annette Barrett from Warner Chappell Music rang us to say we had a cover version of the song in Japan sung in Japanese. This excited us as much as someone telling us we had a number one in Ulan Bator; that's the capital of Mongolia for those who missed their geography classes.

Imagine our surprise, however, when two months later the single went to number one in Japan. It was sung by a girl called Akina Nakamori, a big cheese in Japan. Then, as luck would have it, the song went on her album and the album went to number one as well. As if this was not enough, a few months later it went on her Best of… album, which, at the risk of sounding monotonous, also went to number one. The cash till of our royalties was ringing ever so sweetly again. If you include the number ones I had with the Tigers and Carl

Douglas, this was my third big hit in Japan. I'm not a betting man, but I'm sure no other boy from Bangalore has had this distinction. But I digress.

Nazia's songs had a seismic impact on Asian kids, who were starved of a youth culture. They, for the first time, saw this young, pretty, iconic figure as someone they could look up to. She was nineteen or twenty at the time. They put her posters up on their bedroom walls and teenagers would swoon over her and play her songs over and over again till they knew every single phrase by heart. Zoheb was no slouch either with the girls, with his velvet-toned voice and smouldering looks. India Today magazine went so far as to vote Nazia one of the fifty people who helped change the face of India. Certainly, her songs were instrumental in the genesis of the pop culture in this part of the world.

BUT EVERY HIGH HAS A LOW AND, IN THE CASE of the duo, they did not want to do live concerts. I kept getting offers from promoters in Dubai, Thailand, South Africa and even one from America, but frustratingly, I had to turn them down. Till one South African Indian promoter asked me if I would come and perform at Sun City in South Africa. I had heard of Sun City which, at that time, was more a Forbidden City, as the Musician's Union in the UK did not like its members to play in South Africa, because of the system of apartheid in force at the time. Legislation classified people into racial groups – whites, coloureds, Indians and blacks. The blacks were deprived of their citizenship and all public services given to them, including education, were inferior to those provided to whites.

In this dangerous mix, a pleasure dome and casino complex had been created in Bophuthatswana, a Bantustan or homeland (for black Africans), which was granted self-rule in 1971. It was a client state of South Africa that allowed foreigners to come, gamble and have a good time without the stigma of having been to a country with such a repressive regime. When asked by the promoter if I would tour, my immediate answer was a 'no', because of the system of governance.

'If people don't come to South Africa, it is only the common man who misses out,' the promoter told me. 'You think the bastards in government give a toss? How does it affect them? We people in South Africa need to interact with people from other nations. Otherwise it's another form of apartheid, isn't it?'

It made me think.

He went on, 'Sanctions of any kind only hit the man on the streets, no one else, my friend. Please come, there are so many people dying for some entertainment. They'll come from Zambia, Tanzania and even Uganda to see you. Indians are everywhere you know.'

Sod it, I thought. I'm going, and bugger what the Union says.

'Okay,' I said to him. 'I'll come.'

'You will love the country and the people. They are very warm and hospitable. It will be such an honour to have you,' he said, sounding ambassadorial.

So I decided to play two dates at Sun City. It would be my first live gig since that show with Gladys Knight. But first, I had to work on a two-hour act for the show. I decided to get a spunky young singer from Bombay called Sharon Prabhakar, who knew all the Nazia and Tina Charles songs. She had great stage presence, a friendly disposition and I knew we could work in tandem. For my part, I would do songs like 'Kung Fu Fighting' and 'I'll Go Where the Music Takes Me' plus a lot of the songs that Zoheb had sung for Star. Throw in a couple of instrumentals, and I had an act even I wouldn't mind seeing. I had six musicians, including Winston Sela, and four rehearsals later, we were winging it to South Africa.

Sun City was a hedonistic and decadent playground set in the African bushveld; a massive complex of hotels, restaurants and entertainment centres. It made Vegas look stylish and upmarket. I played my two shows in the main auditorium to a packed house, predominantly made up of Indians who had travelled from all parts of southern Africa to see the show. That they were desperate for entertainment was evident in the fact that even a stand-in like me could pull in the crowds. In the audience I saw my old school friend Larry Dozey; she was married to a German engineer working in South Africa. It was a real surprise and pleasure to see her after nearly twenty years.

I got back from South Africa, thrilled by the concerts, the crowds and the local Indian diaspora I met who were desperate to keep in touch with their motherland. The only avenue open to them was films and music. I saw the gratefulness and appreciation in their faces. For this I was glad I did not toe the line laid down by the Union. So once again my career picked up with calls from promoters in other countries to come and perform. But I began to find it a struggle to focus on work. What had started as a niggle many, many years ago was now turning into a physical nightmare.

OVER THE YEARS I HAD BEEN INCREASINGLY TROUBLED WITH A backache that was getting worse by the day. All the sitting hunched over a guitar and hours spent in front of a computer wasn't helping either. It certainly affected my work. There were times when getting out of a car was sheer agony and I couldn't straighten up for at least ten minutes. Even at dinner parties, friends always made sure my chair had a couple of soft cushions to rest my back against, and during the meal, between every course, I would get up and walk around for a minute or two to give myself a little stretch. I was healthy but this back trouble was extremely debilitating. I'd seen osteopaths, chiropractors, surgeons, healers, mediums, acupuncturists and charlatans. You name it and I'd tried it, clutching at any line of hope, but the problem wouldn't go away.

My wife suggested swimming, as it's a great all-over stretch. Until then, because of the sedentary nature of my work and my dodgy back, the only exercises I was involved in were running up bills and jumping to conclusions. Those days of schoolboy athleticism were definitely over. So I joined a health club in Kensington, which had a decent-sized pool. My new routine was to take our dog Sheba for a quick walk at 6 a.m. and then head for a swim half an hour later, before I sat down to do a day's music. Over the space of a few weeks I managed to increase the amount of lengths I was swimming. I began with six lengths a day and progressed to sixty. A few years later I, along with a young friend called Namrita Bachchan, who happened to be the niece of the Bollywood legend Amitabh Bachchan, raised £7000 for various charities in India by doing a marathon swim. I began to enjoy this daily workout and my back pain did improve, although only marginally.

Some time later, our friend Jane Coulson recommended a chiropractor called Howard Lamb of Pinner in Middlesex who through the magic of his hands and a few sessions healed me almost completely. The relief after thirty years of pain was akin to a Buddha-like enlightenment.

MEN ARE HISTORICALLY CONDITIONED TO BEING CREATURES OF ROUTINE OR a regular pattern of activity, whether it was hunting mastodon or mammoths for food, going to the office jogging or lazing around the house watching soaps on daytime television. The habit seeps into you till it becomes a part of your everyday life. I kept up my swimming routine at the health club, so age or a bad back would not let me wither away. I'd meet a regular bunch of morning people; some worked out in the gym and a few would swim while others came just for the sauna. There was one youngish man I'd see in the changing room at regular intervals. He worked the gym and would come back to the locker dripping with perspiration like he had just been under a shower. I was impressed because, to me, there is nothing more monotonous than running on a treadmill or pumping iron like some Neanderthal.

Eventually, as it often happens, we got to nodding a greeting at one another. Further down the line – I think it was six months later – the nod became a few words of pleasantries. A year later, the exchange of greetings became lengthier, till one day we actually had a conversation.

'What do you do for a living,' I asked, 'that allows you to come here every morning and spend a couple of hours?'

'I work at Whitehall,' my new-found friend replied.

For the uninitiated, Whitehall is a street in London where many of the most important British government departments are based. The word Whitehall is often used to denote the central government apparatus and bureaucracy. So I knew my friend was some kind of bureaucrat.

'I see,' I said, not wishing to prod him further on this and he did not bother to elaborate. Could the man in front of me, wearing just a towel around his midriff, be a spy or, perhaps, be working with MI 5, or, then again, be something more mundane such as a pen-pusher with a desk job? I quite liked the ambiguity of the thought.

We briefly discussed politics and religion in a superficial manner. This was the sweat-drenched, testosterone-induced atmosphere of a men's changing room after all, with guys coming in and taking off one set of clothes for another, while others went past us, headed for the pool, the steam room or shower area.

SOMEHOW THE CONVERSATION DREW US TO AYATOLLAH KHOMEINI. I THINK I mentioned the fact that the face of Islam had changed with the appearance of Khomeini in Iran. Until then, he had been an unknown person seeking refuge in France. I felt he had hijacked the religion and taken it back to medieval times. We spoke about it for a minute or two, when suddenly my half-naked friend said something that astonished me. In layman's terms, I was gobsmacked.

'You know, Khomeini was half-British and half-Indian,' he said, ever so matter-of-factly.

'Pardon?' I said, my voice rising in surprise.

'Ayatollah Khomeini was half-British and half-Indian,' he repeated slowly so the words sunk in.

'You're joking,' was all I could say.

'No.' He looked at me, smiling at the effect his disclosure had on me. Then he went into some detail, some of which I still remember, because of the uniqueness of the story.

'Ayatollah Khomeini's father was an Englishman called William Richard Williamson, born in Bristol of British parents and his mother was a Kashmiri Indian woman.'

'I don't believe this,' I replied, totally flabbergasted. 'You're making this up.'

'It's true. Why would I want to make this up?' he replied, with a gentle shrug of his bare shoulders. 'Williamson ran away to sea and finally joined the police force in Aden, Yemen.'

'Go on,' I said, intrigued.

'Well, Williamson left that job and went to live among the

Bedouins for many years and converted to Islam. He even went to Mecca and finally took on an Arabic name. He married this Kashmiri Indian woman and they had four sons. He became a very strict Muslim, which often happens with converts.'

'So one of the boys was Khomeini?' I asked.

'Yes. Khomeini means one who comes from Khomein. But most of his life was spent outside Iran, mainly in Turkey and Iraq. In fact he could hardly speak Persian and was more conversant in Arabic. You know, in Iran, you're not allowed to ask questions about the Ayatollah's birth.'

'Fascinating,' I said, not sure if I should believe what the gentleman was telling me.

'There you go,' he replied smiling. 'Hard to believe, eh? But it is true, my friend. Check it out for yourself.'

I did, many years later with the advent of Google. What my health club friend told me was true. So, like he said, there you go, I just thought I'd share this little gem with you.

34

INDIAN AT HEART

THE YEAR WAS 1991 AND A DRAMATIC CHANGE WAS about to take place in the Indian economy.

Right after independence, India had, under its first prime minister, Jawaharlal Nehru, followed an economic system that was inspired by the Soviet Union. Pandit Nehru created an economy whose key characteristic was a Planning Commission that centrally administered the economy of the country. In other words, it was a command economy and not a free market one. Over time the system degenerated into a licence-permit raj, marked by blatant political corruption and economic stagnation. By the early 1990s, the country was broke, with just two weeks of foreign currency reserves available. It had its back to the wall, so to speak, and there was only one thing to do – burn at the pyre of decay and inertia or rise from the ashes like a phoenix and soar towards economic prosperity. India had a pool of talented people and entrepreneurs who were handcuffed to an age-old system which allowed corrupt politicians to bleed the country for all it was worth. The joke was that the only time India progressed was at night, when politicians were asleep.

In 1991, the then prime minister, P.V. Narasimha Rao, started the liberalization of the economy, spearheaded by Dr Manmohan Singh, his finance minister. Slowly, the country awoke from its slumber of socialism and the wheels of the economy started their sluggish move forward as the green shoots of progress began to sprout. Gradually, the mood of the country turned upbeat. India was open to the rest of the world.

Lest you assume that the publishers have made a horrendous error, and text from a book on Indian economy has found its way into my story, rest assured. There's a reason for this dummies' guide to the economy in that the change in the economy was marked by change in cultures and attitudes. A new India was shaping, so to speak. A metamorphosis from its old insular and isolated ways to its present emergence and development as a world power.

Back in London, I got a call from a friend in Bombay who had just started his own record company called Magna Sound. The man's name was Shashi Gopal and he had this vision of starting a record company devoted to pop music in the new and reborn India. He surrounded himself with like-minded young people including his right-hand man, a young chap called Atul Churamani. They were hoping to create a pop industry much like we have in the West.

At the time, film songs dominated the music scene even though the genre of music itself had become repetitive, with archaic arrangements, prehistoric productions and inferior quality. Hindi film music had seen a golden period in the 1950s and 1960s, when some fine musicians and lyricists created ever- lasting gems which are still hummed by the Hindi film lover. In fact, songs were the backbone of almost all successful films and many stars like Shammi Kapoor and Rajendra Kumar became icons solely on the strength of songs in their films. In the 1970s people like R.D. Burman had brought in a new and exciting Western sensibility to film songs which had found acceptance with a youth starved for modern beats. But by the 1980s, amongst the few pearls, Hindi film music was marked by mediocrity, plagiarism and downright vulgar lyrics.

Shashi wanted me to make a pure pop album with a spunky

young Indian girl called Shweta Shetty. I was excited for two reasons. Work had dried up in London and so the idea of doing an album for India would keep me occupied. It would also bring in revenue. Plus, I'd keep my hand at programming songs, because when you're in the barren plains of non-creativity, you lose touch with your instruments, your ideas lack the spark of a daily exercise of getting your brain to create something new, inspiring and special, and before you know it you're sent out to grass. You become a has-been.

It is an unforgiving industry, this business of music. Success welcomes you with open arms, yet failure can leave you with the coldness of a lover's rejection. I wondered if my passion and desire for music had ebbed with time. I felt like the footballer who takes his eye off the ball or the hunter who blinks just when he is about to fire and in that nanosecond, his prey has disappeared.

APART FROM THE NAZIA HASSAN ALBUMS, NOTHING ELSE HAD COME out in India with any measure of success. So I set about writing for Shweta's album, hoping the creative juices would flow again. She had a strong powerful voice, more Western than Eastern, but suited to the sound of the day. If I could replicate my Disco Deewane formula, maybe lightning would strike twice. The album Johnny Joker came out and the title song did rather well. India, by now, had a music channel called Channel V, and they played the video of the song on a continuous rotation, allowing the song to reach out to millions of homes. It wasn't an out-and- out smash but it was a beginning that augured well for this new music label pioneering pop against the giant machinery and hype of Bollywood.

A few months later, in November 1994, I got a call from Pakistan. It was from a pop group called Vital Signs who wanted me to produce an album with them. Vital Signs were apparently big parathas in Pakistan, and knew of my past work in connection with Nazia Hassan. They made me an offer I could refuse. Basically, they were offering me crumbs, but it was the best they could do. The boys persevered and since they had written most of the songs, I would only have to contribute a song or two. This made the workload infinitely easier. Not that I had much on, anyway. The rest of the album would be composed by the four boys in the band and the lyrics would be written by their mentor. So, in the end, I agreed to do it. The boys and their mentor turned up at my place to rehearse.

During the working of the album I noticed how patriotic these guys were. It was always Pakistan this and Pakistan that. There was a flag-raising fervour in them which I found missing in other nationalities, maybe not among the Americans, but certainly amongst Indians and the Brits. In India most people thought of themselves in terms of caste or region, and rarely as Indians. Listening to these boys talk among themselves, I wished I could come up with something that Indians could be proud of as a nation. I put my focus on this particular thought. I completed the album with Vital Signs and duly handed them the master tapes, which they took back to the 'Land of the Pure'.

ONE MORNING WHILE TAKING OUR DOG SHEBA FOR ITS MORNING walk, an idea for a song popped into my consciousness. I came up with a title 'Made in India'. I loved it and thought it would make a great title for a song. Each morning I would repeat the title like a mantra as I walked Sheba. What she thought of me, I'll never know, as she is now in doggie heaven. Then a musical riff came to me and slowly, over a number of days, a melody began to form. This happened every morning when I took the dog for a walk. If the mutt was smart, it would have got itself an agent and asked for co-writer credits.

I started programming the song on my computer, giving it a bhangra, samba and a straight Western four-four beat. I loved the pot-pourri of rhythms. The arrangement sat on this groove and the lyric idea was about an Indian girl who wishes to marry, and meets many suitors from around the world, but finally settles for someone 'Made in India'. The song had a subtle patriotic theme.

I wrote the basic lyrics in my schoolboy Hindi, knowing a record company would get a professional lyric writer to spruce it up and correct all the grammatical errors I had made. When the song was ready, it sounded like a sure-fire hit to me. I got the same feeling as I had on some of the earlier songs I had produced which went to number one.

I MADE A DEMO OF THE SONG WITH MY GUIDE vocals and sent it to Shashi Gopal in India. My initial idea was to cut the song with Nazia Hassan, an idea which Shashi bought. On reflection it was not a clever one. Nazia, being Pakistani, was worried how people in her country would take to her singing a song that was basically an anthem for India. So she turned it down.

Then Shashi came up with a brilliant suggestion. He had just signed a singer called Alisha, dubbed the Madonna of India, and he thought I should cut the song with her. An album was on the cards. I had so much faith in my song that suddenly the passion and desire came back. I composed all the songs for the album, working feverishly on the arrangements and sounds and felt I had two certain hits with 'Made in India' and another song called 'Lover Girl'. Alisha came over to London and we rehearsed the songs. She was a lovely girl, attractive and with a delightfully bouncy voice; pop at its best.

We worked at a small studio in Dollis Hill, North London. It was a cheap and cheerful place, owned by a buddy of mine called Noel Ram, who also engineered the session. For the backing vocals on 'Made in India', I used a West Indian singer and a young Indian girl called Sophie Chaudhary. They, along with Alisha, did all the bee vees (backing vocals). Using Sophie was a master stroke. I had met this young girl and her mother Yasmin a few months ago. Sophie wanted to be a singer and I thought she needed to train her voice, learn some vocal techniques and get some experience in the studio before embarking on a full-time music career. These sessions were a perfect learning ground for her. As for the master stroke, you ask? Well, her mother was a fabulous cook and used to bring us home-cooked biryani and other Indian delicacies every day at lunch. This kept the engineer and me in a satisfied and contented mood and the recordings went swimmingly.

I sent the finished product to Atul Churamani at Magna Sound and they were delighted with the tapes. A video of a song was planned and for the record company it was a toss-up between 'Made in India' and 'Lover Girl'. I was emphatic it should be the former and they decided to go with the voice of experience; that's one of the pluses of ageing. Ken Ghosh, a director of television ads, was roped in to make the video.

FOUR WEEKS LATER I FLEW TO BOMBAY FOR THE RELEASE of the album and for the first time, I saw the video that Ken had shot. To say it was fabulous is an understatement. I was bowled over by the colours, pageantry and beauty of the video. Ken had used an elephant, snakes, holy men, a palace – the works. Alisha looked stunning sitting on a throne playing the part of a princess in search of a husband. Men from foreign lands are brought to her court and she rejects them till finally – and this was the pièce de résistance of the video – in a cloud of dry ice and smoke, this tea chest is brought to her, carried by four eunuchs, and suddenly this bare-bodied hunk of a man bursts out of it. Alisha drools on seeing him and Mr Hunk lifts her up as she melts in his arms and is taken away to seventh heaven.

A former swimming champ turned model called Milind Soman played the hunk and he was every Indian woman's idea of Brad Pitt. On seeing this video, I knew for sure that the album would be a beast of a hit; only Armageddon could stop it from being one.

A WEEK LATER, IN APRIL 1995, THE MUSIC WAS RELEASED and it took the country by storm, aided by this phenomenal video. The song stayed in the charts for over thirty-five weeks and became the anthem I had hoped for, selling over three million copies in India alone. The song made people proud again. It was played at cricket matches when India played a visiting team; it was used at fashion shows where models sashayed along the ramp and it was used to highlight goods created or made in India. The term 'Made in India' became a brand and the song title became synonymous with a vibrant and emerging country. Once again, through sheer good luck, talent, or a combination of both, I had hit the mother lode. The incredible success of Made in India would allow me the privilege of working with emerging new artists like the enormously talented Sonu Nigam and Shaan, and that evergreen songbird of India, Asha Bhonsle.

Now, a sense of pride took over me. I had left this country over twenty-eight years ago and although I had remained in touch with it through the years, I never felt totally at home, never fully accepted and never totally relaxed with its heart-breaking poverty, its myriad rules, bureaucracy, lack of basic infrastructure and rampant corruption. I was caught in that familiar juxtaposition between head and heart. A friend of mine jokingly chided me by calling me a coconut, an affectionate but derogatory term meaning brown on the outside but white within.

I was truly fond of Britain as a nation. I had left India with the flickering flame of hope. Britain had welcomed me as an immigrant and allowed me the freedom of my career and it gave me a very good living. I had set down ties within this new country; my wife Sue was English and Zak and ZaZa were born and educated there. But what is feeling British? If England were playing India in a Test match, whom would I root for? Would I pass the Norman Tebbitt test and cheer on my adopted country? (Norman Tebbitt was a Tory minister in the Thatcher government who stated that people from ethnic backgrounds – like West Indians, Pakistanis and Indians – should support the English cricket team rather than a team from their country of origin as a barometer of whether they were truly British.)

I have a British passport, but I could just as easily have had an American or a Spanish one. These are documents more for the ease of travel. An Englishman will always be an Englishman no matter how alien the culture or climate he is in. So also a Scotsman, a Chinaman or a Frenchman. So why not an Indian? A chameleon changes only its colour, its outward appearance, to blend with the surroundings. At the end of the day, you belong to where the roots of your culture and heritage are. You may despise some of it, admire aspects of it, or even be infuriated by all of it, but it is what represents and embodies you. Draw away the curtain and beneath the façade, the pull of your inheritance, your ancestry and your inner soul is too powerful to be forgotten, ignored or washed away. A rock will always remain a rock no matter the countless times the lapping of waves may kiss, caress or pummel it.

I am a citizen of the world, but inside, truly deep inside, I am still made in India.

Acknowledgements

My sincere thanks go to Jaya Vasudevan and Priya Doraiswamy, my erstwhile agents at Jacaranda Books.

Also, a big thank you to my editor, Shantanu Ray Chaudhuri, for his masterly and seamless editing on the manuscript.

Cover design: Rishad Patel.

Many thanks to all my friends. Although I haven't been able to mention all of them in the course of writing this book, they and so many others have brightened and lightened my journey through life. Friends like Patsy and Stuart Reid, Frank Coachworth, Jane and David Coulson, Pauline and Abbas Arbabzadeh, Cathy Hawthorn, Esther and Victor Fieldgrass, Peta and Henry Armitage, Barry and Ruth Berman, Clive and Alex Limpkin, Prady and Sally Balan, Nigel and Layla Watling, Paul and Anthea Spyropolous, Robert and Brigitte Bloeme, Kartar Lalvani and family, Lynne Coachworth (my book-keeper), David Driver (my accountant, for his creative accounting).

T.W. Bhojwani and Hira Bhojwani, Suresh and Deveika Bhojwani, Mr and Mrs Rajendra Kumar, Kumar Gaurav, Zarine and Sanjay Khan, Malavika Sanghvi, Dimple Uberoi, N. Radhakrishnan, Rakhi Kapur, Parmeshwar and Adi Godrej, Ashok and Anne Daryanani, Ash and Gita Tandon, Atul Churamani, Bina and Prakash Mistry, Shashi Gopal, the Gandhis of Los Angeles, Yasmin and Sophie Choudhary, Mrs Oswal and her son Shail, the artists Alisha Chinoy, Sonu Nigam, Shaan and Sagarika, and Shweta Shetty, and Mr and Mrs Hassan and Zoheb, Mr Arora and the staff at Sun 'n' Sand Hotel, Juhu.

I'd also like to thank my family, Richard and Phillip Collard (the dangerous brothers-in-law) and my wife's numerous Meher Baba followers. My brother and sister, nieces and nephews, because in India the family is number one. Thanks also to my sister-in-law Jamuna for always being there for my mom.

Made in the USA
Middletown, DE
25 January 2018